1500125   M
'08

D0220552

DATE DUE

GAYLORD   PRINTED IN U.S.A.

BREVARD COMMUNITY COLLEGE
MELBOURNE CAMPUS LIBRARY
3865 N. WICKHAM ROAD
MELBOURNE, FL 32935

MASTERPIECES OF NON-WESTERN WORLD LITERATURE

Recent Titles in
Greenwood Introduces Literary Masterpieces

Masterpieces of French Literature
Marilyn S. Severson

Masterpieces of Modern British and Irish Drama
Sanford Sternlicht

Masterpieces of 20th-Century American Drama
Susan C.W. Abbotson

Masterpieces of Classic Greek Drama
Helaine L. Smith

Masterpieces of Philosophical Literature
Thomas L. Cooksey

Masterpieces of American Romantic Literature
Melissa M. Pennell

Masterpieces of British Modernism
Marlowe A. Miller

Masterpieces of Beat Literature
Michael J. Dittman

Masterpieces of Jewish American Literature
Sanford Sternlicht

MASTERPIECES OF NON-WESTERN WORLD LITERATURE

Thomas L. Cooksey

BREVARD COMMUNITY COLLEGE
MELBOURNE CAMPUS LIBRARY
3865 N. WICKHAM ROAD
MELBOURNE, FL 32935

Greenwood Introduces Literary Masterpieces

GREENWOOD PRESS
Westport, Connecticut • London

Library of Congress Cataloging-in-Publication Data

Cooksey, Thomas L.
  Masterpieces of non-western world literature / Thomas L. Cooksey.
    p. cm. — (Greenwood introduces literary masterpieces, ISSN 1545–6285)
  Includes bibliographical references and index.
  ISBN-13: 978–0–313–33858–8 (alk. paper)
    1. Developing countries—Literatures—History and criticism. I. Title.
PN849.U43C66 2007
809—dc22   2007026799

British Library Cataloguing in Publication Data is available.

Copyright © 2007 by Thomas L. Cooksey

All rights reserved. No portion of this book may be
reproduced, by any process or technique, without the
express written consent of the publisher.

Library of Congress Catalog Card Number: 2007026799
ISBN: 978–0–313–33858–8
ISSN: 1545–6285

First published in 2007

Greenwood Press, 88 Post Road West, Westport, CT 06881
An imprint of Greenwood Publishing Group, Inc.
www.greenwood.com

Printed in the United States of America

The paper used in this book complies with the
Permanent Paper Standard issued by the National
Information Standards Organization (Z39.48–1984).

10   9   8   7   6   5   4   3   2   1

Copyright Acknowledgments

The author and publisher gratefully acknowledge permission to reprint the following:

Passages from *The Tale of Genji* by Shikibu Murasaki, translated by Royall Tyler. Copyright © 2001 by Royall Taylor. Used by permission of Viking Penguin, a division of Penguin Group (USA) Inc. and Penguin Group (UK) Ltd.

Excerpts from Kovacs, Maureen Gallery, translator, *The Epic of Gilgamesh, with an Introduction and Notes*, Copyright © 1985, 1989 by the Board of Trustees of the Leland Stanford Junior University. All rights reserved. Used with the permission of Stanford University Press, www.sup.org.

Passages from Jayadeva's *Gītagovinda* are reprinted from *The Gītagovinda of Jayadeva: Love Song of the Dark Lord*, translated by Barbara Stoler Miller. Copyright © 1977 Columbia University Press. Reprinted with the permission of the publisher.

Passages from Nguyen Du's *The Tale of Kieu* are reprinted from *The Tale of Kieu: A Bilingual Edition*, translated by Huynh Sanh Thong. Copyright © 1983 by Huynh Sanh Thong. Reprinted by permission of Yale University Press.

To my Elizabeth
Teacher, tender comrade, wife,
A fellow-farer, true through life.
—Robert Louis Stevenson

Contents

Introduction

Through art alone are we able to emerge from ourselves, to know what another person sees of a universe which is not the same as our own and of which, without art, the landscapes would remain as unknown to us as those that may exist on the moon.

—Marcel Proust

compare the methods, materials,
languages of the enterprise.
A great living Library of people,
trillions of brain cells indexed
from the heart, cross-referenced
through usefulness to life, powered
by the stuff of life itself.

—Robert Sullivan

This book offers in one volume 10 interpretive essays, introducing and discussing 10 "classical" masterpieces of non-Western world literature. With two exceptions, each chapter centers on a single work, at the same time ever mindful of the words of the Argentine writer Jorge Luis Borges that "a book is not an isolated being: it is a relationship, an axis of innumerable relationships" (Borges, *Other* 164). Each chapter provides an overview and assessment of the importance of the work, relating it to similar works in its culture. In turn each chapter explains relevant historical and cultural contexts, outlines the plot, describes major characters, discusses central themes, and points to later influences in the indigenous culture and in the larger world. A "Suggested Readings" section at the end of each chapter offers guidance to readily available translations in English and lists primary and relevant secondary sources as the jumping-off place for further study. As such, each essay attempts to fill a gap between the brief entries found in encyclopedias, single-volume handbooks, or anthology headnotes and the comprehensive treatments found in individual monographs devoted to a single work, period, or national literature. This book is intended for the serious reader who wants something more substantial than can be found in the handbooks, but who lacks the time or available research facilities to wade through the vast scholarship that these works have generated.

The title of this book is simply *Masterpieces of Non-Western Literature*, not *The Masterpieces of Non-Western Literature*. The limits of space mean that the works selected for inclusion do not begin to exhaust the rich possibilities, and although each chapter mentions additional works and other authors, I am deeply aware that this book can at best only begin to entice and orient the reader with various promising directions for further reading and study. The 10 chapters include the following:

Chapter 1. The *Epic of Gilgamesh*, the Babylonian epic, recounting the adventures of the ancient king of Sumer and his friend, the wild man Enkidu.

Chapter 2. The *Mahābhārata*, the great epic of ancient India. This work also contains the famous *Bhagavad-Gītā*, one of the masterpieces of moral philosophy.

Chapter 3. The *Gītagovinda* of Jayadeva, a verse play about the love of the blue god Krishna and his beloved Radha, is a work of profound beauty and psychological insight, often compared to the Song of Songs.

Chapter 4. *Sundiata* (also known as *Sunjata* or *Son-Jara*), a great epic of West Africa, chronicles the rise and early triumphs of the founder of the Empire of Mali.

Chapter 5. The poetry of Li Po, among the greatest poets of Tang Dynasty China. His work has also exercised a profound influence on Western modernism.

Chapter 6. *The Tale of Genji* by Murasaki Shikibu is sometimes called the first novel in world literature and is certainly one of the great psychological novels in all literature.

Chapter 7. *The Journey of the West* (also known as *Monkey*) by Wu Ch'êng-ên is regarded as one of the five classic novels of China, tracing the adventures of the Monkey king in his quest for the Buddhist scriptures.

Chapter 8. *The Conference of Birds* by Farīd al-Dīn ʿAttār is an allegorical work of Sufi spirituality and a work of narrative art in the tradition of the *Thousand and One Nights*.

Chapter 9. *The Tale of Kieu* by Nguyen-Du is the national poem of Vietnam, recounting the suffering, betrayals, and endurance of a young woman.

Chapter 10. The *Quetzalcoatl* is a collection of literary fragments about the plumed serpent of Mesoamerica, one of the masterworks of Native American literature.

In addition to the 10 chapters, there is also a general selected bibliography at the end of the book.

Inevitably, the works that I have selected to write about reflect my own tastes in world literature and my own interest in the relationships among literature, philosophy, and religion and in comparative mythology. Nevertheless, I have been guided by five criteria. First, each work selected for inclusion is universally recognized as a canonical masterpiece in its own national literature, as an important contribution to national and cultural identity. As such, each has exercised a profound influence on later work in its respective world, not merely transmitting the values and assumptions of its world, but being itself an artifact of that world. Accordingly, an appreciation of these works and their cultural status is crucial to any subsequent understanding of the national character and its cultural productions. Second, I have tried to cover a diverse range of non-Western cultures and literary types, including works from Africa, East Asia, the Asian subcontinent, the Middle East, and Mesoamerica. Third, each work predates any significant contact with the Western world, or where there was such contact, it was only peripheral (the case of *Quetzalcoatl* is a bit more complicated and will be addressed in that chapter). The point is that each work is the product of a developed, articulate, and highly sophisticated civilization that existed without any reference to the West. Fourth, each of the works under examination represents an achievement that resonates beyond its own national and linguistic boundaries. It has achieved the status of world literature. It is this quality that transforms a masterpiece of national literature into one of world literature. Thus the great German poet Goethe composed his *West-Östlicher Divan* under the inspiration of the Persian poets Hafiz and Rumi, and the Chinese novelist Lu Xun (1881–1936) found a new voice for challenging a corrupt society in the novels of Gogol and Zola. Fifth, by masterpiece I do not mean something that necessarily transmits perennial or eternal truths. Rather it is a work that retains the enduring power to provoke and enrich, whether within its culture or without. Philosopher Kwame Anthony Appiah puts it concisely when he writes of the cultural value of the Nok sculptures and to whom they "belong": "While the government of Nigeria reasonably exercises trusteeship, the Nok sculptures belong in the deepest sense to all of us." Appiah explains, "I just mean that the Nok sculptures are of potential value to all human beings" (Appiah 120). They possess some power that connects or resonates beyond their narrow historical and cultural boundaries. This may point to the perception of shared humanity or simply to the fertile suggestiveness that comes from looking at things from a different perspective. Thus, for instance, within the Western tradition, Homer's *Odyssey* remains vividly alive in James Joyce's *Ulysses* or Derek Walcott's *Omeros*. By contrast, works such as the *Argonautika* of Apollonios of Rhodes, a literary epic about Jason and the Argonauts, and itself a very conscious response to Homer, is an acquired taste largely limited to specialists. Somehow it lacks the spark to ignite much later response.

The comments of Paula M. Varsano, a scholar of classical Chinese literature, are relevant here. Describing the practice of modern Chinese peasants to recall and recite memorized passages or whole poems by Li Po to commemorate special occasions, she writes, "With each such encounter, both the poem and the person who carried it would be enriched: the poem rekindled by the present and the particular, the person firmly anchored in the past and the communal" (Varsano 300). Whether or not they are resurrecting the actual Li Po is less important than that they identify themselves as belonging to a historically grounded community signified by him, and through this identity, they endow him with a modern relevance; they make him a living presence. "In so far as a man or woman is susceptible to *poiesis*, to meaning made form," writes the critic George Steiner, "he or she is open to incursions and appropriations by agencies of delight or of sadness, of assurance or of dread, of enlightenment or of perplexity, whose modes of operation are, finally, beyond paraphrase" (Steiner, *Real* 187).

From the beginning, I should acknowledge the limitations of this project. This is most evident in the problem of language and the necessary recourse to translations. "To imagine a language," said the philosopher Ludwig Wittgenstein, "is to imagine a way of living" (qtd. in Rhees 290). Our language, and by extension our narratives and our art, construct how we understand our world, how we describe things or express ourselves. Correspondingly, to truly get into the culture means understanding the relevant language. Ideally, everything should be read in the original languages. For this book that would include some familiarly with Sanskrit, Chinese, Japanese, Vietnamese, Manding, Nahuatl, and Persian. Falling short of that, we must rely on translations, several if possible. Ultimately, however, it is only through translation that different worlds are able to speak beyond their borders. The Czech writer Milan Kundera notes that Gide did not know Russian, yet was profoundly influenced by Dostoevsky; that Shaw did not know Norwegian, yet considered himself an apostle of Ibsen; and that Sartre did not read Dos Passos in English, but learned much of the art of the novel from him. Kundera adds, "If the books of Gombrowicz and Danilo Kiš had depended solely on the judgment of people who read Polish and Serbo-Croatian, their radical aesthetic newness would never have been discovered" (Kundera 36–37). The Russian poet and novelist Boris Pasternak, himself a translator of some note, says it well: "Translation is not a method of getting to know isolated works, it is the channel whereby cultures and peoples communicate down the centuries" (Pasternak 12).

In its deepest sense, world literature (Western and non-Western) is not so much a body of works or a canon, writes critic David Damrosch, but "a mode of reading" (Damrosch 281). By this he means "a detached engagement with a world beyond our own" (297). There are two aspects here. The first pertains to detachment, a suspension of the judgments and expectations that come with the assumptions of our own culture. Inevitably, of course, we must start from the perspective of our own world and what we know. The challenge is not to hang onto that perspective with white-knuckled dogmatism, but to be open to the possibility that there are ways of thinking about things other than our own. This does not necessarily mean agreeing, but it does mean acknowledging. In his *Georgics*, an attempt to civilize and domesticate the pastoral, to imagine the happy union of man and nature, the Roman poet Virgil recalled Ethiopian cotton, Chinese silk combed from leaves, "foliis depectant tenuia Seres" (2.121), and other products of human production foreign to Italy. Although Virgil's actual understanding of how these things were cultivated is doubtful, and although he wishes to celebrate Italy's own agricultural accomplishments, he acknowledges the value of these cultures foreign to his own, acknowledges that each contributes things that are unique to itself, yet precious to all.

The second aspect of Damrosch's mode of reading involves engagement, being open to reconnecting, the willingness to explore possible fruitful insights gained from comparing and contrasting different works, an often productive conversation. Thus we might compare Li Po or Bashō with Wordsworth, Odysseus and Demodocus with Sundiata and Balla Fasséké, or the *Divine Comedy* with the *Conference of Birds*.

In the end, lacking understanding of the relevant languages is not a valid excuse for not pursuing the study of cultures and literatures outside our own. It is essential to remind ourselves that there is a world beyond our own and that we are enriched by our acknowledgment and appreciation of this otherness. It is the very key to our own self-knowledge, for we only receive a clear appreciation of our own culture, its limits, its values, and its point of view by looking at it from the distance and perspective of another. There is nothing like the study of a foreign language to give one an understanding of our own. There is nothing like the study of different cultures to enhance the understanding of our own. My own profound commitments to the masterpieces of

Western literature also entail a serious commitment to the masterpieces of the rest of the world. My claims to understand my own world are meaningful only against my ability to situate it into the larger context. "Who," asked the poet Goethe in his *West-Östlicher Divan*, "without three thousand years on the account book, does not remain inexperienced, in the dark, living day to day" (Goethe 49, my translation). I share the convictions described by Mircea Eliade, noted historian of religious ideas, that "the study of Dante or Shakespeare, and even of Dostoevsky or Proust, is illuminated by a knowledge of Kalidasa, the Noh plays, or the *Pilgrim Monkey*." "This is not," Eliade explains, "a matter of a vain and, in the end, sterile pseudo-encyclopedism. It is simply a matter of not losing sight of the profound and indivisible unity of the history of the human mind" (Eliade xvi).

Trying to explain how to write a script, the famous Japanese director Akira Kurosawa, who created such classic films as *Rashômon* (1950), the *Seven Samurai* (1954), and *Ran* (1985), wrote that we must first "study the great novels and dramas of the world. We must consider why they are great" (Kurosawa 193). Such a process requires grasping both the emotional resonance in the audience and that of the author. It also involves grasping the skill and meticulousness of the author in creating characters and events. "You must read thoroughly, to the point where you can grasp all these things" (Kurosawa 193). Kurosawa's injunction is very much related to the goals of *Masterpieces of Non-Western World Literature*.

SUGGESTED READINGS

Apollonios Rhodios. *The Argonautika: The Story of Jason and the Quest for the Golden Fleece*. Trans. Peter Green. Berkeley: University of California Press, 1997.

Appiah, Kwame Anthony. *Cosmopolitanism: Ethics in a World of Strangers*. New York: W. W. Norton, 2006.

Borges, Jorge Luis. *Other Inquisitions, 1937–1952*. Trans. Ruth L. C. Simms. Austin: University of Texas Press, 1965.

———. *Seven Nights*. Trans. Eliot Weinberger. New York: New Directions, 1984.

Cheah, Pheng, and Bruce Robbins, eds. *Cosmopolitics: Thinking and Feeling Beyond the Nation*. Minneapolis: University of Minnesota Press, 1998.

Damrosch, David. *What Is World Literature?* Princeton: Princeton University Press, 2003.

Eliade, Mircea. *From the Stone Age to the Eleusinian Mysteries*. Vol. 1 of *A History of Religious Ideas*. Trans. Willard R. Trask. Chicago: University of Chicago Press, 1978.

Garcia, Jorge J. E., Carolyn Korsmeyer, and Rodophe Gashé, eds. *Literary Philosophers: Borges, Calvino, Eco*. New York: Routledge, 2002.

Goethe, Johann Wolfgang von. *West-Östlicher Divan*. *Gedichte*. Vol. 2. Ed. Erich Trunz. Hamburg: Fischer Bücherei, 1964.

Kundera, Milan. *The Curtain: An Essay in Seven Parts*. New York: HarperCollins, 2007.

Kurosawa, Akira. *Something Like an Autobiography*. Trans. Audie E. Bock. New York: Vintage Books, 1983.

Lott, Sandra Ward, Maureen S. G. Hawkins, and Norman McMillan, eds. *Global Perspectives on Teaching Literature: Shared Visions and Distinctive Visions*. Urbana, IL: National Council of Teachers of English, 1993.

Pasternak, Boris. *Selected Poems*. Trans. Jon Stallworthy and Peter France. New York: W. W. Norton, 1982.

Proust, Marcel. *In Search of Lost Time*. 6 vols. Trans. C. K. Scott Moncrieff, Terence Kilmartin, and D. J. Enright. New York: Modern Library, 1993.

Steiner, George. *After Babel: Aspects of Language and Translation*. Oxford: Oxford University Press, 1975.

———. *Real Presences*. Chicago: University of Chicago Press, 1989.

Sullivan, Robert. *Star Waka*. Auckland: Auckland University Press, 1999.

Varsano, Paula M. *Tracking the Banished Immortal: The Poetry of Li Bo and Its Critical Reception*. Honolulu: University of Hawai'i Press, 2003.

Virgil. *The Eclogues and Georgics of Virgil*. Trans. C. Day Lewis. New York: Anchor Books, 1964.

Walcott, Derek. *Omeros*. New York: Noonday Press, 1990.

Xun, Lu. *Diary of a Madman and Other Stories*. Trans. William A. Lyell. Honolulu: University of Hawai'i Press, 1990.

1

Epic of Gilgamesh
(c. 1600–1000 B.C.E.)

(Stoop) if you are abcedminded, to this claybook, what curios of signs (please stoop), in this allaphbed! Can you rede (since We and Thou had it out already) its world?
—James Joyce, *Finnegans Wake* (18)

Fänden auch wir ein reines, verhaltenes, schmales
Menschliches, einen unseren Streifen Fruchtlands
zwischen Strom und Gestein.
[If only we too could find some defined, narrow,
purely human place, our own small strip of fertile soil
between stream and stone].
—Rainer Maria Rilke, *Duino Elegies* (15)

"Attended Meeting to hear Mr. Smith's Paper read on the Babylonian account of the Deluge," the British prime minster William Ewart Gladstone laconically recorded in his diary on December 3, 1872 (Gladstone 252). The meeting was of the Biblical Archaeological Society, and the lecturer was the archeologist George Smith, who had pieced together and deciphered clay tablets excavated earlier by Austen Henry Layard at the site of the palace of the Assyrian King Ashurbanipal (6th century B.C.E.). The reconstructed tablets recounted the story of a man named Utanapishtim, who is warned that the gods plan to destroy human life with a great flood. He builds a great boat by which he will save himself, his family, and the animals of the world. Later, in order to test for dry ground, Utanapishtim sends forth first a dove, then a swallow, and finally a raven. "The raven went off, and saw the waters slither back. / It eats, it scratches, it bobs, but does not circle back to me" (Kovacs 102). Gladstone and the assembled company were, of course, struck by the parallels with the account of Noah in Genesis 6:5–6, parallels that would spark sharp controversy over the authority of the biblical version. What they did not realize at the time was that the account they had heard derived from the *Epic of Gilgamesh*, its first appearance after nearly three thousand years.

The *Epic of Gilgamesh* stands as both the oldest extant masterpiece of world literature and one of the newest. The 1,500-year history of the narrative, coupled with the relative stability of the text among extant versions, testifies to its early status as an important canonical work in Assyrian literature. The sustained interest and admiration set off by its recovery is ample evidence of its enduring power. The text that first emerged through the efforts of George Smith is the so-called late Babylonian version and dates from about the first millennium. It survives in 12 baked clay tablets, written in Akkadian, a Semitic language found in Babylonia and Assyria, and inscribed in cuneiform. It recounts the adventures of the Sumerian hero Gilgamesh, king of the city-state of Uruk (identified as Erech in Genesis 10:10). Other archeological evidence recounts the existence of a historical Gilgamesh who lived between 2700 and 2500 B.C.E. The 12-tablet version is well attested in relation to other surviving versions that have since been recovered, indicating that by the first millennium, the text had achieved such a high status that few later scribes were tempted to make significant modifications. A catalog dating from the first millennium records that "the series Gilgamesh (is) according to Sin-lequi-unninnī the ex[orcist-priest]" (qtd. in Tigay 246), which is generally interpreted to mean that Sin-lequi-unninnī is either the author or the editor who established the standard version.

In a very real sense, the *Epic of Gilgamesh* is a three-dimensional jigsaw puzzle, spanning both space and time. Just as George Smith had to piece together the fragments of the "late" version, so later scholars have had to piece together the genesis of the text over some 1,500 years of composition and development. The first 11 tablets of the 12-tablet version assembled by Smith articulate a well-ordered thematic and narrative whole. By contrast, the 12th tablet seems out of place, crude, and repetitive in style and theme. This difference led scholars to argue that it represents a later addition, at the same time pointing to the likelihood that the narrative as a whole was the product of a long history of accretion and revision, a hypothesis confirmed by the subsequent discovery of earlier texts and by linguistic analysis. The exact genesis must necessarily remain tentative given the remoteness of the materials, but scholars have established a number of likely stages along the way.

A historical core can be shown from surviving inscriptions, hymns, and omen literature. The Sumerian King List identifies the historical Gilgamesh as the fifth ruler of the First Dynasty of Uruk, placing him somewhere between 2700 and 2500 B.C.E. He is known as the *en* ("lord"), pointing to both a priestly and a warrior function. Other nonliterary documents from around 2400 to 2000 B.C.E. trace the transformation of his status from a figure of ancestral veneration to a divinity, from the subject of funeral offerings placed at the "Riverbank of Gilgamesh" to an identity as the judge of the Netherworld. In this later context he is often conflated with the dying god Dumuzi (Tammuz), the consort of goddess Ishtar (Inanna), a motif that takes an ironic twist in the epic itself. Other surviving inscriptions and hymns trace his transformation from warrior-hero to divine deputy in Uruk's war of independence against Kish.

Parallel with the historical core, scholars identify the contribution of at least five separate Sumerian court poems about Gilgamesh that survive in various fragments, themselves the product of an earlier oral tradition. These stories include Gilgamesh and Huwawa; Gilgamesh and the Bull of Heaven; Gilgamesh, Enkidu, and the Netherworld; the Death of Gilgamesh; and Gilgamesh and Agga. An Old Babylonian version of the epic (1900–1600 B.C.E.), composed in the Akkadian language, selectively adapts and combines these narratives along with several separate and unrelated folktales, including the story of the Wild Man, the Quest for Life, the story of the Deluge, and the story of the snake. Although textually related to its sources, the Babylonian version represents an original composition. Enkidu, originally a courtier and servant in the Sumerian narratives, is conflated with the Wild Man, becoming the friend and equal of Gilgamesh. Whereas the Sumerian and historical sources emphasized the divinity and immortality of Gilgamesh, the Babylonian version moves in the opposite direction, treating the themes of human mortality and the rites of passage. Overall, transcendence comes only through fame and the achievement of great works, a process that also desacralizes kingship. The Babylonian version also plays on a tension between civilization and nature. The narrative itself divides into three parts, each spanning a period of six or seven days, each symbolizing the rites of passage signified by eating or dressing. Thus, in the first part, Enkidu the wild man becomes Enkidu the man, entering the human community by learning to eat and drink, wash his body, and put on clothes. In the second part, Gilgamesh mourns the death of Enkidu, leaving the human community by fasting, refusing to wash, and replacing his clothes with animal skins. Finally, in the third part, Gilgamesh falls asleep before the house of Utanapishtim, a weakness that underlines his human mortality. Thus finally accepting his humanity, he again

washes, puts on clothes, and again reenters civilization. Hurrian and Hittite
translations survive from about 1500 B.C.E., and the standardizing text of
Sin-lequi-unninnī dates between 1300 and 1000 B.C.E. Out of this version the
11-tablet *Epic of Gilgamesh,* sometimes called the Nineveh Recension, grew,
elaborating and expanding the earlier works to over 3,000 lines. One copy
found its way into the library of the Assyrian king Ashurbanipal (668–627
B.C.E.) in his capital of Nineveh, near Mosul in modern Iraq. Other copies
have been excavated in Assur, on the west bank of the Tigris in Iraq; Calah,
on the Tigris, south of Mosul; and in Svetantepe, in southern Turkey.

PLOT AND CHARACTER DEVELOPMENT

The epic opens with the narrator inviting some companion (the reader or
auditor) to marvel at the foundations and brickwork of the walls of Uruk. "Is
not (even the core of) the brick structure made of kiln-fired bricks, / and did
not the Seven Sages themselves lay out its plans?" (Kovacs 3). Closing the
narrative frame at the end of the 11th tablet, Gilgamesh echoes these words,
addressing the ferryman of Utanapishtim. The present converges the narrator's past with Gilgamesh's future, expressed in the image of baked bricks. The
narrator further invites the companion or reader to open the copper tablet
box and then take and "read out" "how Gilgamesh went through every hardship" (Kovacs 4).

The epic traces several interconnected patterns. On one level, the semi-
divine Gilgamesh learns about his mortality. Through two quests, he tests
himself and discovers his limits, ultimately returning sadder but wiser. In the
first quest, to kill the monster Humbaba and cut down the cedar tree, he
projects outward in his assertion of pride and accomplishment. Gilgamesh is
establishing his identity as a hero. In the second quest, to seek Utanapishtim,
he draws inward, in comprehension of his boundaries and limits. Together
these outward and inward movements represent a quest for religious wisdom,
a coming to terms with the human condition and human mortality. On another closely related level, the narrative is about the process of civilization,
at its most literal level in the creation of cities, a movement away from the
state of nature, yet at the same time, the narrative acknowledges that civilization cannot cut us off from nature, that inevitably we are bound to its cycles
of generation and decay. It is only in the "kiln-fired bricks" of cities, or the
baked clay tablets of epics, that humankind achieves a sort of immortality.
We survive in the deeds worthy to be recorded and later "read out" to future
generations.

Beginning his story, the narrator explains that Gilgamesh is "supreme
over other kings," the most lordly in appearance, the most heroic. He was

formed by the Great Goddess, Aruru, to be two-thirds divine and one-third human. Compared to a wild bull, he possesses restless energy that torments and oppresses his people. He "does not leave a son to his father"; he "does not leave a girl to her mother!" (Kovacs 5), which is generally interpreted to mean that he involves all of the young men in constant adventures or battles and that he exercises his sexual prerogatives with all of the young women. Hearing the complaints of the people, the gods reply by creating an equal to be Gilgamesh's companion and to match his "stormy heart." (Kovacs 5). Thus the goddess Aruru takes some clay, throws it into the wilderness, and creates Enkidu, a wild man, who is covered with hair, the embodiment of nature. The name signifies "Lord of the good place" (Lambert 38). Enkidu's creation from clay underlines his humanness, a motif that runs through a number of archaic myths and religious traditions. In the Indo-European context, the word *human* is cognate with "humus," distinguishing the creatures of and out of the earth from those of the sky. In the context of Semitic languages, it is also relevant that the name of Adam (from the Hebrew '*adām*, probably from the root '*dm*, meaning "red") generically signifies "humankind," as well as the first male in the creation narrative found in Genesis 2:4–3:24. It is probably etymologically related to the Akkadian *adamu*, meaning "red" or "blood," and *adamā*, meaning "dark red earth" or "clay." Humans are clay plus blood or the spirit of life.

At first Enkidu lives as an animal among the other animals, moving on all fours, grazing on grass, and drinking at the watering hole. To protect the other animals, he begins to fill in the pits dug by the hunter to trap them. To save his livelihood, the hunter sets a trap for Enkidu, baited with the harlot (*harimtu*) Shamhat, whom he instructs, "Expose your sex so he can take in your voluptuousness. / Do not be restrained—take his energy!" (Kovacs 8). The lure is successful, and Enkidu has intercourse with the harlot for six days and seven nights. The result is a self-awareness that separates and alienates him from the other animals, who now run from him in fear. No longer one with nature, he realizes that he needs a friend as a substitute. The harlot now tells Enkidu about Gilgamesh and takes him to Uruk, where he challenges the king, blocking him just as he is about to exercise his royal prerogative over a young bride. Gilgamesh and Enkidu grapple, fighting to a draw. Their anger abated, "they kissed each other and became friends" (Kovacs 18). Although some extant stories make Enkidu a courtier and servant, the epic emphasizes his equality with Gilgamesh.

Enkidu represents the earliest surviving literary representation of the wild man, a complex but recurrent figure in myth and folklore, expressing variously the primitive or natural man, the uncivilized barbaric man, or the lapsed man (the insane or the regressive). One way or the other, he is juxtaposed with the civilized, "normal," or orthodox. Typically, the sign of his wildness is his hairiness, whether he has long locks or an entire body covered with matted fur. Also typical of the mythic pattern is the way that he is tamed by a woman, in Enkidu's case the role played by Shamhat. Parallels might be drawn with Samson (Judges 13–16) or with the figures of the Anglo-Saxon *wuduwasa,* the *wodwo* found in *Sir Gawain and the Green Knight,* or the temporary fate of Chrétien de Troyes' Yvain. Also of relevance is the tension between the hairy Esau, a hunter, and his brother Jacob over their birthright (Genesis 25:29–34). In his hairy form, natural origins, and sexual transformation, Enkidu typifies the wild man as primitive being. Similarly, Gilgamesh's later distraught wandering in the wilderness after his friend's death is commensurate with the pattern of the wild man as a lapsed man, someone whose mental state has taken him out of the civilized "human" norm. At a deeper level, the wild man distinguishes the human from the divine. The *Enūma eliš* ("When on high"), an Akkadian creation epic, makes the point explicit. When its hero Marduk slays the primal goddess Ti'āmat, he dismembers her body, creating from the various pieces the heavens and the earth. "Blood I will mass and cause bones to be," he declares. "I will establish a savage, 'man' shall be his name. Verily, savage-man I will create. He shall be charged with the service of the gods" (Pritchard 1.36). The savage or wild man *is* man, defined in binary opposition to the gods as their earthly servants. The meaning and function of Enkidu is summarized in anthropologist Roger Bartra's comments about the figure of the European wild man. "The wild man was created to answer the questions of civilized man; to reveal to him the meaninglessness of life in the name of the cosmic unity, thereby sensitizing him to the tragic and terrible compromise brought on by his individuality and loneliness" (Bartra 204). In short, the earthly Enkidu teaches Gilgamesh that despite his spark of divinity, he is a mortal earthly being, and he is not the center and meaning of the cosmos, but the servant of the gods, beholden to that cosmos.

Now possessing a suitable companion, Gilgamesh is prepared to pursue fame and adventure. In the first of two major adventures, Gilgamesh and Enkikdu travel to the great Cedar Forest (in Lebanon) to challenge its ogre guardian Humbaba (Humwawa). "Humbaba's roar is a Flood, his mouth is Fire, and his breath is Death!...Enlil assigned him as a terror to human beings" (Kovacs 19). With much difficulty the heroes manage to capture the monster. Humbaba, however, who seems to know Enkidu from some previous time, begs him to intervene with Gilgamesh. Instead, Enkidu advises his friend to make haste in destroying the monster. The surviving text is damaged and partially garbled, but its sense is clear.

My friend, Humbaba, Gilgamesh, Guardian of the Forest,
grind up, kill, pulverize (?), and ... him!
Before the Preeminent God Enlil hears,
and the ... gods are full of rage at us. (Kovacs 45)

Gilgamesh finally slays the monster, but not before Humbaba puts a curse on Enkidu. "May he not live the longer of the two, / may Enkidu not have any 'shore'(?) more than his friend Gilgamesh" (Kovacs 46). Gilgamesh now cuts down the great cedar, taking it back to Uruk where it will make a huge door.

The second adventure comes to Gilgamesh in the form of the goddess Ishtar, who is attracted by his beauty. "Come along, Gilgamesh, be you my husband," she pleads, "to me grant your lusciousness" (Kovacs 51). Gilgamesh, however, recollecting the fate of her other mortal consorts, violently rejects the offer. "Where," he asks ironically, "are your bridegrooms that you keep forever?" (Kovacs 52). The lover of her youth, Tammuz (sometimes known as Dumuzi), is now the subject of annual lamentations. Another time, she broke the wing of her lover, the shepherd bird, who must evermore stand in the forest crying "*kappi, kappi*" (Sandars 86), an onomatopoetic pun signifying both the call of a bird and the expression "my wing, my wing!" In turn her lover the lion received "seven and again seven pits" (Kovacs 52), and her lover the stallion received the whip, the goad, and the lash. Another lover, the master herder, she turned into a wolf, so that now his own dogs snap at him, and yet another paramour was turned into a dwarf.

Angered over Gilgamesh's rejection, Ishtar flies to the heavens to seek the help of her divine parents, Anu and Antum. "Father, Gilgamesh has insulted me over and over," she cries. "Gilgamesh has recounted despicable deeds about me, / despicable deeds and curses!" (Kovacs 53). In order to avenge herself, she asks use of the Bull of Heaven, in order to kill Gilgamesh, threatening to smash open the Gates of the Netherworld and release the dead if they do not comply with her wish. Anu relents to these threats, giving her the Bull of Heaven. The bull is recurrent throughout the Middle Eastern and Mediterranean worlds as a figure of power, strength, and violence. The Bull of Heaven's first snort is so strong that it opens a pit in the earth that swallows a hundred men. With a second snort, two hundred men fall in. Finally with the third, Enkidu falls into the pit. He is, however, able to extricate himself, seizing the Bull by the horns. Holding it while twisting its tail, he instructs Gilgamesh to stab it with a sword between the nape and the horns. When Ishtar realizes that the Bull has been killed, she mounts the wall of Uruk: "Woe unto Gilgamesh who slandered me and killed the Bull of

Heaven!" (Kovacs 55). Hearing this, Enkidu tears the hindquarter from the Bull carcass, throwing it at the face of the goddess. Given Ishtar's designs on Gilgamesh, the reference to the Bull's hindquarter may be a euphemism for the Bull's genitals. Indeed the phallic character of the Bull's "thigh" and later "horns" is reinforced when Ishtar and the temple-harlots, priestesses of the cult of Ishtar, begin mourning it.

Gilgamesh's encounter with Ishtar reflects a complex response to the mythic and religious dimensions of his world. Ishtar (or the Sumerian Inanna or the Phoenician Astarte) was the Babylonian goddess of love, fertility, and war (the Hellenic Aphrodite, goddess of love, and her lover, the war god Ares, suggest a parallel conception). The epic's reference to Ishtar's lover or consort Tammuz (or his Sumerian counterpart Dumuzi or the Syrian Adonis) points to a deeper religious connection. Tammuz is an example of what anthropologists term a "dying" god, the mythopoetic center of a pattern in which the god must suffer death, descend into a netherworld, and finally return or rebirth. Typically an annual occurrence, this pattern of death and rebirth relates to fertility and the cycles of nature, especially in relation to the agricultural seasons of harvest, fallowness, and new growth. In the Babylonian context, this involves the ritual murder of the god at the end of spring, the end of the planting season. It is then followed by a period of lament, which in turn is followed by the search for the god by his sister or wife, depending on the version. The process culminates when the sister or wife returns alone. Nevertheless, this reaffirms the fructifying principle of nature, signified by the harvest. In the end the god merely appears again. Analogous patterns also inform such ancient divinities as Osiris, Baal, Dionysius, and Mithra. In the context of religion practice, the pattern shapes various rituals, including what anthropologists term the *hieros gamos*, or sacred marriage, the sexual union of the goddess and her consort, symbolizing the fruitfulness of the earth, followed by the sacrificial death and mourning of the consort to ensure the earth's fertility. In the Babylonian religion the *hieros gamos* of the goddess and consort was performed ritually or literally between the priestesses of Ishtar (through the mediation of the temple harlots, or *harimtu*) and the king, a form of sympathetic magic to assure fertility. Critical of these practices, the biblical prophet Ezekiel complained of the women "weeping for Tammuz" (Ezekiel 8:14).

Given the underlying religious practice, the *Epic of Gilgamesh* dramatizes a number of striking ironies. The hermetically closed relationship between Enkidu and Gilgamesh disrupts the cycles of nature. Enkidu's sexual initiation with the temple harlot (the mortal avatar of the goddess) parallels on the human level the *hieros gamos*, whereas Gilgamesh's rejection of Ishtar breaks the ritual pattern on the cosmic level. Enkidu's defiant act of throwing the thigh of the Bull of Heaven at Ishtar is a futile gesture, as though nature could be contrary to nature, an irony underlined by Ishtar's curse. In turn, the subsequent death of Enkidu, followed by Gilgamesh's lament, search, and eventual return alone inverts the mythic pattern in a sort of parody of the ritual practices. Here instead of the bride seeking her lost husband, it is Gilgamesh searching his lost sense of immortality. The fructifying principle that he sustains is not about the fertility of the earth, but the nourishment of fame. In the end, the walls that signify civilization cannot protect humans from the cycles of nature. They carry their nature with them in the clay that constitutes their being.

Enkidu's primary role in the death of Humbaba and the Bull of Heaven evokes the wrath of the gods. Falling ill, he dreams that a convocation of the gods has met, condemning him to death. Despairing over what seems to him the unfairness of the situation, he first curses the great cedar door, associated with Humbaba, and then the hunter and harlot who gave him the self-awareness that made him a human instead of a mere animal living from moment to moment. Paradoxically, his anguished appreciation of his own death, his mortality, makes him most fully human. This almost seems to anticipate the existential concept that humans are "beings-toward-death," that we are most human only when fully and authentically aware of our dying. In a deep sense, Enkidu's state of mind captures what it means to be a human confronting existence without himself.

Enkidu now dreams of the Netherworld, *Kur* (originally the word signified "mountain," but came to mean "remote foreign land [mountainous]" and finally an underground realm of the dead, the ultimate alien land). In one of the surviving Sumerian fragments, the servant Enkidu travels to the underworld to retrieve some lost object for Gilgamesh, only to become trapped. In the epic version, he dreams that he is seized and taken to the "House of Dust" (Kovacs 65). "Everywhere I looked," he says, "there were royal crowns gathered in heaps, / everywhere I listened, it was the bearers of crowns who in the past had ruled the land" (Kovacs 65). So go the glories of the world, the fate of earthly power. He is then taken before Ereshkigal, the Queen of the Netherworld. Here the text is damaged, but we may infer from Gilgamesh's response that Enkidu is condemned. "My friend has had a dream that bodes ill (?)" (Kovacs 65). Awakening from his dream, Enkidu lies down to die, expiring in 12 days, despairing that he has been abandoned.

The conception of the afterlife represented in Enkidu's dream is consistent with what scholars term a pre-Axial worldview, a view found in many archaic religions and civilizations. Here there is little difference between the mundane and the transmundane worlds. Death is in large part a return to the earth, ashes to ashes, dust to dust. Parallels may be found in the subterranean oblivion of *Shoel* in pre-rabbinic Judaism, Vedic Hinduism, and early Daoism, as well as in some of the traditional religious views found in Africa, in which the soul of the dead shifts from "living-dead," in which it possesses some personal identity, to a condition of nonexistent, collective immortality. By contrast, Axial and post-Axial religions, including Zoroastrianism, Brahmanic Hinduism, Buddhism, Christianity, Islam, and other salvation religions, are characterized by a move toward transcendence and a separation between the mundane and transmundane, between the conception of the human and the deity. The fate confronted by Enkidu is similar to that encountered by Odysseus in Homer's *Odyssey*, when he finds his fallen comrade Achilles among the shadowy figures of the Netherworld:

> No winning words about death to me, shining Odysseus!
> By god, I'd rather slave on earth for another man—
> some dirt-poor tenant farmer who scrapes to keep alive—
> than rule down here over all the breathless dead. (11.554–558)

Reduced to a cold and shadowy state of existence, Achilles finds consolation only in the achievements of his son, the lesson being that transcendence is not personal, but in the record of one's deeds or those of one's progeny. It is also the lesson that Gilgamesh must learn.

Confronted with the death of his friend—and by extension, himself—Gilgamesh initially denies anything is wrong, coming to his friend's side only when he hears the death rattle. Still refusing to acknowledge Enkidu's death in the face of the evidence, he sits by the body for six days and seven nights, preventing it from being buried until a maggot falls out of its nose. Only then does he finally give way to lamentation: "Hear me, O Elders of Uruk, hear me, O men! / I mourn for Enkidu, my friend, / I shriek in anguish like a mourner" (Kovacs 70). Gilgamesh's anguish soon turns to the condition of his own mortality. Wandering about the wilderness, he cries, "I am going to die!—am I not like Enkidu?! / Deep sadness penetrates my core, / I fear death, and now roam the wilderness" (Kovacs 75). He finally decides to go on a quest, seeking the advice of Utanapishtim the Faraway, a man reputed to have survived the great flood and who now lives at the end of the earth. Gilgamesh hopes to learn the secret of eternal life from this ancient being.

Many encounters finally lead Gilgamesh to the edge of the sea, across the "waters of death," and finally to the presence of Utanapishtim. At first, supposing the ancient man would look extraordinary, Gilgamesh does not recognize him, only slowly comprehending with whom he is talking: "But your appearance is not strange—you are like me! / You yourself are not different—you are like me!" he says incredulously, then asking, "How is it that you stand in the Assembly of the Gods, and have found life?" (Kovacs 97).

Utanapishtim explains that the gods were once moved to inflict a cataclysmic flood on the world in order to destroy the human race. The reasons for this are not entirely clear, but separate surviving texts from the Old Babylonian period, most notably the Akkadian *Atrahasis Epic* (Atrahasis is another name for Utanapishtim), attribute the cause to the gods' wrath over increasing population and the noise of the human race. Utanapishtim tells Gilgamesh that the gods took an oath not to warn the humans, but the trickster Ea (the *nissiku* or "Clever Prince") gets around the letter of this oath by warning Utanapishtim's reed house and wall. "Hear, O reed house! Understand, O wall!... Tear down the house and build a boat!... Spurn possessions and keep alive living beings!" (Kovacs 98). Because of this ruse, Utanapishtim, his family, and a sampling of the creatures of the world survive the deluge. Indeed, the devastation is so terrible that even the gods are frightened, "cowering like dogs, crouching by the outer wall" (Kovacs 101), soon regretting their actions, especially when they realize that there are no longer people to make sacrifices to them. Utanapishtim's boat finally lodges on Mt. Nimush, and when the waters recede, he makes a burnt offering to the gods, earning their appreciation. By way of thanks, Utanapishtim and his wife are granted immortality and allowed to reside at the Mouth of the Rivers.

Utanapishtim advises Gilgamesh that eternal life is impossible for humans. Only the gods are sleepless, troubled, and restless. To prove his point, he challenges Gilgamesh to stay awake for seven days. Gilgamesh accepts the challenge, but instantly dozes off, sleeping for seven days, exhausted by his many hardships in the wilderness. For each day that he sleeps, Utanapishtim's wife places a newly baked loaf of bread beside his head, leaving the old ones as well. When the hero finally awakes on the seventh day, insisting that he had not slept, but merely rested his eyes, Utanapishtim points to the seven loaves of bread, the oldest hard and desiccated, the next oldest stale, the next soggy, the next covered with white mold, the next sprouting gray mold, and the newest still fresh. The succession of loaves suggests the stages of human aging, from the youth in full vigor to the grey-haired, to the white-haired, to the decaying corpse, and finally to the hard dry bones of one who has returned to the elements.

Chagrined, Gilgamesh despairs. By way of compensation, Utanapishtim tells him about an underwater plant that though it will not give immortality, will produce rejuvenation, making one young again. With the aid of the ferryman who earlier carried him over the water to Utanapishtim's house, Gilgamesh dives and gets the plant, only to have it stolen by a snake, which sloughs off its old skin in the process, presumably part of its rejuvenation. (Some scholars see parallels with the serpent and the fruit in Genesis 3:1–13.) With nothing left to do, Gilgamesh has the ferryman transport him back to Uruk, where he points to the brickwork of the walls, closing the epic narrative on the same note with which it began: "is not (even the core of) the brick structure of kiln-fired brick, / and did not the Seven Sages themselves lay out its plan" (Kovacs 107). He adds, "One league city, one league palm gardens, one league lowlands, / the open area (?) of the Ishtar Temple, / three leagues and the open area (?) of Uruk it (the wall) encloses" (Kovacs 108). In the end, Gilgamesh acknowledges that the boundaries that mark civilization also include the forces of nature signified by Ishtar and her temple. Generation and decay are an integral part of what it means to be human. The clay used to form Enkidu or Gilgamesh must inevitably return to its source in the House of Dust. The only immortality that clay beings have is that of kiln-fired brick, signifying the walls that mark civilization, or the clay tablets that mark great deeds and accomplishments. It is this immortality that Gilgamesh enjoys.

SUBSEQUENT INFLUENCE

The story of Gilgamesh is part of the common ground that nurtures Judaism, Christianity, Islam, and beyond. The influence of the *Epic of Gilgamesh* falls into two periods. The first relates to before it was "lost" after a succession of conquests that submerged the Mesopotamian culture, and the second period came after the work's recovery and translation in 1872. The prevalence of versions and copies of the epic, albeit fragmentary, as well as the relative stability of the text testify to the popularity of the *Epic of Gilgamesh* within the Mesopotamian world. Perhaps taking the lesson of Gilgamesh to heart, the Assyrian king Ashurbanipal (685–627 B.C.E.), a scholar as well as a warrior, built a huge library in Nineveh to house and preserve the great works of Assyrian literature, his own hedge against mortality. The most complete Sumerian and Akkadian versions of the *Epic of Gilgamesh*, including those excavated by Austen Henry Layard and deciphered by George Smith, emerge from this collection. After Ashurbanipal's death, the Assyrian empire began to disintegrate. With the sack of Nineveh in 612 B.C.E., power first shifted to Babylonia, then to Persia and the formation of the Achaemedian empire (559–330 B.C.E.) after the conquest of Cyrus the Great, and then to the formation of Hellenistic Persia (the Seleucid empire, 330–150 B.C.E.) after the conquest of Alexander the Great.

The influence of the *Epic of Gilgamesh* on other works in its world is more difficult to ascertain with any confidence. Striking similarities between the account of the flood in the epic and that in biblical Genesis, as well as other references, suggest the possibility that Jewish scribes were familiar with it or other Babylonian versions; this exposure might have occurred during the

Babylonian exile between the fall of Jerusalem in 587 B.C.E. and the construction of the "second" Temple and a new Jewish state after the liberation granted by Cyrus the Great in 538 B.C.E. Some scholars think they see a reference to Gilgamesh and Humbaba in the Aramaic *Book of Giants,* found among the Dead Sea Scrolls. Others argue that an allusion to a King Ganmagos, found in the Syriac writings of Theodor Bar Qoni, a Nestorian Christian of the seventh century, may also refer to Gilgamesh (see Kovacs xxxiii). In both these cases, the links to the epic are at best tenuous.

After the epic's reconstruction and recovery, the initial interest in the *Epic of Gilgamesh* centered on its relationship to the Bible, especially as it related to the authority of the biblical account of the deluge. Most scholars now concur that it was the Babylonian material, whether the epics of Gilgamesh or Atrahasis or some similar account, that contributed to Genesis, rather than the other way around. Since then, however, writers and artists have been intrigued and stimulated by the epic for its own sake. In addition to influence on literature, artistic responses range from anime and graphic novels to music and film. Many of the earlier writers drawn to the *Epic of Gilgamesh* were struck by the themes of life, death, and sexuality. The Austrian poet Rainer Maria Rilke expressed an enthusiasm for it, reading first Georg Burckhardt's 1916 German translation and later Arthur Ungard's more literal 1911 version. In a letter to Helene von Nostitz, he wrote, "Here is the epic of death-fear [*Todesfurcht*], descended from time immemorial to mankind, especially the definitive and fatal separation of death and life" (qtd. in Moran 209, my translation). Although Rilke had not yet apparently read the *Epic of Gilgamesh* when he commenced the *Duino Elegies* (1911), the sympathies that would attract him to it are readily apparent: "denk: es erhält sich her Held, selbst der Untergang war ihm / nur ein Vorwand, zu sein: seine letzte Geburt [Remember: the hero lives on. Even his downfall / was only a pretext for attained existence, a final birth]" (Rilke 7). The American poet Charles Olson was drawn to the *Epic of Gilgamesh* and Sumerian literature in general as an "objective" alternative to what he considered the subjective Hellenic tradition. "MASONRY," he declared, "is especially associated with MYTH in man," taking a cue from the Sumerian and other non-Western cultures (Olson 85). They represented for Olson an aesthetic liberation, much the same role that Chinese literature played for Ezra Pound. "As I read it," said Olson, writing on Gilgamesh in his essay "The Gate and the Center," "it is an incredibly accurate myth of what happens to the best of men when they lose touch with the primordial & phallic energies & methodologies which, said this predecessor people of ours, make it possible for man, that participant thing, to take up, straight, nature's, live nature's force" (Olson 173). Several of his poems, including "La Chute"and "Bigmans II," as well as the *Maximus*

Poems, paraphrase passages from the *Epic of Gilgamesh*. Similarly, the poet A. R. Ammons, also attracted to Sumerian culture, alludes to Gilgamesh, most notably in his poem "Gilgamesh Was Very Lascivious."

> Because he sought the mate
>   of his physical divinity
> Gilgamesh
> let many usurp the missing one
> and went
> singly in his tragic excellence. (Ammons 26)

A number of novelists have also used the myth of Gilgamesh. Writer Rhoda Lerman's *Call Me Ishtar* (1973) alludes both to Olson's famous study of Melville, *Call Me Ishmael*, and to the story of Gilgamesh. Equally playful is Philip Roth's 1973 novel, *The Great American Novel*, set in 1933 and featuring a baseball pitcher named Gil Gamesh. In a Borgesian twist on books, libraries, and what it means to be human, the Polish science fiction writer Stanislaw Lem includes a fictitious review of a nonexistent novel based on Gilgamesh in his *A Perfect Vacuum* (1971). Satirizing James Joyce's *Ulysses* and *Finnegans Wake*, and the notion of open-ended rewritings and interpretations that derive from them, he imagines a novel ostensibly retelling the epic, featuring a "GI Joe" Maesch and N. Kiddy, thus making *Gilgamesh* both the oldest and the "crowning achievement of modern literature" (Lem, *Perfect* 40), immortality predicated on the postmodern reinterpretation of texts. Lem also draws on *Gilgamesh* in his 1981 collection *Golem XIV*, available in English as *Imaginary Magnitude* (1984). Here Gilgamesh is the name of a supercomputer with "Self-perfecting Intelligence" (Lem, *Imaginary* 105), a modern variation on the theme of mortality in the life-infused clay, the ghost in the machine.

The epic has also enjoyed a number of adaptations. The novelist John Gardner, famous for his oblique treatment of the Old English epic *Beowulf*, telling the story from the perspective of the monster in his novel *Grendel* (1971), completed a translation of the *Epic of Gilgamesh* in collaboration with the Assyriologist John Maier (1981). Similarly, African American poet Yusef Komunyakaa, winner of the 1993 Pulitzer Prize for his collection *Neon Vernacular*, has prepared a verse adaptation of the *Epic of Gilgamesh* for the stage, working with playwright Chad Gracia. "This road is neither ahead / nor behind, and now the days / of darkness turn into blindness / and my eyes refuse to set / on any path, where ascension / is descension and / descension is a bottomless pit / in the sky," says Gilgamesh, lost in the wilderness after the death of Enkidu (Komunyakaa 62).

Scholars have found a variety of references or allusions to *Gilgamesh* in a number of works of modern fiction, especially in the treatment of the hero. Some of these include Joseph Conrad's *Lord Jim* (1900), Willa Cather's *The Professor's House* (1925), William Faulkner's *Absalom, Absalom!* (1936) and *Go Down, Moses* (1942), J.R.R. Tolkien's *The Return of the King* (1955), Joseph Heller's *Catch-22* (1961), Italo Calvino's *Invisible Cities* (1972), Kurt Vonnegut's *Breakfast of Champions* (1973), and Michael Ondaaje's *In the Skin of a Lion* (1987). Also of interest is the stop-action animated interpretation by the Quay Brothers in their 11-minute 1985 film *The Unnameable Little Broom*, a surrealistic take on the hermetic world that Gilgamesh tried to create, suspended from the flow of nature. The enduring attraction of the epic is well summarized by David Damrosch: "Today as in antiquity, Gilgamesh's story underwrites explorations of issues of tyranny and justice, love and death, and art and immortality" (Damrosch 256). After 3,600 years, Gilgamesh is very much alive and well.

SUGGESTED READINGS

Ammons, A. R. *Collected Poems: 1951–1971*. New York: W. W. Norton, 1972.

Bartra, Roger. *Wild Men in the Looking Glass: The Mythic Origins of European Otherness*. Trans. Carl T. Berrisford. Ann Arbor: University of Michigan Press, 1994.

Collon, Dominique. *First Impressions: Cylinder Seals in the Ancient Near East*. Chicago: University of Chicago Press, 1987.

Damrosch, David. *The Buried Book: The Loss and Rediscovery of thee Great Epic of Gilgamesh*. New York: Henry Holt, 2006.

Eisenstadt, S. N., ed. *The Origins and Diversity of Axial Age Civilizations*. Albany: State University of New York Press, 1980.

Eliade, Mircea. *From the Stone Age to the Eleusinian Mysteries*. Vol. 1 of *A History of Religious Ideas*. Trans. Willard R. Trask. Chicago: University of Chicago Press, 1978.

Foster, Benjamin. "Gilgamesh: Sex, Love and the Ascent of Knowledge." *Love and Death in the Ancient Near East*. Ed. John H. Marks and Robert M. Good. Guilford, CT: Four Quarters Publishing, 1987. 21–42.

Gardner, John, and John Maier, trans. *Gilgamesh*. Translated from the Sîn-leqi-unninnī version. New York: Vintage Books, 1985.

Gladstone, William Ewart. *The Gladstone Diaries*. Vol 8. Ed. H. C. G. Matthew. Oxford: Clarendon Press, 1982.

Hughes, Joseph J. "Echoes of *Gilgamesh* in Vonnegut's *Breakfast of Champions*." *Publications of the Missouri Philological Association* 16 (1991): 93–97.

Jacobs, Robert G. "*Gilgamesh*: The Sumerian Epic that Helped *Lord Jim* to Stand Alone." *Conradiana* 4.2 (1972): 23–32.

Jacobsen, Thorkild. *The Treasures of Darkness: A History of Mesopotamian Religion*. New Haven: Yale University Press, 1976.

Joyce, James. *Finnegans Wake*. New York: Viking Press, 1959.

Kirk, G. S. *Myth: Its Meaning and Function in Ancient and Other Cultures*. Cambridge: Cambridge University Press, 1973.

Komunyakaa, Yusef, and Chad Gracia. *Gilgamesh: A Verse Play*. Middletown, CT: Wesleyan University Press, 2006.

Kovacs, Maureen Gallery, trans. *The Epic of Gilgamesh*. Stanford: Stanford University Press, 1989.

Kramer, Samuel Noah. *History Begins at Sumer*. Garden City: Doubleday Anchor Books, 1959.

Lambert, Wilfred G. "Gilgamesh in Literature and Art: The Second and First Millennia." *Monsters and Demons in the Ancient and Medieval Worlds*. Ed. Ann E. Farkas, Prudence O. Harper, and Evelyn B. Harrison. Mainz: von Zabern, 1987. 37–52.

Lem, Stanislaw. *Imaginary Magnitude*. Trans. Marc E. Heine. New York: Harcourt Brace Jovanovich, 1984.

———. *A Perfect Vacuum*. Trans. Michael Kandel. Evanston, IL: Northwestern University Press, 1979.

Lerman, Rhoda. *Call Me Ishtar*. Syracuse: Syracuse University Press, 1973.

Maier, John R. "Charles Olson and the Poetic Uses of Mesopotamian Scholarship." *Journal of the American Oriental Society* 103.1 (January–March 1983): 227–235.

———. *Gilgamesh: A Reader*. Wauconda, IL: Bolchazy-Carducci Publishers, 1998.

Micale, Jennifer. "The Walls of Uruk: Cather's *The Professor's House*, the Universal Hero, and *The Epic of Gilgamesh*." *Willa Cather Pioneer Memorial Newsletter* 42.3 (Winter–Spring 1999): 67–73.

Mobley, Gregory. "The Wild Man in the Bible and the Ancient Near East." *Journal of Biblical Literature* 116.2 (Summer 1997): 217–233.

Moran, William J. "Rilke and the Gilgamesh Epic." *Journal of Cuneiform Studies* 32.4 (October 1980): 208–210.

Olson, Charles. *Collected Prose*. Ed. Donald Allen and Benjamin Friedlander. Berkeley: University of California Press, 1997.

Oppenheim, A. Leo. *Ancient Mesopotamia: Portrait of a Dead Civilization*. Chicago: Chicago University Press, 1977.

Pritchard, James B., ed. *The Ancient Near East: An Anthology of Texts and Pictures*. 2 vols. Princeton: Princeton University Press, 1968.

Rilke, Rainer Maria. *Duino Elegies*. Trans. Edward Snow. New York: North Point Press, 2000.

Roth, Philip. *The Great American Novel*. New York: Holt Rinehart and Winston, 1973.

Sandars, N. K., trans. *The Epic of Gilgamesh*. London: Penguin Books, 1972.

Tigay, Jeffrey H. *The Evolution of the Gilgamesh Epic*. Wauconda, IL: Bolchazy-Carducci Publishers, 2002.

Van De Mieroop, Marc. *Cuneiform Texts and the Writing of History*. London: Routledge, 1999.

Weiner, Steve. "The Quay Brothers' *The Epic of Gilgamesh* and the 'Metaphysics of Obscenity.'" *A Reader in Animation Studies*. Ed. Jayne Pilling. Sydney, Australia: John Libbey, (1997): 25–37.

Westling, Louise. "Women, Landscape, and the Legacy of Gilgamesh in *Absalom, Absalom!* and *Go Down, Moses*." *Mississippi Quarterly: Journal of Southern Culture* 48.3 (1995): 501–521.

2

Attributed to Krishna Dvaipāyana Vyāsa *Mahābhārata*

(c. 350 B.C.E.–400 C.E.)

That which concerns the soul shall be heard here, and that which consists in the five Elements and the three Properties: the unmanifest cause and its products are sung here, and the One who transcends it—that which the greatest of mystics, yoked and possessed of the vigor of the Yoke of meditation, see lodged in their own selves, as an image in a mirror.

—*Mahābhārata* (van Buitenen 1.31)

There is nothing outside of the text.

—Jacques Derrida, *Of Grammatology*, 158

The *Rāmāyana* and the *Mahābhārata* are the great epics of India. The first is about the romance and adventures of the young hero Rama and his wife Sitā, especially with regard to the rescue of Sitā from the multiheaded Rāvana, the demon-king of Ceylon. The second is about the character of India. The title of the *Mahābhārata* itself means the Epic or History of the (descendants) of Great Bharata, a legendary founder of India. At some 88,000 verse couplets (19 volumes in the Poona critical edition) written in the ancient language of Sanskrit, the *Mahābhārata* stands as one of the longest works in world literature, about eight times the combined length of Homer's *Iliad* and *Odyssey*. Only the Sino-Tibetan *Epic of Gesar of Ling,* based on an open-ended tradition of oral ballads, claims to be longer. *Mahābhārata*'s greatness, however, rests not in its size, but in its status as the center and repository of Indian traditions and rituals. Just as the *Iliad* and the *Odyssey* provided a common point of identity that linked the diverse Greek-speaking peoples scattered around the Aegean, so the *Mahābhārata* provides a unifying center around which coalesce the legends, myths, and wisdom traditions of the vastly more diverse regions, languages, and cultures of the Asian subcontinent. It is not so much the foundational text of Hinduism as a melding of legends, mythology, cosmology, wisdom literatures, and philosophical parables that inform the subsequent art, literature, and culture of Hinduism, Jainism, and Sikhism—and to a slightly lesser degree, Buddhism—down to the present. Among the works embedded in the *Mahābhārata* is the *Bhagavad-Gītā*, universally recognized as one of the masterworks of moral and philosophical literature. Comparing the *Rāmāyana* with the *Mahābhārata*, scholar and poet P. Lal observes that the former arouses compassion, the later "cosmic awe" (qtd. in Nandan 201).

The *Mahābhārata* is ostensibly authored by one Krishna Dvaipāyana Vyāsa, who repeatedly appears throughout the text as progenitor of the major characters and an important director of the action as well as the author. As Vyāsa tells his mother, "When you think of me, I shall appear to you if any task needs to be done" (*Mahābhārata*, van Buitenen 1.134). His dual identity as author and character conflates reality with text, equating the narrative fiction with cosmic history, with the *Mahābhārata* as the sum of reality. "Know that Krishna Dvaipāyana Vyāsa is Nārāyana the lord [Vishnu the preserver], for who other than the lord could be the author of the *Mahābhārata*," declared an ancient commentator (qtd. in Hiltebeitel, *Rethinking* 89).

The work reduced to writing that comes down to us derives from the combination, accretion, appropriation, reconfiguration, and interpolation of different regional traditions and historical periods. The resulting whole is often repetitive, digressive, and even at times inconsistent or contradictory. One critic called it a "jungle," with its dense overgrowth of tradition upon tradition. Another called it a "literary unthing [*literarisches Undig*]" (qtd. in Hiltebeitel, *Rethinking* 1). Sanskrit scholar and translator J.A.B. van Buitenen prefers the metaphor of a "library of opera" (xxv). Nevertheless, there is a coherent core. The *Mahābhārata* centers on the heroic exploits and struggles between two sets of cousins, the Pandavas family and the Kauravas family, a struggle that culminates in an apocalyptic war. The Pandavas are helped by their loyal ally Krishna, one of the 10 incarnations of the god Vishnu. Much of the enduring power of the *Mahābhārata* is in the resonance of its characters, not only in their fantastic feats of heroism and military prowess and in their profound nobility, but also in their failings and very recognizable human weaknesses. Their origins are symbolic of what is attractive about them. Each of the five Pandavas brothers has a divine father and a mortal mother, a suggestion that all mortals despite their limitations and flaws share some eternal spark of the divine and that there is a divinity in the ordinary rituals of life. In turn, each confronts the perplexity of finding moral certitude in what seems a morally ambiguous world.

HISTORICAL AND CULTURAL CONTEXT

The word "Hindu" derives from the Persian (Old Iranian) version of the Sanskrit name of the Sindhu River (the Indus) and in its original sense signified a person from India (the Asian subcontinent). Hinduism as it relates to the *Mahābhārata* involves a complex and layered history that can be outlined here only briefly. Scholars of religion distinguish several periods. The earliest is the so-called Vedic period (1400–500 B.C.E.) and involves the migration of Indo-Aryan–speaking cattle herders into the Indus Plain from the Indo-Iranian borderlands in the northwest. (The theme of exile, wandering in the wilderness, or migration is recurrent in the *Mahābhārata*.) The Indo-Aryan language is closely related to Old Iranian, and many of the names of Vedic gods are linguistically similar to those of figures found in the Iranian *Avesta*, the sacred scriptures of Zoroastrianism. Working backward from cognate languages and consistent patterns of sound shifts, linguists have reconstructed Indo-European as a source language and culture for both modern European and Indian languages. It also accounts for some shared concepts and mythic patterns. These Indo-Aryan–speaking cattle herders were polytheistic, though their ritual practice centered on the cult of the fire sacrifice (*yajña*), related to the continual regeneration of the universe. Their hymns and prayers were later written down as sacred scriptures, the *Vedas* (literally knowledge or wisdom), including the *Rig-Veda*, with the philosophical and religious aspects of these elaborated in the various *Upanisads*.

Already present on the Indus Plain was a civilization that archeologists call the Harappa culture, after the excavation of the cities Harappa and Mohenjo-Daro. Little can be said about this culture aside from the facts of an extended urban civilization and settled agriculture. Ancient accounts say that they were dark complexioned, which may contribute to why Krishna and Vyāsa are dark skinned. It is also suggests that the Hindu god Śiva, though deriving from the Vedic god Rudra, owes much of his form and character to Harappa culture.

The interaction of these cultures led to the next phase of development: Brahmanic Hinduism, or the Brahmanic synthesis (500 B.C.E.–467 C.E.). This involved the rise of a priest class (the Brahmans) and social structure (the caste system), undergirded by an elaborate cosmology. Two tendencies were at work, a drift toward monism, seeing the diversity of reality as unified by some underlying principle, and theism as the focus of ritual devotion (*bhakti*). The various gods became more concrete in their form (hierarchy and theogony), while at the same time understood as part of a larger unity. As one hymn in the *Rig-Veda* declares, "They call him Indra, Mitra, Varuna, Agni, and he is heavenly nobly winged Garutmān. / To what is One, sages give many a title" (*Hymns* 1.164.46). Out of this comes the codification of the Hindu trinity coupled with their respective consorts: Brahma the creator with Sarasvatī, Vishnu the preserver with Lakshmī, and Śiva the destroyer-transformer with variously Parvati, Kālī, and Durgā. This trinity is somewhat artificial, however. Brahma tends to shift to the background, and Hindu devotion and cult practice, down to the present, tends to center on Śiva (the ascetically minded Saivites), Vishnu (the Vaishnavites), or their consorts or incarnations. In addition to these, there is a large assortment of *Devi* ("shining ones," a word cognate through Indo-European roots with our words "divinity" and "divine"). These include gods such as Indra (a king-warrior god), Agni (god of fire), Kama (god of love), and Varuna (god of the sea).

The later phase of the Brahminic synthesis related to the rise and decline of the Mauryan dynasty (324–184 B.C.E.), reaching its high point with the reign of the Indian emperor Asoka c. 273–232 B.C.E.), who patronized Buddhism, and to the rise and decline of the Gupta dynasty (320–467 C.E.). This period is sometimes referred to as the "golden" or "classical" age of Hinduism and represents the emergence of a distinct Hindu identity forged from the various diverse cultures and religions. It was during this period that the Sanskrit language and literature reached a high level of sophistication. It was also during this period that the great epics the *Rāmāyana* and *Mahābhārata* emerged.

PLOT AND CHARACTER DEVELOPMENT

As it stands in its written form, the *Mahābhārata* is divided into 18 books (*Parvans*), beginning with the *Ādi-parvan*, the "Book of Beginnings," an account of the origins of the families, their problems, and their early exploits, and culminating with the *Svargārohana-parvan*, the "Book of the Ascent to Heaven." It takes in the entire course of human life and relates that to the cycles of nature and the cosmos. The epic is contained in an elaborate narrative frame in which it is supposedly recited by the bard (*Sūta*) Ugraśravas at a festival in honor of King Pariksit of Hastinapura ("City of the Elephant"), who had heard it recited by Vaiśampāyana at a festival hosted by Pariksit's son Janamejaya, a descendent of the Pandavas. In turn, Vaiśampāyana had learned it from Krisna Dvaipāyana Vyāsa, ostensibly both a witness to the original events and the author of the *Mahābhārata*. Whether or not we give much literal credence to this explanation, it suggests how the tales that make up the epic were transmitted orally from festival to festival, from royal court to royal court, layering on and incorporating local legends as it moved from one bard to the next.

Scholars argue that the *Mahābhārata* represents the synthesis of at least four classes of materials. At the center are various hero songs, the accounts of warriors and battles. Some of these stretch back into antiquity and may even share sources with some Western myths. Thus, for instance, the blind Kauravas king Dhritarāstra and his one hundred sons may point to common origins with the (figuratively blind) Trojan king Priam and his one hundred sons, as do some similarities in the feats of the Pandavas hero Arjuna and the Greek Odysseus. Then there are various didactic treatises on law, philosophy, and ethics that derived from the priest class, the Brahmans. This process, sometimes referred to as brahmanization, often gave a religious tone or interpretation to what were otherwise secular stories. To this were added the *Purana*, literally the "old things." These included local myths and legends, the stories of the gods Vishnu and Śiva, and the different cosmologies. Finally, there were materials related to saintly hermits and mendicants, the so-called "forest dwellers" who had renounced life and taken up a life of asceticism and meditation in the forests. These tales include the lives and the sayings of these saints. Not surprisingly, the heroes of the epic eventually abdicate power and retire to the forests at the end of their lives.

Although it is easy to get lost in the tangled genealogies, going into some detail about the beginnings is important for appreciating the intertwined webs of fate and cosmic allegory at play in the *Mahābhārata*. In turn, many of the episodes have achieved an iconic status in Indian culture that make them instantly recognizable. The story proper begins with the virtuous king Santanu, who weds a beautiful woman who turns out to be the human incarnation of the river Gāngā. This celestial woman marries under the proviso that Santanu never question her actions. Then she throws the first seven of their newborn sons into the river. Horrified and perplexed by this, Santanu finally intervenes, asking her not to drown their eighth. The lady grants the wish, but departs because of the broken proviso, explaining that these children were really gods that had been forced to assume human form because of a curse. Her action in bearing and throwing them into the river was to speed them through the cycle of reincarnation and back to their divine form. The eighth son, now forced to remain in human form, is eventually known as Bhīshma ("The Terrible"), because of a vow of celibacy that he takes. In the epic he becomes the wise, grandfatherly guardian of both Pandavas and Kauravas.

Santanu next encounters Satyavati, the beautiful daughter of a fisherman. Struck by her celestial beauty, Santanu wishes to marry, but the fisherman will not grant permission unless Santanu guarantees that only his daughter's children will inherit the throne. Santanu despairs because this would mean cheating Bhīshma out of his birthright. Bhīshma, however, in an act of nobility, renounces any claim to the crown so that his father might marry Satyavati. Further, he takes a vow of celibacy that he might not have children who would later dispute the crown. For this vow he receives the name Bhīshma. He also receives the boon of dying only when he chooses it, a sort of quasi-immortality.

The union of Santanu and Satyavati results in two sons, with Bhīshma serving as their guardian on the death of their father. When the eldest son dies in battle, Bhīshma arranges the marriage of the younger, Vicitravīrya, by kidnapping the three daughters of the neighboring King of Kāśī: Ambā, Ambikā, and Ambālikā. Ambā, the eldest, begs to be returned to her fiancé, so is released by Bhīshma. (Ironically, this gesture will eventually come back to haunt him, causing him to call in his boon to choose the time for his own death.) The other two, however, marry Vicitravīrya, living with him without issue until he suddenly dies of consumption. Despairing how to save the dynasty, Satyavati reveals that she previously bore another son by an ascetic sage. When young, she was afflicted with a disorder that gave her the odor of fish. In exchange for a sexual favor, the sage cured her. The result of this union was none other than Vyāsa, the author of the *Mahābhārata*. He is also called Krishna because of his dark complexion (the word means black or dark). Because he is his mother's other son, he is allowed by the code of the warrior class (the *ksatriyas*) to substitute for his dead half-brothers, thereby preserving the bloodline. The liasons are arranged, but because of his dark complexion, and because he was a forest dweller, he is covered with grime and matted hair, making him a frightful sight. Thus, when Ambikā sees Vyāsa, she closes her eyes in terror, and as a result, their son, Dhritarāstra, is born blind. When Ambālikā sees Vyāsa, she blanches with fear, with the result that their son, Pandu, is born pale. The subsequent children of blind Dhritarāstra form the Kauravas line of the family (the Kuru), and those of Pandu form the Pandavas line. Vyāsa also fathers a son, Vidura, by one of the lady's maids. By a complex symbolism, Vyāsa becomes both the literal progenitor of the conflicting parties of the epic as well as the author recounting it.

Dhritarāstra marries the virtuous Gāndhari, who because of her father's devotion to the god Śiva, was granted the boon of bearing one hundred sons. Discovering that her husband is blind, Gāndhari bandages her eyes with a cloth in an act of devotion and sacrifice, so that she will not excel him. Gāndhari becomes pregnant, but after a two-year gestation gives birth to a hard spherical mass of flesh. In accordance with Vyāsa's instructions, this mass is divided into one hundred pieces and placed into jars of ghee (clarified butter). By this means, the one hundred sons and one daughter of Dhritarāstra and Gāndhari are produced. The two oldest are the princes Duryodhana and

Duhsasana, both consumed by envy and ambition. Dhritarāstra is warned that the portents are dire and that Duryodhana should be abandoned: "Your son [Duryodhana] will be the exterminator of your race" (*Mahābhārata*, Narasimhan 19). Figuratively as well as literally blind, Dhritarāstra ignores these warnings, preferring his loyalty to blood and thereby contributing to the fulfillment of the prophecy.

At the same time, Pandu has married a woman known as Kuntī. Pandu, however, suffers under a curse. Hunting in the forest, he sees two deer mating. Shooting them with five arrows, he learns that the deer were really a forest dweller and his wife in disguise. Thus, Pandu is condemned to die the moment he ever has sexual relations. Kuntī, however, knows a magical incantation that will allow conception through divine mediation. By this way she produces five sons, one for each arrow. Yudhisthira, the oldest, and the embodiment of wisdom, is fathered by Dharma (god of wisdom). Bhīma, the second, a hero of mighty strength and stature, is fathered by Vayu (god of the wind). Arjuna, the greatest of all warriors, is fathered by Indra (king of the celestials). Finally, the twins, Nakula and Sahadeva, are fathered by the twin Asvins (physicians of heaven). In addition to these, it turns out that the Pandavas have a half brother unbeknownst to them, analogous to Vyāsa's relationship with the sons of Santanu. Before her marriage to Pandu, Kuntī had used the magic incantation to produce, by Surya (the Sun-god), a son known as Karna. Karna, who was born with armor and earrings, was thrown in the river by Kuntī, to hide her transgression, but was rescued and raised by a charioteer. Disguised as a Brahman, the god Indra once approached the young Karna, asking for his armor and earrings as alms. In an act of spontaneous generosity, Karna (whose name means the cutter) hacked them off of his body and gave them still dripping with blood to Indra. Duly impressed by this act, Indra gave him the Sakti, a celestial weapon of cataclysmic power.

Even in their conception and gestation, there is a fierce and increasingly rancorous competition between the two sets of cousins. With the untimely death of Pandu, Bhīshma assumes guardianship, arranging for all of the cousins to be educated together, putting them under the tutelage of Drona, master of the arts of war. Among the various early adventures and conflicts between the cousins, two are of special note. One day Drona is teaching archery. Setting up a straw bird target, he tells Yudhisthira to take aim, asking him to say what he sees. Yudhisthira replies, "The tree and the bird, the bow and the arrow, and my arm, and you" (Buck 24). Drona tells him to stand aside, and one by one, he asks the others the same question, each time receiving a similar answer. He finally asks Arjuna, "Tell me what you see." Arjuna replies, "a bird." Drona then asks him to describe the bird, to which Arjuna replies, "I cannot, I see only his neck" (*Mahabharata*, Buck 24). Pleased with this expression of single-minded concentration, Drona tells Arjuna to shoot. Having made him the best of all archers, Drona compels Arjuna to promise him one thing: "if ever I come against you, along or with many, you will fight to win" (*Mahabharata*, Buck 25).

The superior abilities and accomplishments of Bhīma and Arjuna continually rankle the wicked-minded Duryodhana, nourishing his jealousy and wrath. Uncertain of his prowess against them, however, he is restrained from seeking revenge. One day in the arena, Karna suddenly appears, challenging Arjuna to a contest of skill. Not knowing Karna's real identity as a half brother, and invoking the rule that only another prince would be worthy to fight him, Arjuna refuses the challenge. Sensing an opportunity, Duryhodhana declares that he will install Karna as the ruler of one of his kingdoms, thereby making him socially worthy. This cements Karna's friendship with Duryhodhana and his resentment against Arjuna. Now allied with Karna, Duryhodhana feels emboldened to plot the destruction of the Pandavas.

The first attempt involves the "fire house," or Palace of Lac. The Pandavas travel to a festival. Duryhodhana, however, arranges that the palace prepared for them be constructed of flammable materials and saturated with ghee (in a cattle culture, clarified butter was the chief combustible fuel, just as olive oil was in the Mediterranean world) and lacquer. Sensing that they are being sent into a firetrap, the Pandavas have a tunnel excavated. Setting the house on fire themselves, the five brothers and their mother Kuntī escape, the charred bones of six others misidentified as them. This initiates a series of adventures as the brothers and mother abandon Hastinapura and wander the forest, fighting various demons and keeping themselves concealed.

One day, Arjuna attends a *svayamvara*, or marriage festival, staged for Draupadī, daughter of King Drupada. To win her hand, the successful contestant must perform the feat of stringing a magic bow and then shooting five arrows at a target through a small aperture. The motif of this contest occurs in various epic traditions. Rāma must do something similar to win the hand of Sitā in the *Rāmāyana*, as does Odysseus at the end of Homer's *Odyssey* in order to establish his identity and recover the hand of his wife Penelope. These similarities point either to a common source or to the conflation of several traditions into each other. Arjuna is successful in the contest, thereby winning the hand of Draupadī. Returning home, he announces jokingly to his mother Kuntī that he has won "alms" that day. Kuntī, the archetypal mother, not realizing to what Arjuna is referring, declares, "Share equally, all of you, whatever you have got" (*Mahābhārata*, Narasimhan 37). Soon realizing that the "alms" means Draupadī, Kuntī regrets her words, but this maternal declaration has the irrevocable force of law. Vyāsa justifies the polyandry by explaining that in an earlier incarnation, Draupadī had prayed for a husband five times, so is now rewarded with five husbands. Thus Draupadī becomes the bride of all five of the Pandavas brothers and thereafter the symbol of veneration in Indian culture as the virtuous wife. "Draupadī," the wise Yudhisthira declares, "shall be the queen of us all, as ordained by our mother" (*Mahābhārata*, Narasimhan 39).

The Pandavas make themselves known to the cousins but, at the urging of Kuntī, resist seeking revenge. Rather than challenging the Kurus for their inheritance, the Pandavas set up a separate kingdom, and their capital, Indraprastha (near modern Delhi), soon exceeds Hastinapura in splendor. Duryhodhana feels humiliated and diminished by the Pandavas' success. "I am filled with envy which burns me day and night," he confesses to Śakuni, his maternal uncle. "I feel dried up like a small pond in the summer" (*Mahābhārata*, Narasimhan 48). This time Duryhodhana challenges Yudhisthira to a dice game with unlimited stakes. Because Yudhisthira naively supposes himself an expert at dice games, and forgetting the counsel of the *Rig-Veda* that playing games of chance is a betrayal of the will (*Hymns* 7.86.6), he is easily manipulated. Śakuni, an expert at cheating, plays for Duryhodhana. When Śakuni wins the first round, Yudhisthira tellingly responds, "You won that take by cheating. Fie on you, O Śakuni! Let us play staking thousands" (*Mahābhārata*, Narasimhan 50). A true gambling addict, however, he supposes he can beat the odds by increasing the stakes, with the result that he soon loses all of his wealth, his kingdom, and then one by one each of his brothers. In one last desperate throw of the dice, he finally loses the Pandavas' wife, Draupadī. Ignoring all warnings of honor and propriety, and drunk with success, Duryhodhana orders that Draupadī be brought before the men, her hair disheveled and her single garment spotted with menstrual blood, a shameful act deeply offensive to her virtue. Only Duryhodhana, Śakuni, Duhśāsana, and Karna are delighted by Draupadī's humiliation. The rest of the court is shocked and saddened, but to their discredit, they remain silent. Duhśāsana tries to disrobe her, but in a miracle wrought by the god Lord Krishna, her garments are instantly replaced the moment they are ripped off, with Duhśāsana finally dropping from exhaustion, the floor of the hall covered in cloth. In response to this attempt on Draupadī's honor and dignity, Bhīma swears the prophetic oath that he will one day tear open Duhśāsana's chest and drink his blood. In continued defiance, Duryhodhana bares his left thigh before Draupadī and her husbands, a ritual gesture of rape. To this Bhīma swears the prophetic oath that he will one day smash that thigh in battle.

At long last shamed by his sons' dishonorable actions, and spurred to action by Draupadī's enduring virtue, the blind king Dhritarāstra finally intervenes, granting Draupadī three wishes. She accepts the first two, thereby winning the freedom of her husbands, but refuses the third. "O best of kings, avarice kills virtue; I do not wish to be greedy.... These my husbands, having been rescued from the miserable state of slavery, will win prosperity by their good deeds" (*Mahābhārata*, Narasimhan 55). After being challenged and losing one last throw of the dice, Yudhisthira, his brothers, and Draupadī are sent into exile, condemned to wander the forests for 12 years and then in the 13th year to hide among the people.

The years of wandering are the occasion for assorted pilgrimages, adventures battling demons and monsters, and even the rescue of the ungrateful Duryodhana and Karna from the iron meshed net of the Gandharvas, celestial musicians. Toward the end of the 12 years, Yudhisthira comes upon a crystal lake, and discovers his four brothers, who had preceded him, lying dead. A voice in the air explains that they had tried to drink the water without answering his questions. Yudhisthira, himself now challenged to answer the voice's questions, readily accedes. What follows is a long catechism of philosophical riddles: for instance, "What is swifter than the wind?" "The mind is swifter than the wind." "Who is the guest that all life is host to?" "Fire." "What is the most valuable possession?" "Knowledge." "What is not thought of until it departs?" "Health." "What is the best happiness?" "Contentment." "What is honesty?" "That is to look, and to see every living creature as yourself, bring your own will to live, and your own fear of death." "What is the rarest thing?" "To know when to stop." "What is true wealth?" "Love and kindness are better than gold; honor is more valuable than rooms full of jewels" (*Mahābhārata*, Buck 120–122). The voice is pleased with Yudhisthira's answers, identifying himself as none other than his divine father Dharma (god of wisdom) and bringing the others back to life. This contest of riddles is the thematic counterpart and contrary to the game of dice, success depending on wisdom, rather than cheating or chance.

Having completed their 12 years of forest exile, the Pandavas begin their 13th year in disguise, taking residence in the court of the neighboring Virāta, king of Matsya. Each takes on an identity that represents a wry and ironic squint at his or her conventional persona. Thus, Yudhisthira presents himself as a Brahman expert in dice games; Bhīma, the fierce giant, as a cook and animal trainer; Arjuna, the warrior and embodiment of masculinity as a eunuch and dance master; the twins Nakula and Sahadeva as, respectively, horse keeper and cowherd; and finally, the matronly Draupadī as a ladies maid and hairdresser. The year nearly passes without incident, until the general of king Virāta's army tries to seduce Draupadī, his unwelcome attentions resulting in his being crushed beyond recognition by Bhīma. The death of Virāta's general leaves his lands unprotected and emboldens Duryodhana and Karna, still wondering about the whereabouts of the Pandavas, to raid

Virāta's cattle. King Virāta's young son, Uttara, accompanied by Arjuna, still
in the feminine disguise of the eunuch, drive off the Kuru. The Pandavas now
make themselves known, and the lines for a final showdown with the Kuru
are drawn.

Both sides make preparations for war, drawing up elaborate rules of engagement, all of which will eventually be violated. One of the profound
paradoxes is that Krishna keeps pressing Yudhisthira to victory by cheating
or deceit—*jihmopayas* (crooked stratagems). They also seek allies. Of special
importance is an alliance with Krishna, son of Vasudeva, renowned for his
wisdom and steadfastness; it will eventually be learned that this Krishna is
none other than the god Lord Krishna, one of the 10 incarnations of the god
Vishnu. At dawn one morning, both Duryodhana and Arjuna enter the tent
of the sleeping Krishna, Duryhodhana taking a plush seat near Krishna's head
and Arjuna sitting on the ground at Krishna's feet. This choreography is symbolic of their respective characters. Krishna offers them a choice. They can
have either his vast army or himself as an unarmed noncombatant. Although
Duryhodhana may have arrived first, Krishna saw Arjuna first, so he is granted
the first choice. Showing the same wisdom that informed Yudhisthira's earlier
riddle contest, Arjuna selects Krishna without the slightest hesitation. Duryhodhana takes the army, claiming he would have selected it had he been first.
Their choices are expressive of the inner personality.

The *Mahābhārata* devotes some seven books to the great battle that lasts
18 days and culminates in the annihilation of the Kurus. Grandfather Bhīshma
will lead the Kauravas army for nine days until he chooses death. When Yudhisthira asks Bhīshma what will vanquish him, the old man willingly explains
that he can defeat all warriors except one named Śikhandi. This is because
Śikhandi is really a woman, and the warrior code will not allow him to fight
a woman. In fact, she is none other than Ambā, whom he had kidnapped
and then released when he sought out brides for Vicitravīrya. Ambā, upon
returning to her fiancé, was met only by his rejection, judged by him unclean
and compromised. She thus temporarily assumed the form of a man to avenge
herself. With this knowledge, Arjuna uses Śikhandi as a shield to get close
enough to Bhīshma to pierce him with a fusillade of arrows. Under these circumstances, Bhīshma decides to invoke his long-held boon and wills to die.
(His actual death occurs after the battle and a lengthy sermon on the nature
of reality.) The preceptor Drona now assumes the generalship of the Kauravas
army for the next six days, until by the Pandavas' trickery, he supposes that
his son has been killed, and he allows himself to be killed by Arjuna, who redeems his earlier promise to fight Drona to win. On the sixteenth day, Karna
takes command, until killed by Arjuna when Karna's chariot becomes mired
in the mud. When Karna complains bitterly that the code of the warrior class

does not permit killing a warrior who is down this way, Arjuna reminds him that he betrayed the code when he allowed Draupaudī to be humiliated; thereupon, Arjuna beheads him with his arrow. On the last day, Duryodhana is cornered, hiding under a lake. In a final figurative throw of the dice, he challenges Bhīma to a duel to the death using maces, his skill and practice pitted against Bhīma's raw strength, as with the famous dice game earlier. In the end, however, victory comes from trickery, an ironic comeuppance for Duryodhana's cheating. Following Krishna's advice, Bhīma triumphs by a low blow, shattering Duryodhana's thigh, a fulfillment of his oath, as he had earlier fulfilled his oath to drink the blood of Duhśāsana. The last offensive of the battle occurs when the last three surviving Kuru warriors stage a night raid on the camp of the victorious Pandavas army, killing and burning thousands in their sleep, a final act of treachery blessed by the dying Duryodhana. The Pandavas brothers and Krishna survive because they are away at the time.

The most famous episode of the *Mahābhārata* is the section known as the *Bhagavad-Gītā, The Song of the Lord,* or more literally the *Exalted One.* It occurs in Book 6, the *Bhīshma-parvan* ("The Book of Bhīshma's General-ship"). Before the battle, the two armies line up across from each other, vast arrays of soldiers, war chariots, horses, and elephants. With Krishna serving as charioteer, Arjuna rides between the two armies to blow a conch shell, signaling the start of the battle. Seeing friends and relatives on both sides, Arjuna is consumed with anguish, dropping his weapons and sitting down in his chariot: "Krishna, when I see all my family poised for war, my limbs falter and my mouth goes dry" (*Bhagavadgītā* 71). He explains, "With the destruction of family the eternal family Laws are destroyed. When Law is destroyed, lawlessness bests the entire family" (*Bhagavadgītā* 73). What fol-lows is a debate between Arjuna, who argues that the meaning of our actions comes from the consequences, and Krishna, who counters that it is about duty and devotion *(bhakti).* Krishna argues that the death and destruction are illusion. "There is no becoming of what did not already exist, there is no unbecoming of what does exist" (*Bhagavadgītā* 76). We cannot remain virtuous by refraining from action. That itself is a moral betrayal. Rather we must not give into our desires and love the objects of the illusory world. We must act out of pure duty, renouncing the fruits of our actions. Thus one acts "without hatred of any creature, friendly and compassionate without posses-siveness and self-pride, equable in happiness and unhappiness, forbearing, contented, always yoked, mastering himself" (*Bhagavadgītā* 123). After lis-tening to a lengthy discourse on metaphysics and the social implications and the various ways we show devotion, Arjuna asks to see Krishna in his divine form and is struck with awe:

I see all Gods in your body, O God,
And all creatures in all their varieties—
On his lotus seat the sovereign Brahmā,
The seers all and the snakes divine.
Your own infinitude stretching away,
Many arms, eyes, bellies, and mouths do I see
No end do I see, no beginning, no middle,
In you, universal in power and form. (*Bhagavadgītā* 113)

Asked to identify himself, Krishna answers in words later quoted by the physicist J. Robert Oppenheimer, upon witnessing the first atomic bomb blast:

I am Time grown old to destroy the world,
Embarked on the course of world annihilation. (*Bhagavadgītā* 117)

Finally regaining his equanimity, Arjuna returns to his chariot and blows the conch shell, and the battle begins.

The last books of the *Mahābhārata* are devoted to the aftermath of the war and to the treatment of various rituals and philosophical themes. Of particular interest are the last two books, the *Mahāprasthānika-parvan* ("The Book of the Great Departure") and the *Svargārohana-parvan* ("The Book of the Ascent to Heaven"). These books tell how after many years, the Pandavas brothers and Draupadī renounce secular power and set out on one last pilgrimage. One by one, each dies, falling by the wayside, until only Yudhisthira and a dog who has been following them are left. The god Indra appears to Yudhisthira in a chariot, explaining that his brothers have already renounced their bodies and gone to the celestial realms. Indra now invites Yudhisthira to join them, though with the proviso that he must abandon the dog who has been keeping him company. Yudhisthira balks. "I do not wish for prosperity if I have to abandon a creature who is devoted to me" (*Mahābhārata*, Narasimhan 209). Upon these words, the dog is transformed into Dharma, who declares that no one in heaven is Yudhisthira's equal. Yudhisthira is now translated to the celestial realms where he is appalled to discover Duryodhana and the other Kauravas in radiant spender. He is next shown a dark, infernal realm where he sees his brothers and Draupadī in torment. Confronted with a cosmos in which the wicked prosper and the virtuous suffer, the indignant Yudhisthira chooses the companionship of those he understands to be virtuous, even though it means going to hell. Suddenly, Indra and the other celestials appear, and the dark scene dissipates to reveal a pleasant spot. Indra explains that all of this was illusion, that his wife and brothers enjoy heaven. "Hell,

O son, should be seen by all kings. There is some good and bad in all things. You once deceived Drona concerning his son, and have therefore been shown hell by an act of deception" (*Mahābhārata*, Narasimhan 213). Thus, in the end, the virtuous Pandavas achieved the celestial regions by the merit of their "word, thought, and deed" (*Mahābhārata*, Narasimhan 215).

THEMES

Nobel laureate Amartya Sen (Economics, 1998) jokes that prolixity and loquaciousness are not alien to India, pointing to the length of the *Mahābhārata* as evidence (Sen 3). On a more serious level, he suggests that this points to a willingness in the Indian character to weigh all the opposing arguments and counterarguments with care and sympathy. Such an open-mindedness is central to the meaning of the *Mahābhārata*. In its vastness, the text attempts to unfold and assess an array of interconnected problems in cosmology, metaphysics, epistemology, morality, ethics, politics, social order, and gender. The debate between Krishna and Arjuna in the *Bhagavad-Gītā* is a microcosm that informs the whole.

The central debate not only of the *Bhagavad-Gītā*, but of the *Mahābhārata* as a whole, relates to the nature of dharma. Yudhisthira is known by the epithet the *dharma-rāja*, and in a very real sense, the epic is about his education in dharma. The meaning of the word is difficult to grasp, a difficulty that underlines Yudhisthira's own perplexity. Literally, dharma means "what holds together." It signifies the moral or canonical laws and traditions that give society its order and cohesion. At the same time, it signifies the principles that give order and meaning to the cosmos and, because humans are part of the cosmos, an order that is inscribed into their inner being. The problem of dharma centers on the dilemma of when our intuition of righteousness comes into conflict with the external traditions, the problem of resolving the conflict between the spirit and the letter of the law, between general principles and particular circumstances. The goal is *moksha* (liberation, release, spiritual freedom), to achieve a perfect harmony between inner and outer, to become one with the great spirit. Krishna tells Arjuna, "When he sees me in everything and sees everything in me, I will not be lost to him and he will not be lost to me. He who shares in me as living in all creatures and thus becomes one with me, he is a yogin" (*Bhagavadgītā* 97). There are no easy formulas, no guarantees. The wisdom that Yudhisthira seeks is one that we must constantly seek, an unending negotiation between the intuition of inner dharma and the laws of outer dharma. D. S. Sarma articulates the essence of dharma and the *Mahābhārata* as a whole when he writes, "*dharma* is *moksha* in the making. If *moksha* is complete divinity, *dharma* is divinity under human conditions" (qtd. in Morgan 21).

Hinduism with its myriad gods and elaborate cosmology can be sustained on a number of levels. For the less educated or sophisticated, the gods may be taken as literal. For the more philosophically or spiritually inclined, they can be read as symbolic of metaphysical forces or iconically as the ritual focus of devotion, the expression of divine presence. We might say that the *Mahābhārata* is the site of many levels of argument. At an outermost level, it is about the interplay of cosmic forces. These are manifest or personified in the struggles between the various gods. In turn, the gods and their struggles are incarnated in the heroes and human institutions and history. The conflicts and factions among the heroes express the *psychomachia*, the internal debate within the mind of Vyāsa. Finally, all of this finds form in the text of the *Mahābhārata*. The world envelops the text and the text the world. Or, as Krishna tells Arjuna, "the most accomplished man of yoga [the liberated man]...shares in me in good faith, with his inner self absorbed in me" (*Bhagavadgitā* 99).

SUBSEQUENT INFLUENCE

Given the *Mahābhārata*'s definitive role, its prominence in the popular culture of India, Sri Lanka, Indonesia, and wherever Hinduism has reached cannot be overstated. The epic has been mined for stories, themes, characters, and images, finding expression in sculpture, painting, dance, plays, puppet theater (including the famous Wayang Kulit shadow puppets of Indonesia), and more recently fiction, film, animation, and even comic books and graphic novels. Inscriptions and sculpted scenes reach as far as Angkor-Wat in Cambodia and Candi Jago in East Java. The fifth-century Sanskrit playwright Kālidasa developed his masterpiece, *Shakuntalā*, from an episode in the *Mahābhārata* (see *Mahābhārata*, van Buitenen 1.62–70), a practice followed by many of the great writers of classical Sanskrit. Rabindranath Tagore (1861–1941), the Bengali poet, playwright and novelist and winner of the 1913 Nobel Prize for Literature, drew explicitly on the *Mahābhārata* for his verse plays *Chitra* (1892), *Karna and Kuntī* (1900), and *Gāndhāri's Prayers* (1928). In turn, his 1924 novel *Gora* explored many of the spiritual, social, and political paradoxes found in the epic. The poet and philosopher Aurobindo Ghose (1872–1950) based his epic *Savitri* with an eye on both the *Mahābhārata* and Dante's *Divine Comedy*. Sivaji Savanta offers perceptive insight into the character of Karna in his novel *Mrityunjaya, the Death Conqueror* (published in Bengali in 1968 and English in 1989), as does Buddhadeva Bose in his *Three Mahābhārata Verse Plays* (1992). S. L. Bhyrappa's *Parva: A Tale of War, Peace, God, and Man* (1994) offers a realistic and naturalistic take on the epic and its characters. At the same time, Shashi Deshpande looks at many of the women, such as Amba, Draupadi, and Kuntī, in "The Stone Woman" and other of her short stories. In turn, many modern Indian writers, whether on the Asian subcontinent or dispersed around the world, draw on it as a point of common reference. Many of the characters in the novels of the Indo-Trinidadian writer V. S. Naipaul (Nobel Prize in Literature, 2001) allude to material from the epic. Writing as an Indian woman in the Transvaal of South Africa, Muthal Naidoo takes on the traditional assumptions of gender in her 1995 play *Flight from the Mahabareth*.

Developing the themes of truth, *ahimsā* (nonviolence), and *brahmacaryā* (continence or renunciation), Mohandas Gandhi (1869–1948) deliberately identified himself with Yudhisthira and the quest for dharma. By contrast, Shashi Tharoor uses the *Mahābhārata* ironically to recast the history of modern India in his novel *The Great Indian Novel* (1989), turning Gandhi into Bhīshma, Jawaharlal Nehru (1889–1964) into Dhritarāstra, Indira Gandhi (1917–1984) into Duryodhana, and the conflict between the Pandavas and the Kauravas into that between Pakistan and India.

The *Mahābhārata* has found its way into film, including several attempts at a comprehensive adaptation. Of special note, directors B. R. Chopra and Ravi Chopra produced a 94-episode series (*The Mahabharat* in Hindi) that appeared on Indian television from 1988 through 1990, earning the accolade of the most popular series ever to appear on Indian television. In addition, British director Peter Brook, working with French writer and director Jean-Claude Carrière, produced a marathon theater experience, which they condensed into a 318-minute, six-episode miniseries (1989) featuring an international cast, aspiring to popularize the *Mahābhārata* as universal myth. Several other adaptations are of interest. Japanese director Shoji Kawamori produced an anime series *Arjuna* (1999) about the heroic adventures of a 15-year-old girl, Juna, and her wheelchair-bound friend Chris, not very subtle allusions to Arjuna, Krishna, and the chariot. In passing, an episode of the *Twilight Zone*, written by Earl Hamner Jr. and titled "The Hunt" (episode 84, January 26, 1962), translates the story of Yudhisthira and the dog to Appalachia and the story about an old hillbilly hunter and his hound dog.

The *Mahābhārata*, and more specifically the *Bhagavad-Gītā*, entered Western consciousness at the end of the eighteenth century. The *Bhagavad-Gītā* was first translated into English by Charles Wilkins in 1785. This in turn was translated into Latin, French, and German. European and British scholars, infused with a historical awareness of language, were led to Sanskrit, and by extension to its literature, as part of a Romantic search for the linguistic origins of Indo-European languages and mythic patterns and a corresponding quest for spiritual unity, especially among German poets and philosophers—of special note, Friderich and August von Schlegel, Wilhelm von Humboldt, Georg Wilhelm Friedrich Hegel, and later Arthur Schopen-hauer. By the middle of the nineteenth century, French critic Sainte-Beuve could declare in his influential essay "What Is a Classic?" that Vyāsa, Valmiki (the traditional author of the *Rāmāyana*), and Firdousi (the author of the Persian epic *Shahnama*) should be included with Homer in the pantheon of epic poets. In America, Emerson and Thoreau took deep inspiration from the *Bhagavad-Gītā*. In his poem "Brahma," Emerson is drawn to quest for the unity of opposites:

> Far or forgot to me is near;
> > Shadow and sunlight are the same;
> The vanished gods to me appear;
> > And one to me are shame and fame. (Emerson 471)

In the twentieth century, poet and critic T. S. Eliot, himself a student of Sanskrit and the *Bhagavad-Gītā*, looks at the primacy of action in "The Dry Salvages" from his *Four Quartets:*

> So Krishna, as when he admonished Arjuna
> On the field of battle,
> > > Not fare well,
> But fare forward, voyagers. (Eliot III)

Finally, bringing things full circle, Leo Tolstoy, writing on pacifism, was deeply influenced by his reading of the *Bhagavad-Gītā*, and these writings in turn deeply influenced Gandhi, recalling him to his native traditions. Sub-sequently, Martin Luther King looked to both Tolstoy and Gandhi for his own conception of nonviolence. Vyāsa still appears when a task needs to be done.

SUGGESTED READINGS

Bhagavadgitā: A Bilingual Edition. Trans. J. A. B. van Buitenen. Chicago: University of Chicago Press, 1981.

Bhyrappa, S. L. *Parva: A Tale of War, Peace, Death, God, and Man*. Trans. K. Ragha-vendra Rao. New Delhi: Asia Publishing House, 1994.

Bose, Buddhadeva. *Three Mahābhārata Verse Plays*. Trans. Kanak Kanti De. Calcutta: Writers Workshop, 1992.

Brockington, John L. *The Sanskrit Epics*. Leiden: Brill Academic Publishers, 1998.

Buck, William, trans. *Mahabharata*. New York: New American Library, 1973.

van Buitenen, J. A. B., trans. *Mahābhārata, Books 1–5*. 3 vols. Chicago: University of Chicago Press, 1973–1978.

Carrière, Jean-Claude. *The Mahābhārata*. Trans. Peter Brooks. New York: Harper and Row, 1987.

Coomarasaswamy, Ananda K. *History of Indian and Indonesian Art*. New York: Dover Publications, 1985.

Dange, Sadshiv A. *Myths from the Mahābhārata*. 3 vols. New Delhi: Aryan, 1997–2002.

Deschpande, Shashi. *Collected Stories*. 2 vols. New Delhi: Penguin, 2003, 2004.

Dimock, Edward C., et al. *The Literatures of India: An Introduction*. Chicago: University of Chicago Press, 1974.

Dumezil, Georges. *The Destiny of a King*. Trans. Alf Hiltebeitel. Chicago: University of Chicago Press, 1988.

———. *Mythe et épopée*. Paris: Gallimard, 1995.

Eliot, T. S. *Four Quartets*. New York: Harcourt Brace, 1971.

Emerson, Ralph Waldo. *Selected Writings of Ralph Waldo Emerson*. New York: New American Library, 1965.

Ganguli, Kisari Mohan, trans. *Mahabharata of Krishna-Dwaipayana Vyasa*. 4 vols. New Delhi: Munshiram Manoharlal Publishers, 2000.

Ghose, Aurobindo. *Savitri: A Legend and a Symbol*. Pondicherry: Sri Aurobindo Ashram, 1993.

Griffith, Ralph T. H., trans. *Hymns of the Rgveda*. Ed. J. L. Shastri. Delhi: Motilal Banarsidass, 1973.

Grimes, John. *A Concise Dictionary of Indian Philosophy: Sanskrit Terms Defined in English*. Albany: State University of New York Press, 1989.

Hiltebeitel, Alf. *The Cult of Draupadī*. 2 vols. Chicago: University of Chicago Press, 1991.

———. *Rethinking the Mahābhārata: A Reader's Guide to the Education of the Dharma King*. Chicago: University of Chicago Press, 2001.

———. *The Ritual of Battle: Krishna in the Mahābhārata*. Albany: State University of New York Press, 1990.

Hopkins, E. Washburn. *The Great Epic of India: Its Character and Origin*. New York: Charles Scribner's Sons, 1901.

Long, J. Bruce. *The Mahābhārata: A Select Annotated Bibliography*. Ithaca: Cornell University Press, 1974.

Morgan, Kenneth W., ed. *The Religion of the Hindus*. New York: The Ronald Press, 1953.

Naidoo, Muthal. *Flight from the Mahabharath*. In *Black South African Women: An Anthology of Plays*. Ed. Kathy A. Perkins. London: Routledge, 1998. 113–141.

Naipaul, V. S. *A House for Mr. Biswas*. New York: Vintage Books, 1989.

Nandan, Satendra. "The Mahābhārata and Modern Fiction." In *Myths, Heroes, and Anti-Heroes: Essays on the Literature and Culture of the Asia-Pacific Region*. Ed. Bruce Bennett and Dennis Haskell. Nedlands: Centre for Studies in Australian Literature, University of Western Australia, 1992. 201–209.

Narasimhan, Chakravarthi V., trans. *Mahabharata: An English Version Based on Selected Verses*. New York: Columbia University Press, 1998.

Narayan, R. K. *Mahābhārata: A Shortened Modern Prose Version of the Indian Epic.* Chicago: Chicago University Press, 2000.

Nooten, Barend A. Van. *The Mahābhārata of Krishna Dvaipayana Vyasa.* New York: Twayne Publishers, 1971.

Parmar, Arjunsinh K., ed. *Critical Perspectives on the Mahābhārata.* Sarup: New Delhi, 2002.

Rajagopalachari, Chakravarti, trans. *Mahābhārata.* Bombay: Bharatiya Vidya Bhavan, 1985.

Savanta, Sivaji. *Mrityunjaya, the Death Conqueror.* Trans. P. Lal and Nandini Nopany. Calcutta: Writers Workshop, 1989.

Sen, Amartya. *The Argumentative Indian: Writing on Indian History, Culture and Identity.* New York: Farrar, Straus and Giroux, 2005.

Sharpe, Eric J. *The Universal Gita: Western Images of the Bhagavad Gita, A Bicentennial Survey.* La Salle: Open Court, 1985.

Tagore, Rabindranath. *The Collected Poems and Plays of Rabindranath.* New York: Macmillan Company, 1949.

———. *Gora.* New York: Macmillan, 1980.

Thapar, Romila. *Early India from the Origins to AD 1300.* Berkeley: University of California Press, 2003.

Tharoor, Shashi. *The Great Indian Novel.* New York: Arcade Publishing, 1989.

Zaehner, R. C. *Hinduism.* New York: Oxford University Press, 1966.

Zimmer, Heinrich, Joseph Campbell, and Eliot Elisofon. *Art of Indian Asia: Its Mythology and Transformation.* 2 vols. Princeton: Princeton University Press, 1960.

potential to take us out of ourselves and our sense of autonomous individual identity, to seek union with the other, and ultimately to seek the divine. Not surprisingly, the connection between the erotic and the religious is a common motif among mystics and religious poets around the world, informing the relationships of Rumi and Shams, Dante and Beatrice, and the Bridegroom and Shulammite. Among many in India, and especially the Vaishnava—those whose worship centers on the preserver god Vishnu, his consort Lakshmī, or his ten incarnations, including Krishna—the *Gītagovinda* represents an important part of devotion. Describing the measure of a great poet, the tenth-century critic Rājaśekhara declared, "A poet's composition is praise worthy if it does not belong to this world alone. It should live on ever after the poet's death. It should be praised even by critics who come from far off places" (Rājaśekhara 152). Jayadeva fully satisfies this standard.

BIOGRAPHICAL AND CULTURAL CONTEXTS

Jayadeva combines a double identity in Indian culture as both poet and saint. Most of the facts of his life are a mixture of conjecture and legend. In broad terms we can say that he flourished in the twelfth century. Throughout the *Gītagovinda* he terms himself a professional poet (*Śrī-jayadeva-kaver*). Such repeated self-references are part of a literary convention, a way of signing one's work, a gesture that still persists in much modern Indian and Middle Eastern poetry. In one couplet, he identifies himself as "Jayadeva— / The poet from Kindubilva village, / The moon rising out of the sea [*varnitam jayadevakena harer idam pravanena / kindubilva-samudra-sambhava-rohini-ramanena*"]) (Miller 111; Siegel 294). This has led Bengali scholars to argue that he comes from the west Bengali village of Kenduli on the Ajayr River, and Oriyasan scholars to contend that he is from Kenduli on the Praci River in Orissa. Others locate his place of birth in Gujarat, Mahrashtra, or Bihar (Siegel 209). One way or the other, we may reasonably conjecture, given the strictures of traditional Indian society, that his father, whom he identifies by the name of Bhouadeva, had also been a professional poet and would have first initiated Jayadeva into the linguistic and rhetorical tricks of the trade. We may also infer that he was a member of the educated Brahman class and would have been trained in the philosophical and poetic classics of Sanskrit literature.

What is a poet in Jayadeva's world? Rājaśekhara describes the discipline of poetry in terms that resemble a priestly vocation, combining purity, devotion, and scholarship. "Thus, for the poet who practices with single-minded devotion, Sarasvatī (goddess of learning and wisdom) takes up the vow of the only wife for him...for ever" (Rājaśekhara 159). He also notes in his *Kāvyamīmāmsā*, one of the classics of Sanskrit poetics, that women are as qualified as men to be poets, his explanation offering insight. "Poetic power is born of *samskāra* (traces or impressions). These impressions are a part of the inner soul," he writes. "Thus there need be no discrimination between men and women...there are any number of princesses, daughters of ministers and performing artistes who are endowed with ability born of knowledge of the *śāstras* [the sacred scriptures] and with the ability to compose poetry" (Rājaśekhara 157). A professional poet's function was to entertain and instruct the elite, requiring the patronage of a king or some wealthy householder. This would involve traveling to various courts around India and participating in assorted literary festivals and poetry contests. Promoting his abilities in the *Gītagovinda*, Jayadeva writes,

> Umāpatidhara is prodigal with speech,
> Śarana is renowned for his subtle flowing sounds,
> But only Jayadeva divines the pure design of words.
> Dhoyī is famed as king of poets for his musical ear,
> But no one rivals master Govardhana
> For poems of erotic mood and sacred truth. (Miller 69)

The names he cites are not at random, but a group of poets known collectively by the title "jewels of Laksmanasena's assembly-hall" (Siegel 209n), linking them with the court of the Bengal king, Laksmanasena (1179–1209). This has led many scholars to conclude that the *Gītagovinda* was probably composed under Laksmanasena's patronage. The king himself was considered a devotée of the god Vishnu and is thought to have composed some verses of his own about the love between Krishna and Rādhā.

Because of the prominent role that the *Gītagovinda* takes in the devotion to the god Krishna (also known as Hari, "the tawny one") and its role in Vaishnava, Jayadeva is also described as a Hindu saint. Indeed, the classic *Marathi Bhatavijaya* of Mahipati (1715–1790), a compendium of saints' lives, cites him among the first. A number of interesting if questionable legends have grown up around Jayadeva and the composition of his masterpiece. Two are of special interest here. Early in the text, Jayadeva describes himself as the king (or emperor) of wandering bards "who sing at Padmāvatī's lotus feet" (Miller 69), a reference to either his wife or the goddess. One legend pertains to the composition of the *Gītagovinda*. According to the story, Jayadeva had reached the climax of the poem, a point at which Rādhā puts her foot on Krishna's head, a gesture that signifies her triumph and his complete submission to her. Disturbed by the thought that it might be disrespectful to represent the god this way, Jayadeva hesitated. Unable to resume writing, he went off to the baths. While he was away, Krishna appeared disguised as Jayadeva and, asking Padmāvatī for Jayadeva's writing book, Krishna completed the lines:

> Place your foot on my head—
> A sublime flower destroying poison of love!
> Let your foot quell the harsh sun
> Burning its fiery form in me to torment Love. (Miller 113)

Later returning from his ablutions, Jayadeva was astonished to discover the new lines. He asked Padmāvatī about them and was incredulous when she replied that he himself had written them. Realizing the true significance of what had happened, Jayadeva told her that she was truly blessed for having had a vision of the Lord (Krishna). The effect of this legend is to sacralize the lines, adding authority to the work as a whole. It might not be too far to suggest, as the twelfth-century Italian poet Guido Guinizelli does in his "Al cor gentil rempaira sempre amore" ["I truly wish to give my lady praise"], that one loves God through loving the lady (or gentleman).

Several legends are linked with Jayadera's wife Padmāvatī, one being that she was a dancer either in the court of Laksmanasena or in the Jagannātha temple in Purī. The cult of Jagannātha, literally "Lord of the World," was highly syncretic and cosmopolitan in nature, assimilating various strands not only from Hinduism, but from Jainism and Buddhism as well. According to legend, the young Jayadeva leaves home, entering the life of a wandering ascetic, and finds himself in Puri, where he encounters a Brahman who has promised his daughter to the god Jagannātha because of her resemblance to Lakshmī. In a dream, Jagannâtha appears to the Bhrahman, declaring that because he is currently in the form of the Buddha, the daughter should be married to Jayadeva, who "is a portion of me, an *avatar* of mine" (Abbott 15). Delighted by this, the Brahman arranges the marriage between Jayadeva and Padmāvatī. The name of Padmāvatī is often glossed as one of the names of Lakshmī, the consort of great god Vishnu. It may be that marriage to Padmāvatī is also a signification for initiation into the cult of Śrīvishnava in Puri, which had been established under the influence of the philosopher Rāmānuja. (Śrī is an honorific in Sanskrit that is sometimes translated "lord," but it also often carries a feminine connotation, and thus, Śrīvishnava pertains either to the worship of Lord Vishnu or to Lakshmī.) Aesthetically, the strong linkage between Jayadeva and the dancer Padmāvatī points to the profound role of music and especially dance in our appreciation of the *Gītagovinda*. Modern performances typically involve dance, and many of the visual representations draw on the iconography of dance movement. Philosophically, all of this underlines the religious and spiritual dimensions of Jayadeva's work, the symbolic union of cosmic forces. Śrīvishnava cult owes much to the religious philosopher Rāmānuja (C.E. 1017–1137). The erotic stages of love, loss, and reunion between Krishna and Rādhā allegorize themes central to Rāmānuja's doctrine. Although Jayadeva is doing significantly more than simply dramatizing this philosophy, a brief examination of its general outlines deepens our appreciation of the religious dimensions of the *Gītagovinda*.

Vedānta, literally the "end of the Vedas," is one of the orthodox traditions of Indian philosophy. It attempts to give a rigorous and systematic coherence to the epigrammatic and often ambiguous statements found in the Vedic scriptures, especially the *Upanisads*. Vedānta in general is concerned with clarifying our knowledge of the ultimate ground of reality, Brahman, as the key to salvation. The philosopher Śankara, developing a system known as *Advaitins* (non-dualism), argues that *Brahman* (pure being) is one with *Ātman* (ultimate consciousness), that the perceived plurality of the world is illusion— a confusion of "this for that," "the snake for a piece of rope," he says in a famous example. Deploying an argument reminiscent of Descartes' "I think, therefore I am," in which I say that I exist because I cannot without absurdity doubt that I am conscious that I am conscious, Śankara argues that it is logically incoherent to be conscience of unconsciousness, that there can be nothing beyond consciousness. Thus ultimate consciousness, Ātman, is none other than the undifferentiated ground of being, Brahman. The personal and the divine dissolve into absolute union, a view that, although philosophically satisfying, offers little comfort or consolation for those with religious or spiritual yearnings. "The individual's religion may be egotistic, and those private realities which it keeps in touch with may be narrow enough," writes the philosopher and psychologist William James, addressing the tension between a personal religion and science (or philosophy), "but at any rate it always remains infinitely less hollow and abstract, as far as it goes, than a science which prides itself on taking no account of anything private at all" (James 500). It is exactly this psychological need for a more personal religious experience that impels Rāmānuja's Viśistādvaita Vedānta ("qualified non-dualism"), a school of philosophy that seeks to preserve the identity of Ātman and Brahman while at the same time preserving the reality of the individual self and the notion of a personal relationship with the divine.

Rāmānuja develops his position through what philosophers call identity-in-difference. Thus, for instance, although I might say that soul and body are distinct orders of being, if they interact, and body is entirely controlled by soul, then effectively they form a unity (a qualified non-dualism). Rāmānuja makes an analogous argument. Brahman informs the world as soul informs the body. "The individual self is a part of the highest Self; as the light issuing from a luminous thing such as fire or the sun is a part of that body" (Radhakrishnan 555).

There is therefore an identity between being and the diversity of the world. The individual self has real qualities and can be understood as a mode of Brahman. Just as knowledge requires both a knower and the known to be meaningful, two separate realities form an identity-in-difference, so glancing toward Jayadeva's aesthetic vision, love requires the lover and the beloved. For Rāmānuja, devotion to God (*bhakti*) involves the real individual surrendering himself completely to God, not in the sense of dissolving the self, but in a willing surrender (*prapatti*), a form of communion. "The selves, on their side, endowed with all the powers imparted to them by the Lord and with bodies and organs bestowed by him...apply themselves on their own part, and in accordance with their own wishes, to works either good or evil," writes Rāmānuja (Radhakrishnan 553). In turn God completes the communion. "The Lord, then recognizing him who performs good actions as one who obeys his commands, blesses him with piety, riches, worldly pleasures, and final release" (Radhakrishnan 553). In their reciprocal relationship, God and the individual form a unity, but a unity that preserves the individual and acknowledges the personal nature of the religious experience.

PLOT AND STRUCTURE DEVELOPMENT

A dramatic lyric, the *Gītagovinda* can be described as the libretto for a dance-drama, a song cycle such as Schubert's *Winterreise* ("Winter Journey"), or a Mozartian opera composed of recitatives that advance the horizontal movement of the narrative and arias that allow the singer to express emotional depth and complexity, a vertical movement. It unfolds in 12 cantos or sections (*padāvalās*), each one titled by one of the many epithets used to name Krishna and a description of the god's state of mind. The recitatives are in a classical Sanskrit verse form known as *kāvya*, and they set the scene, advance the plot, or establish themes. The 12 cantos bring together 24 songs, some cantos containing one or two, others up to four. Traditional Indian music plays on a system of improvisation circumscribed by strict conventions. Thus, each song is labeled with a characteristic *raga* (*rag* in Hindi and Urdu); the word is cognate with the Sanskrit *ranj* (to color). Thus, a raga represents a melodic pattern, an acoustic method for "coloring" the listener's reception of the song, adding emotional depth or complexity. Each traditional raga has a characteristic series of notes, modal structure, and ascending and descending structure that governs the limits of the performer's improvisations. The typical raga takes about half an hour and involves first the establishment of the basic pattern, followed by an ornamentation around its mode. In turn, many traditional ragas are conventionally associated with seasons or times of day. For instance, the first song in the *Gītagovinda* is marked to be sung with a

Raga Malava (or *megha*), which is derived from the classical symbol of the monsoon and used traditionally to evoke rain in times of drought. It is also associated with songs sung at twilight. The choice of this type of raga takes its cue from the opening *kāvya*: "Clouds thicken the sky. / Tamāla trees darken the forest. / The night frightens him" (Miller 69). Some 12 ragas are employed in the *Gītagovinda*, though scholars of music note that the ragas associated with the various songs probably postdate Jayadeva, and further, despite the continuity of traditions, we cannot be sure that his understanding of certain ragas is the same as our present understanding of them. That said, the ragas now associated with each song have effectively become fixed.

The 12 cantos and 24 songs of the *Gītagovinda* dramatize an emotional and psychological arc, tracing the emotions of Rādhā and Krishna as they move from calm, to longing, to languishing, to anger, to reunion, and finally to consummation, a movement that N.S.R. Ayengar describes musically in terms of a gradual development from lower notes to crescendo and then denuendo (Ayengar 69). On the erotic level, each step dramatizes the subtle gradations and emotional complexities of love, especially codified in the conventions of classical Sanskrit drama. On a philosophical level, it traces the soul's desire to be one with the divine, the sexual union of Krishna and Rādhā allegorizing the union of the divine soul with that of the individual in a way that also preserves the separation of each, a relation commensurate with Vaishnava devotion and the philosophical position described by Rāmānuja. As one of the early songs declares, "You [Krishna] free us from bonds of existence, / Preserving life in the world's three realms" (Miller 72).

Canto 1, titled "Joyful Lord" (the untranslated title is "Sāmoda-Dāmodarah," and the word *Dāmodarah* literally means "one who has a rope around his waist," an epithet for Krishna that refers to a rope tied around the infant god to control him like a baby harness), sets the scene with nightfall and an impending storm. Nanda, Krishna's foster father and the chief of the cowherds, instructs Rādhā to look after Krishna. Thereupon, Jayadeva hymns an invocation of 10 incarnations associated with the god Vishnu, a move that identifies Krishna with Vishnu and situates the action of the drama into the larger cosmic contexts. The first incarnation is the Fish, Matsya, who protected the wisdom of the Veda at a time of an apocalyptic deluge. The second is the Tortoise, Kūrma, who signified the postdeluvian restoration of the Vedas. Next is the Boar, Varāha, who held the earth on its tusk, preserving the balance between chaos and order. From this cosmic balance came the tension between human and beast in the figure of the Man-Lion, Narasimha. This is followed by the Dwarf, Vāmana, who destroyed arrogance, tricking the demon by taking three cosmic steps. Then is the Axeman (Bhrgu or Rama with the Axe) who purified the world of corrupt rulers with blood. He is followed by Rāma, the hero celebrated in the epic *Ramayana,* who rescued his wife Sitā, slaying the 10-headed demon Ravana. The next incarnation is Balarāma the Plough-holder, traditionally identified as the brother of Krishna, but also a figure of exuberance, drunkenness, and creative chaos. Next is the figure of the Buddha, defined as the incarnation of the present. This figure was incorporated by various sects of Hinduism in response to a need to compete with Buddhism, the Hindus claiming that the Buddha was the current incarnation of Krishna and by extension Vishnu. The 10th incarnation is that of Kalki, the avenger on horseback, a symbol of the final end of the dark ages *(Kali Yuga),* a figure of the future.

Having established the cosmic context of Krishna and the universe contained within his embrace, the narrative turns back to Rādhā. What has begun as an embrace begins to grow to a longing, leading her to wander the forest seeking him. A friend, and confidante, and important mediating character throughout the narrative sings of Krishna's sexual games with the *gopi,* the girls who tend the cattle: "He hugs one, he kisses another, he caresses another dark beauty...Hari revels here as the crowd of charming girls / Revels in seducing him to play" (Miller 77).

The second canto is called "Careless Krishna" ("Aklesa-Kesavah"). Distracted by his love games, Krishna grows negligent of Rādhā. At the same time, envy of the *gopis* causes her to isolate herself in a forest retreat. Despite her efforts, everything in the forest reminds her of love. She admits that she is excited by his wantonness, refusing to admit her rage, refusing to recognize his guilt. Here she pours out her feelings to her confidante, imploring her to go find Krishna and bring him back to her. "I've gone mad waiting for his fickle love to change," she says (Miller 80). Her song, Jayadeva explains, is a fantasy of sexual desire.

In the third canto, "Perplexed Killer-of-Madhu" ("Mugha-Madhu-Sūdhnah"), the god begins to feel bonds with Rādhā, recognizing in her the incarnation of earlier consorts; by this Jayadeva suggests both the individuality and the unity of Krishna and Rādhā. Searching for her in vain, Krishna curses himself and his wanton ways. "Even when the sensuous objects are gone, / My mind holds on to her in a trance" (Miller 85).

The confidante tells Krishna about Rādhā's feelings of dejection in canto 4, "The Affectionate Killer-of-Madhu" ("Snigdha-Madhu-Sūdhnah"), how she curses sandalbalm and moonbeams for making her think of her beloved. "Lying dejected by your desertion, fearing Love's arrows," the confidante sings, "She clings to you in fantasy, Mādhava [another of Krishna's epithets, a complex pun, signifying both springtime or honey-time, and the progenitor of Krishna's clan] (Miller 87). In language akin to the metaphysical conceit, she describes love in terms of sickness and death.

She bristles with pain, sucks in breath,
Cries, shudders, gasps,
Broods deep, reels, stammers,
Falls, raises herself, then faints. (Miller 89)

Distressed by these words, Krishna tells the confidante to return to Rādhā in canto 5, "The Lotus-Eyed-One in a State-of-Longing" ("Sākānksa-Pundarīkāksah"). She is to appease her and bring her to him. Following these instructions, she seeks Rādhā in her retreat, singing of the god's passion and, in explicitly erotic terms, urging her to come to him. "Rādhā, don't let full hips idle! Follow the lord of your heart!" She adds, "Leave your noisy anklets! They clang like traitors in love play" (Miller 92).

In canto 6, "Ardently-Longing Vaikuntha" ("Sotkantha-Vaikunthah"), the confidante despairs when she realizes that exhausted by her passions, Rādhā has become petulant and will not leave her retreat, in order to punish the god. In turn Krishna lies helpless with love. Both have become proud, and each refuses to be the first to budge. The night returns, and the moon rises at the start of canto 7, "Cunning Nārāyana" ("Nāgara-Nārāyanah"), portrayed by Jayadeva in a sensuous imagery that heightens the mood of erotic guilt. "The moon displayed cratered stains, / Seeming to flaunt its guilt / In betraying secret paths / Of adulterous women, / Lightning depths of Brindaban forest / With moonbeam nets" (Miller 97). When Rādhā sees her friend return without the god, she becomes suspicious that he is again with some girl. Love is now a struggle of wills for domination. The poet describes her arrayed for "the battle of love." No longer able to endure the feelings of separation, she begs nature to extinguish her life in oblivion. "Drown my limbs with waves! / Let my body's burning be quenched" (Miller 105).

The following morning, Rādhā awakes to find Krishna leaning over her. Despite (or because of) her desires and suffering, she responds not with affection, but with angry scorn. In canto 8, "Laksmi's Master Vexed" ("Vilaksya-Laksmī-Patih"), she berates the god, sarcastically asking if he still has telltale nail or tooth marks of his lover on his body. "Dark Krishna, your heart must be baser black than your skin" (Miller 107). (Analogously, Beatrice berates Dante when they are at long last reunited in *Purgatorio* 30 of the *Divine Comedy*, a frequent motif in the medieval romance.) Sizing up the situation, the confidante intervenes in canto 9, "Artless Mukunda" ("Mugdha-Mukundah"). "Don't turn wounded pride on Mādhava!" she sings. "He is proud too, sullen Rādhā" (Miller 109). The relationship has taken on a sort of proud perversity. "When he is tender you are harsh, / When he is pliant you are rigid" (Miller 110). In imagery that anticipates the Petrarchan conceit, she explains how her state of mind has transformed ice into fire, joy into hell.

Canto 10, "The Clever Four-Armed-One" ("Catura-Catur-Bhujah"), begins at dusk. Krishna again approaches Rādhā. Her anger has subdued, and she looks at her friend shamefaced while the god expresses his love. Appealing to the elaborate language and conventions of courtship, he flatters and cajoles, even begging her to place her feet on his head, a token of his complete submission.

> Fierce Rādhā, your eyes glower
> Like gleaming dark lotuses;
> You nose is a sesame flower;
> Your teeth are white jasmine.
> Love's flower arms conquer worlds
> By worshipping your face. (Miller 114)

He concludes with a hymn in which he compares her to the various celestial beauties, "Frail Rādhā, as you walk on earth, / You bear the young beauty of heavenly nymphs" (Miller 114). At one level this can be read as a literary convention of courtship; at another, it can be read as signaling the spiritual dimensions of the relationship. Rādhā is both an individual and a part of the Divine, an identity-in-difference.

The relationship finds its fullest consummation in canto 11, "Blissful Dāmodara" ("Sānada-Dāmodarah") and canto 12, "The Very-Delighted Yellow-Robed-One" ("Suprī ta-Pī tā mbarah"). In anticipation, each dresses elaborately. Rādhā approaches Krishna's forest bower, decorated with garlands and golden chains. He is adorned in jeweled bracelets, and she with sounding anklets. At the sight of the other's face, each is enraptured. For Krishna, "all his deep-locked emotions broke when he saw Rādhā's face, / Like sea waves cresting when the full moon appears" (Miller 120). Similarly for Rādhā, "when she saw her lover's face / Graced by arrows of Love, / Even Rādhā's modesty left in shame" (Miller 121). Jayadeva suggests the sexual union discreetly and indirectly, a reminder that, despite India's being the land of the *Kama Sutra*, its traditional society is very conservative and that until recently it was taboo to show even kissing in movies. As part of their love play, Rādhā asks Krishna to ornament her body: "Paint a leaf design with deer musk here on Love's ritual vessel!" (Miller 124). Step by step she describes her body, what each part means, and how she wants it adorned. Correspondingly, step by step, he willingly obliges, decorating her body, moving from face, to hair, to hips, to arms, to legs. From this the poet finally turns discreetly away, summing up.

> His musical skill, his meditation in Vishnu,
> His vision of reality in the erotic mood,

His graceful play in these poems,
All show the master-poet Jayadeva's soul
Is in perfect tune with Krishna—
Let blissful men of wisdom purify the world
By singing his *Gītagovinda*. (Miller 125)

In a subtle analogy, the poet suggests that his poem is performing in language what Krishna is doing with the liquid deer musk, ornamenting and delineating the body of the loved one in an act of devotion. To sing his poem is to worship the god, the aesthetic embracing the erotic, and the erotic, the divine.

CHARACTER DEVELOPMENT

There are four characters in the *Gītagovinda*: Rādhā, Krishna, the friend/confidante (*sakhī*), and the poet/narrator (*gāyaka*). The figures of Rādhā and Krishna are part of a complex history that informs how Jayadeva's audience would receive them. It is useful to our appreciation of them, therefore, to unpack some of this background.

The figure of Krishna is among the most popular in Hinduism and in Indian culture in general, combining and symbolizing the divine attributes of love (*prema*), beauty (*rūpa*), and playfulness (*līlā*), with play here understood as a free action performed for its own sake with no other purpose in mind. Although he is considered one of the *avatra* of Vishnu, one of the earthy incarnations of the god, he largely subsumes Vishnu. The ninth-century C.E. *Bhagavata Puranā*, for instance, declares, "Krishna is God himself ("*Krisnas tu bhagavan snayam*") (1.3.27). By the time Jayadeva composed his poem, the identity between Krishna and Vishnu was well established, supported by a large body of traditions and stories. The figure of Krishna himself has a complex history and probably reflects the synthesis or combination of several different heroes or deities, a point underlined by the many epithets attached to him. Three strands are of special interest here.

One of these strands comes from southern India. By the first millennium C.E., there is evidence among the Tamil-speaking peoples of a hero known as Māyōn, whose name derives from the Tamil for "black complexioned," a figure who may ultimately be traced back to the Dravidian peoples who inhabited the Asian subcontinent before the arrival of the Aryans. The Tamil name Māyōn is equivalent to the Sanskrit Krishna, which also signifies "dark" or "black-complexioned." Māyōn is also Krishna-like in many of his adventures, especially with the gopis, his favorite a milkmaid named Pinnai, for whom he subdued seven bulls. Although the Māyōn/Pinnai pairing resembles that of

Krishna/Rādhā, Pinnai herself enters Sanskrit literature under the name of either Nila or Satya.

Two more strands come from northern India, Vāsudeva Krishna and Krishna Gōpala. Vāsudeva Krishna is a hero-warrior figure, part of the Vrsni clan of Mathura. He liberates the throne of Mathura and eventually establishes a dynasty in the Dvaraka. This Krishna is the friend and counselor of the Pandavas and plays a prominent role in the epic *Mahābhārata* (see chapter 2 on the *Mahābhārata*). Also important is the second-century C.E. epic *Mahabhasya* of Patanjali. Although the overarching structure of the *Mahābhārata* subsumes everything under Vishnu, the famous *Bhagavad-Gītā*, featuring the dialogue between Krishna and the warrior Arjuna, was originally a distinct work, developing a distinctly Krishnavite theology. By contrast, Krishna Gōpala (Krishna the cattle herder) belongs originally to the popular secular culture and was originally associated with the nomadic Abhira people, though he became linked with the Vrsni of Mathura, as the Abhira interacted with the Mathura. This Krishna is known for his mischievousness, trickery, and erotic games played with sixteen thousand gopi worshipers and sixteen thousand wives, engaging in enormous amorous circle dances (*rā sa līlā*) in which he multiplies his form so that each gopi supposes that she is dancing with him alone. Later this becomes an important emblem of the theme of "love-in-separation"—the idea that Krishna belongs to everyone, yet retains his distinctness, a theme closely related to the "identity-in-difference" found in the Śrīvishnava of Rāmānuja. Krishna Gōpala is also linked with a favorite among the gopis, a milkmaid known as Rādhikā. The figure of Krishna Gōpala is represented either by the playful child stealing butter or by the beautiful long-haired youth (*Keśava*) stealing hearts. This is the iconic Krishna with his neck tilted and ankles crossed, playing his flute.

Jayadeva's work shows familiarity with both the pastoral and the heroic conceptions of Krishna, but favors the lover, Krishna Gōpala. The *Gītagovinda* plays a prominent role in making that image the dominant focus of devotion.

The figure of Rādhā is now universally linked with Krishna, celebrated as the god's earthly beloved and eternal consort. Iconically, they are often represented standing side by side (*yugala-mūrti*). Thanks in no small measure to the influence of the *Gītagovinda*, Rādhā has become an important object of veneration, the *prema bhakti*, or object of "loving devotion," a mediator between the human and the divine. Although her name looks back to the Abhira milkmaid Rādhikā, it also may play on the feminine form of the Vedic *rāhas*, "desired object." None of the early Krishnavite works, especially the *Bhagavata Purāna*, the *Harivamśa*, or the epics, make any reference to her. She probably enters in the Krishna canon from elements of the Abhira Rādhikā and the Tamil Pinnai. Both of these figures have designations that were earlier applied to the goddesses Devī and Durgā and characteristics applied to Lakshmī, a set of associations that helps to reinforce the links between Krishna and Vishnu.

In constructing and characterizing Rādhā, Jayadeva draws heavily on the conventions of Sanskrit theater. The *Nātyaśāstra* of Bharata Muni, an important Sanskrit treatise on dramaturgy and histrionics, dating from the second century c.e., describes eight kinds of conventional heroines, five of which readily apply to Rādhā: *vasakasajjakā*, the heroine who dresses up, eagerly expecting her lover; *virahotkanthitā*, the heroine who feels sadness when her lover does not show up; *kalahāntaitā*, the heroine who burns with jealousy, making her quarrelsome; *khanditā*, the enraged heroine; and *abhisārikā*, the heroine overcome by love, shamelessly going to her lover herself (Bharata 196). Bharata Muni also characterizes 10 "stages of love in women," many of which inform Rādhā's behavior. These include *abhilāsā*, the first stage of love, marked by "longing," and then *cintana*, a sort of obsession that grows out of the longing. This is followed by *Anusmrti*, marked by sighing again and again, and then *gunakīrtana*, expressing the happy-unhappy remembrance. The fifth and sixth stages are *udvega*, marked by restlessness, and *vilāpa*, regret. Next comes *unmāda*, hysteria. The last three are *vyādhi*, a delirious and feverish behavior; *jadatā*, insensitiveness; and finally, *marana*, death (Bharata 194). Happily, Rādhā does not reach the final three stages, though her prostration and wish to die (described in canto 8), approach them. It is evident, however, that Jayadeva is playing with a well-developed set of dramatic conventions.

Although all of this is significant to our appreciation of Rādhā, her real importance is most evident where Jayadeva parts from the traditional prototypes and dramatic conventions. Despite the importance of Krishna, Rādhā is the central character in the *Gītagovinda*. It is her transformation that traces the development of the plot, her emotions that drive the action. Although she is eternally linked with Krishna, with no independent identity in the literature or later tradition, it is she who changes Krishna. All of this is especially remarkable given the predominately paternal nature of Indian society and the Hindu religion. Although the figure of Rādhā derives from the gopis, and Jaydeva glances toward that tradition, she is nevertheless portrayed not as a pastoral milkmaid, but as somehow different, separate from the rest. Nanda's instructions to her to take the young Krishna home (1.1) indicate that she is in independent enough to be entrusted with him and is not just a playmate. Many later versions of the story, such as those of Candīdāsa and Vidyāpati, portray her as a married woman. Related to that, a number of poets, theologians, and commentators have debated whether she is *svakīyā*, "one's own woman," or *parakīyā*, "another-man's woman." Although marriage, especially arranged marriage, was very much a matter of duty and social order, illicit love was about passion, devotion freely given, pleasure, and longing, themes consonant with the courtly love traditions of the West. Jayadeva himself, however, is deliberately ambiguous as to whether Rādhā is *svakīyā* or *parakīyā*. Siegel notes that one way or the other, she and Krishna are both under the care and control of Nanda, and their tryst is in defiance of him (Siegel 118–119). Barbara Miller, on the other hand, emphasizes Rādhā's independence, at least in relation to Krishna. She is "neither a wife nor a worshiping rustic playmate," Miller argues. "She is a jealous, solitary, proud female who is Krishna's exclusive partner in a secret love, a union that is contrasted with his communal sexual play" (qtd. in Hawley 13). All of this serves to elevate her status, transforming her into the archetype of the ideal lady.

Brief mention should be made of the friend/confidante and the poet/narrator. On one level, both are conventional stock characters. At the same time, both are important thematically. On a deeper level, although they are separate, each stands in analogous relation to the other. The friend is the go-between, mediating between Rādhā and Krishna, advancing the action, providing a double perspective as both participant and detached observer. In her actions, she expresses no personal passion or attraction for Krishna, only the desire to bring the lovers together. "She mediates and reveals," writes Siegel, "and because it is absolutely without selfish motive, without any desire for joy, it brings infinite joy" (Siegel 135). This is also the role and function of the poet/narrator, serving as the go-between, joining the action of the drama with the audience. It is exactly this role of mediation that endows the poetic treatment of the passion of Rādhā and Krishna with its devotional character. "The Vaisnava poets, headed by Jayadeva, Candīdāsa and Vidyāpati," says S. B. Das Gupta, "placed themselves rather in the position of the Shkhīs, or female companions of Rādhā and Krishna, who did never long for their union with Krishna—but ever longed for the opportunity of witnessing from a distance the eternal love-making of Rādhā and Krishna, which the Vaisnava poets desired to enjoy" (qtd. in Siegel 136). The poem and the poet are engaged in a virtual love-making, an eros that puts them in harmony with the divine.

SUBSEQUENT INFLUENCE

Describing Jayadeva's achievement, Mahipati declared, "He composed a book called *Gītagovinda* which everyone copied and took away with him. They joyfully committed it to memory and sang it in every house. Flowers may be in one place, but their fragrance spreads everywhere" (Abbott 12). This account indicates how this and other works were transmitted in twelfth-century India through a combination of transcription and performance. It also indicates how the *Gītagovinda* became a ready success, inspiring further elaborations of the story of Rādhā and Krishna by later poets and playwrights, as well as many expressions in sculpture, music, and dance, especially in Orissa and Karnataka. It was a particularly fertile subject for paintings, from wall paintings to illustrations to palm leaf manuscripts.

Among writers of note, the sixteenth-century playwright Rūpa Gosvāmī composed a number of plays about Rādhā as the model and object of devotion. This period also saw the composition of the influential *Śrīkrsnakīrtana* by Candīdāsa (1486–1533). At about the same time, the secular songs of Sūr Dās, the *Sūr Sāger*, celebrated the relationship between Rādhā and Krishna. The general tendency was to endow Rādhā with the attributes of a goddess, *prakriti* (primal nature), *śākti* (power or capacity), and *māyā* (illusion or the power of creation). By contrast, the courtly poetry of the seventeenth and eighteenth century, *rīti* poetry, emphasized the themes of courtly love and the erotic. Here she is the ideal heroine *(nāyika)* paired with Krishna the ideal courtly lover *(nāyaka)*.

Although Rādhā remains a central focus of spiritual devotion, the figure of Rādhā as the embodiment of the female ideal has given way in most modern Hindi literature with its strong concern with social reform, replaced with more general images of the universal woman, or the downtrodden woman. Two exceptions attempt to make relevant to the modern reader the story of Rādhā and Krishna, including the long poem *Priyapravās* (1914) by Ayodha-simha Upadyaya (Harioudh) and, more recently, *Kanupriyā* (1966) by Dhar-mvir Bhāratī (Hawley 114). Otherwise, the references are often ironic, as in Laksmīkānt Varmā's "Śri Krishna Looking for Arjuna in an Antique Store," a 1968 poem that interrogates both the heroic and the pastoral images of Krishna. Amid the junk, the god finds the image of Rādhā, but fails to recognize her, "stashed away in a silver casket, / brimming with emotion, swathed in a haze, body tarnished / and worn out" (qtd. in Hawley 89).

In subtle ways, allusions to Rādhā's and Krishna's relationship find their way into modern and contemporary works not otherwise explicitly treating them, works that are using the tradition as a framework to set in relief and question the cultural assumptions of modern society. Consider three examples readily available to an American audience: R. K. Narayan's 1958 novel *The Guide*; the 1988 movie *Salaam Bombay!* by director Mira Nair; and director Deepa Mehta's controversial 1996 movie *Fire*.

Narayan's novel centers on the adventures of a trickster figure named Raju, who finds himself involved in an affair with a *parakīyā* named Rosie, a temple dancer who is married to a scholar studying cave inscriptions. The novel traces various "incarnations" of Raju, from railroad-Raju, to a tea-boy, to a tour guide, and finally to a reluctant guru (like the Buddha stage in the

Gītagovinda). Ultimately, Narayan remains ambiguous. In *Salaam Bombay!*—a film reminiscent of François Truffaut's 1959 *Les Quatre cents coups* ("The 400 Blows")—director Mira Nair, originally from Orissa, explores the life of a dark-complexioned, curly-haired 10-year-old street urchin nicknamed Chaipau, though his real name is aptly Krishna, who finds himself abandoned on the streets of Bombay. Here he survives, taking up a life among the thieves, pimps, pushers, and prostitutes in the red-light district near Bombay's train station. Krishna/Chaipau becomes infatuated with three *parakīyā*/Rādhā figures: a prostitute nicknamed "Sweet Sixteen"; Rekha, the prostitute wife of Baba (ironically "Papa"), a local drug pusher; and Rekha's seven-year-old daughter Manju. Each expresses the various emotions and states of mind through which Rādhā passes. True to form, Krishna is dressed in saffron (here, however a sweatshirt rather than robes) and eventually slays the demonic Baba. The final relationship with the three Rādhās ends on a disturbing, indecisive, and ironic note. By contrast, director Deepa Mehta's *Fire* confronts the cultural contradictions in Indian society with regard to sexual identity, playing the archetype mythically represented by Sita, the ideal wife portrayed in the *Ramayana*, with that of Rādhā, the object of erotic desire. Mehta's story traces the development of a lesbian relationship between a woman named Rādhā and her sister-in-law, Sita, who are living together in a joint household, both in loveless arranged marriages. Sita's husband, a handsome but self-absorbed Rama-like figure, is pursuing an affair with another woman. Rādhā's husband, an ascetic, has responded to her inability to have children by taking a vow of celibacy in pursuit of spiritual discipline, ignoring his wife's emotional needs for warmth and connection. At one level, it as if Jayadeva's spiritual quest were told from the perspective of Padmāvatī. If Nira and Mehta have not rejected Jayadeva's vision, they have certainly fractured, inverted, and complicated it. Nevertheless, despite the many ironies and the ambivalence, Jayadeva's vision persists as a profound pattern in the Indian psyche, and the *Gītagovinda* remains a classic both to India and in world literature.

SUGGESTED READINGS

Abbott, Justin E., and Narhar R. Godbole, eds. *Stories of Indian Saints: Translation of Mahipati's Marathi Bhaktavijaya*. Delhi: Motilal Banarsidass Publishers, 1933.

Archer, William George. *The Loves of Krishna in Indian Painting and Poetry*. New York: Grove Press, 1960.

Ayengar, N.S.R. *Gītagovindam: Sacred Profanities: A Study of Jayadeva's Gitagovinda*. Delhi: Penman Publishers, 2000.

Bharata Muni. *The Nātyaśāstra: English Translation with Critical Notes*. Trans. Adya Rangacharya. New Delhi: Munshiram Manoharlal, 1996.

Candīdāsa, Baru. *Singing the Glory of Lord Krishna: The Śrīkrsnakīrtana*. Trans. M. H. Klaiman. Chico, CA: Scholars Press, 1984.

Dimmitt, Cornelia, and J. A. van Buitenen, eds. and trans. *Classical Hindu Mythology: A Reader in the Sanskrit Purāṇas*. Philadelphia: Temple University Press, 1978.

Dimock, Edward C. *The Place of the Hidden Moon: Erotic Mysticism in the Vaisnava-sahajiyā Cult of Bengal*. Delhi: Motilal Banarsidass, 1991.

Hardy, Friedhelm. *The Religious Culture of India: Power, Love and Wisdom*. Cambridge: Cambridge University Press, 2005.

Hawley, John Stratton, and Donna Marie Wulff, eds. *The Divine Consort: Rādhā and the Goddesses of India*. Boston: Beacon Press, 1982.

James, Williams. *The Varieties of Religious Experience: A Study of Human Nature*. New York: Penguin Books, 1984.

Kālidāsa. *The Recognition of Śakuntalā*. Trans. W. J. Johnson. Oxford: Oxford University Press, 2001.

Kinsley, David. *The Sword and the Flute: Kālī and Krsna: Dark Visions of the Terrible and the Sublime in Hindu Mythology*. Berkeley: University of California Press, 1975.

Miller, Barbara Stoler, ed. *The Gītagovinda of Jayadeva: Love Song of the Dark Lord*. New York: Columbia University Press, 1977.

Narayan, R. K. *The Guide*. New York: Penguin Books, 1980.

Pathy, Dinahath, Bhagaban Panda, and Bijaya Kumar Rath, eds. *Jayadeva and Gītagovinda in the Traditions of Orissa*. New Delhi: Harman Publishing House, 1995.

Plato. *Symposium*. Trans. Alexander Nehamas and Paul Woodruff. Indianapolis: Hackett, 1989.

Puligandla, R. *Fundamentals of Indian Philosophy*. Nashville: Abingdon Press, 1975.

Radhakrishnan, Sarvepalli, and Charles A. Moore, eds. *A Sourcebook in Indian Philosophy*. Princeton: Princeton University Press, 1957.

Rājaśekhara. *Kāvyamīmāmsā: Original Text in Sanskrit and Translation with Explanatory Notes*. Ed. Sadhana Parashar. New Delhi: D. K. Printworld, 2000.

Rao, Jaja. *Kanthapura*. New York: New Directions, 1963.

———. *The Serpent and the Rope*. New York: Pantheon Books, 1960.

Śankara. *A Thousand Teachings: The Upadeśasāhasrī of Śankara*. Trans. Sengaku Mayeda. Albany: State University of New York Press, 1992.

Schweig, Graham M. *Dance of the Divine Love*. Princeton: Princeton University Press, 2005.

Siegel, Lee. *Sacred and Profane Dimensions of Love in Indian Traditions as Exemplified in the Gītagovinda of Jayadeva*. Delhi: Oxford University Press, 1972.

Vatsyayan, Kapila. *Classical Indian Dance in Literature and the Arts*. New Delhi: Sangeet Natak Akademi, 1968.

4

Sundiata

What we properly understand by Africa, is the Unhistorical, Undeveloped Spirit, still involved in the conditions of mere nature.

—G.W.F. Hegel, *The Philosophy of History* (99)

I am the man for the morrow [*sinimogo*].
I am the man of the day to follow [*sini-kini-mogo*].
I will rule over the bards,
And the three and thirty warrior clans.
I will rule over all these people.

—*The Epic of Son-Jara* (Johnson 52)

The *Sundiata*, also known as *Sunjata* or *Son-jara*, is one of the great epics of Africa. Its hero, Sundiata Keita or So'olon Jara ("Sogolon's Lion"), is the historical founder of the West African empire of Mali. Historians date him by the defeat of his great opponent, Soumaoro Kanté, around 1235. This historical battle appears in the climax of the epic. Although a later emperor (*mansa*), Kankan Musa (ruling from 1312 to 1327), had a wider fame outside Mali, especially in connection with his famous pilgrimage to Mecca (1324–1325), Sundiata remains the most celebrated, the undisputed cultural icon, his story a carefully ordered body of teaching.

Saying that the *Sundiata* is one of the epics of Africa immediately elicits two questions: What is meant by Africa? And what is meant by epic? The first question acknowledges the vast cultural, linguistic, and national diversity of the African continent. With regard to what Africa is, we should distinguish among North Africa (Egypt, Sudan, and Morocco, Algeria, and Tunisia); Francophone Africa, south of the Sahara; Anglophone west Africa (including Nigeria, Ghana, Sierra Leone, and Cameroon); east Africa (including Ethiopia, Kenya, Tanzania, and Uganda); and southern and South Africa, as well as the Portuguese-speaking African countries Mauritius and Réunion and finally Diasporian Africa, the complex influence and expression of African cultures beyond the African continent, found especially in the United States, the Caribbean, and South America—what the British sociologist Paul Gilroy terms the "Black Atlantic." Further, reference to the colonial languages in the division of regions should not submerge the fact that there are four major linguistic families in Africa and some 2,000 indigenous languages.

With regard to the *Sundiata*, then, we are discussing a work of the Mande peoples in West Africa. The name signifies speakers of the Manding group of languages (or dialects) in the Niger-Congo family, including Maninka, Bamana, Dyula, and Mandinka, distributed over a region that now includes Mali, Upper Volta, Senegal, and Gambia. In turn, variant and hybrid traditions extend into what are now the modern republics of Guinea and Sierra Leone. Some scholars also find echoes in Togo, Bénin, and northwestern Nigeria. There are versions not only in the Manding languages, but in the Wolof, Tukolor, Soninke, Khassonke, and Zarma languages as well.

As epic, the *Sundiata* assumes an important place among other African epic traditions, including the Mwindo epic of the Banyanga of eastern Zaire; *The Song of Seydou Camara*; Nsonga's *Lianja*, the epic of the Knundo Mongo of Zaire in south-central Africa; the *Dausi epic* of the Soninke people of north-central Africa, which includes the famous *Gassire's Lute*; and the *Ozidi Saga* of the Nigerian Ijo; also of relevance is the *Desturi za Waswahili* ("The Customs of the Swahili People") of Mtooro Bin Mwinyi Bakari; the *Bambara epic*; and the later Zulu works associated with the Emperor Shaka (or Chaka, 1787–1828), of special note Thomas Mofolo's 1925 novel *Chaka* and Mazisi Kunene's *Emperor Shaka the Great* (1979).

The question about epic also raises issues of both form and content. The formal question centers on the nature of oral narrative and the literary status of a work based originally on utterance and hearing instead of writing and reading, what the Kenyan linguist Pio Zirimu terms "orature," to distinguish it from other narrative systems, such as written—that is literature (the word *literature* derives from the Latin noun *litteratura*, "a writing," and ultimately *littera*, "letter [of the alphabet]"). More specifically, with regard to the *Sundiata*, the question of epic means that the work's original and primary existence is in oral performance or recitation by a *jèli* (plural *jeliw*), what is now conventionally designated by the French word *griot*. This complicates both the questions of text and authorship. Although some griots check their recitations against a carefully guarded written version (*tariku*), the griot is not simply performing verbatim a fixed text, the way an actor might perform a play by Shakespeare. Although there is a high degree of continuity and consistency among the variants, the order of some events, the identity of some characters, and matters of local color may vary from version to version. There are, in effect, as many versions of the *Sundiata* as performances. In this context, the notion of a final or definitive version is meaningless. There can be no critical edition as in the case of a novel. That said, none of this diminishes the merits of the *Sundiata*. The situation is analogous to that of Homer's *Iliad* and *Odyssey* or the old English *Beowulf*. The only difference is that in each of these cases, only a handful of versions committed to a written form has managed to survive the ravages of time, and there are no more bards to produce variants.

At the same time, many of these performances of the *Sundiata* have been recorded and transcribed, and some 20 of these have been translated into English. Authorship in this case conventionally identifies both the editor/translator and the griot. Among the versions readily available to the general reader, those edited by William Johnson (griot Fa-Digi Sisòkò), Gordon Innes (griots Bamba Suso, Banna Kanute, and Dembo Kanute), and David C. Conrad (griot Djanka Tassey Condé) represent translations of transcribed recitations. Those of D. T. (Djibril Tamsir) Niane (griot Mamadou Kouyaté) and Camara Laye (griot Babu Condé) are essentially historical novels constructed from the recension of several performances. This chapter will largely focus on D. T. Niane's version, which over the last 40 years has achieved something of a canonical status and which is accessible to most readers, though references will be made to other versions (especially William Johnson's) where relevant.

This brings us to the question of epic content. On one level, historians and anthropologists often treat the *Sundiata* as a historical source, though as with the historical and archaeological elements embedded in the *Iliad* or *Beowulf*, such usage is often problematic and should be employed with caution. Although the Mande people designate the *Sundiata* as history, a number of modern anthropologists and historians have noted the absence of the sort of details about the reign of the emperor that one would expect in a chronicle. It is more accurate to say that it is a work of art built on historical foundations. On a more conventional level, and congruent with Western epics, the *Sundiata* sings of the trials and triumphs of a hero. The word *epic* derives from the Greek *epikos* for songs praising or celebrating heroes whose exploits warrant remembering, and indeed, the *Sundiata* grows out of an African praise song tradition. On a deeper level, related to this, the *Sundiata*, like the *Iliad* or the *Mahābhārata* of India, does not merely incorporate, but embodies the cultural assumptions of its world, becoming a center of cultural identity, a center of focus that creates a sense of unity among often diverse groups. The *Sundiata* does this for the Mande peoples and beyond, transmitting their cosmology, their social structure, their wisdom literature, their linguistic modes and verbal texture, and their sense of themselves in the world. Unlike the *Iliad* or *Beowulf*, however, the *Sundiata* remains the expression of a living epic tradition for the very reason that there is no fixed or final version. Within the performance, the griot may refer to events or circumstances contemporary with the performance. For instance, the griot Fa-Digi Sisòkò, in a recitation recorded on March 9, 1968, made anachronistic references to the Republic of Mali and to airplanes: "Settling the backwoods does not suit the weak, / But he did not make airplanes his shoes / For to travel far and wide" (Johnson 54). More profoundly, the griot Babu Condé (in Camara Laye's *The Guardian of the Word*) delivered a heartfelt apostrophe after the defeat of the tyrannical Soumaoro Kanté that also seems to speak to the condition of suffering caused by some of modern Africa's postcolonial "big men"—from Sekou Touré of Guinea and Mobutu Sese Seko in Zaire to the infamous Idi Amin of Uganda. Such references and allusions are not narrative flaws, but epic vitality. In a very real sense, the words of the griot allow the past to speak to the present, to show the historical continuity between remote times and modern circumstances. For the griot, the *Sundiata* is not the artifact of a dead tradition, but a living presence.

GRIOTS AND ORAL LITERATURE

Between 1352 and 1353, the Moroccan merchant Abu Abdalla Ibn Battuta (1304–1354) traveled to west Africa, visiting the Mali empire and the court of its ruler, Mansa Sulaiman, a descendent of Sundiata. (Earlier adventures had taken Ibn Battuta to east Africa and as far as India and China.) His accounts provide the earliest and most detailed extant eyewitness accounts of Mali by an outsider. On the occasion of a festival, Ibn Battuta describes the performance of the poets—what he terms *julā*, his Arabic transliteration of the Manding word *jēli* or *griot*. It takes place before the king, who sits on a platform (*banbī*): "Each one of them has got inside a costume made of feathers to look like a thrush with a wooden head made for it and a red beak as if it were the head of a bird" (Hamdun 52). The poetry, described as a "kind of preaching," tells of the previous kings who had sat on the *banbī* and their good deeds. "Then the Archpoet mounts the steps of the *banbī* and places his head on the sultan's lap. Then he climbs on the top of the *banbī* and places it on his right shoulder, then on the left, meanwhile speaking in their tongue" (Hamdun 53). Glossing the scene, Ibn Battuta adds, "I was informed that this performance is old amongst them; they continued it from before Islam" (Hamdun 54).

It is debatable whether Ibn Battuta was witness to a performance of the *Sundiata*. Modern accounts cite recitations of four or five hours and sometimes over several days. Nevertheless, his account points to the importance of the griot and the role of oral performance in the culture. In the *Sundiata* the griot Balla Fasséké plays a crucial role, almost next to Sundiata himself. When the boy Sogolon Djata (who will become Sundiata) receives his griot, Balla Fasséké, who is the son of his father's griot, it is explained that "in Mali every prince has his own griot." He is further instructed, "Be inseparable friends from this day forward. From his mouth you will hear the history of your ancestors, you will learn the art of governing Mali according to the principles which our ancestors have bequeathed to us" (Niane 17). The griot of a prince is not an entertainer, but an alter ego and a living link with the past, whose praise songs give voice both to the past and to the future, a role affirmed by the hereditary nature of the position.

In one presentation recorded at the village of Kela (January 24, 1979), on the occasion of the seven-year ritual re-roofing of the Kamabolon (a sacred shrine), the recitation involved a narrator (*kumatigi* or master of the word), a musical accompanist, and a respondent (*naamu*-sayer) on whom the narrator called. In this sort of recitation, the narrator recites, rather than performs per se, speaking in a declamatory tone of voice. There is no interchange or response from the audience. On formal occasions, the *kumatigi* will wear a ritual costume.

One must be born a griot. In Mande society the griot belongs to a hereditary caste and assumes a monopoly over the special knowledge and skills passed down from father to son, uncle to nephew, thus the importance of the griot's pedigree. Mande society as a whole, even down to the present, describes itself as *fa-siya* ("father-lineage-ness") (Johnson, qtd. in Austen 11). The *Sundiata* describes the practices of female griots (griottes) as well, the corresponding voice for the queen or princess. Traditional Mande culture is agricultural, and most members of society are farmers. Within the culture, however, there are four protected hereditary castes, each of which has a monopoly on a specialized body of knowledge or skill: the *numu*, woodcarvers and blacksmiths; the *garangè*, leather workers; the *funè*, mimes and Islamic praise-poets; and the *jeli*, the bards or griots. In this protected role, the griot has control over the character and interpretation of history. He also has a monopoly over the use of musical instruments and certain classes of literature. The griot is also the mediator of social customs and values, his status in the caste giving him license (at least theoretically) to express opinions and judgments in public without fear of reprisal. All of this underlines the central importance of Sundiata's griot Balla Fasséké to the narrative. It also points to the cultural taboo that the tyrannical Soumaoro Kanté (often linked with the blacksmith caste) breaks, singing his own praises while accompanying himself on the balafon (a sort of xylophone). He is guilty not merely of vanity, but of violating caste boundaries.

Within a performance, the griot deploys three styles or modes of vocalization, shifting back and forth according to the need. These are the speech or narrative mode, the song mode, and the recitation or praise-proverb mode. Speaking in the narrative mode, the griot tells the story in his own words. To punctuate and commemorate outstanding events in the action, he will switch to the song mode, singing a traditional song or hymn. Here the words are generally fixed and well known, representing the oldest surviving parts of the work. At other moments, he will shift to the recitation mode, which consists of fixed phrases or formulaic expressions. These tend to be either praise-poems based on the names of ancestors and genealogical lists or general observations on life, involving verbal formulae associated with blessings, incantations, oaths, curses, prayers, praise-names, and proverbs. Throughout the performance by the griot, the respondent (naamu-sayer) interjects comments that affirm, underscore, or encourage what the griot says, most frequently using the words naamu, which roughly translates "yes" or "I hear you"; tinye, "truly"; walahi, "I swear"; and amina, "amen" (Conrad xviii).

PLOT AND CHARACTER DEVELOPMENT

Although the arrangement of episodes may differ among variants, in broad terms, the overall plot of the Sundiata may be divided into three sections or cycles of stories, pivoting around the hero's mother, Sogolon Kedjou (Sugulun Kòndè in Johnson). The first part outlines Manding cosmology and origins and traces the genealogy of the kings up through the marriage of Sogolon Kedjou and Maghan Kon Fatta (Fara Magan, the Handsome, in Johnson). The second part follows the birth of Sundiata and his early trials, triumphs, and exile through the death of Sogolon Kendjou. Her death is the sign that he must seek his destiny, an omen of his future triumph. The third part centers on Sundiata's struggle and defeat of the tyrant Soumaoro Kanté (Sumamuru in Johnson) and from there on the foundation of the empire.

For the sake of narrative smoothness, Niane conflates elements of the first and second parts in his reconstruction of the Sundiata. He first briefly sketches the genealogy of the Manding kings back to Bilali Bounama (Bilal ibn Ribah), a companion of the Prophet Muhammad and the first muezzin, the one who makes the call to prayer (adhan) in Islam. Throughout the epic, and by extension throughout the Manding culture, there is a complex interplay between Islamic and pre-Islamic concepts, especially involving the role of spirits, magic, sorcery, and occult knowledge. The scholar Ivor Wilks notes that many of the traditional songs remain unchanged, but there is an overlay of "Islamization" with regard to the legitimacy of the state, "in accordance with an Islamic vision of what constitutes a Rightful Caliphate" (Wilks, qtd. in Austen 51). Wilks draws a parallel with the Christianization of the pagan bards of medieval Wales. The genealogy that begins with Bilali culminates in Maghan Kon Fatta, of the Keita family, the father of Sundiata. One day, a hunter skilled in the arts of the soothsayer arrives at Maghan's capital, Ni-aniba (Niani). Communicating through Maghan's griot, Gnankouman Doua, he casts cowrie shells, predicting that the king will be approached by two hunters, accompanied by a hideous woman with a disfiguring hump on her back—her ugliness corresponding with his beauty. The hunter admonishes the king to marry this woman, telling him that from this union will be born a son who will rival Alexander the Great, creating a great empire. (The theme of Alexander enters through Islamic influence, in which Alexander—Sekandar or Iskandar—embodied military prowess, and later Sundiata will style himself the last great conqueror after Alexander.) The king is disturbed by this prophecy, but lets it pass.

One day, two hunters arrive from the country of Do, the brothers Oulamba and Oulani, bringing a woman they claim would make a worthy wife for the king. They proceed to tell their story. The kingdom of Do was being rav-aged by a giant buffalo. The king of Do had sent out a call to anyone who could save his people and vanquish the buffalo. Many hunters had tried, but failed. The brothers decided to take up the challenge. Approaching the city, they encountered a wretched, weeping, hungry old woman. Although others ignored her, the brothers felt sympathy and gave her food. Moved by this act of kindness, the old woman explained that she was a sorceress, the sister of the current king of Do, who had cheated her out of her inheritance; she told them that she, in fact, was the buffalo. To reward their generosity, she told them how to kill her, with the added proviso that they take as their reward the ugly and hump-backed Sogolon Kedjou. (Sogolon's humped back shows a correspondence with the powerful spirit of the buffalo, signified by its great hump or crest.) The brothers followed the old woman's advice to the letter, even though the people of Do later mocked them as fools for choosing the ugly Sogolon as their reward. The brothers now consider her worthy of King Maghan, who accepts the offering with trepidation, recalling the predictions of the earlier hunter. Other versions begin the narrative with an extended account of the battle with the buffalo, and some versions have each of the brothers trying to sleep with Sogolon, but prevented by her magical powers.

Sogolon becomes the king's second wife, instigating a jealous response on the part of his first wife, Sassouma Bérété, who wishes to guard the interests of the son she has borne by Maghan. Sogolon at first resists the king's advances with her magical powers, protected by her wraith. Turning to subterfuge, he appears one night with his drawn sword, telling her that he was approached by the protective spirit of the Manding kings and told that he must spill the blood of a virgin. He prepares to strike her with his sword, so terrifying Sogolon that her wraith cannot enter her body to protect her. She submits to Maghan, and on that night, Sundiata is conceived.

The second cycle of stories focuses around the childhood and exile of Sundiata. Sogolon bears the king a son and then later a daughter and another son. The jealous first wife, Sassouma Bérété, arranges that a hex be cast on the baby Sogolon Djata (Sundiata), and it soon becomes evident that he is crippled, spending his first years crawling on all fours, with no ambition but eating. In Naine's version, Sassouma Bérété's son, Dankaran Touman, is 11 years older than Sundiata. In other versions, they are born at the same time, underlining the theme of competition. The griot Gnankouman Doua keeps the faith, reassuring the king that the delayed development is a sign of powerful forces coming together (the spirit of the buffalo, Do, and the spirit of the lion, Manding). The king has his doubts, but arranges that his son be granted his own griot, Gnankouman Doua's son, Balla Fasséké. The king also takes a third wife, who will bear him a daughter, Nana Triban, Sundiata's half sister. When the king finally dies, his first son, Dankaran Touman, is declared king, and the new king's mother, who is made regent, uses her position to persecute Sogolon.

Among the most famous episodes is that of the baobab tree, Sundiata's first great triumph. Sogolon and her children (Sundiata, a sister, and a brother) have been reduced to subsisting on Sassouma Bérété's leftovers. One day, when Sundiata is about seven, Sogolon goes to Sassouma asking for some baobab leaves, used as a condiment in cooking. (Indigenous to Africa and Australia, the baobab is also known by the name "monkey-bread" tree or "upside-down" tree because it looks like the roots are in the air and its branches in the ground.) Sogolon receives them, but must endure the derisive laughter of Sassouma: "As for me, my son knew how to walk at seven and it was he who went and picked these baobab leaves. Take them then, since your son is un-equal to mine" (Naine 19). Finding his humiliated mother weeping, the boy Sundiata declares that he will stand and walk that very day, instructing Balla Fasséké to have an iron rod made for his support. In front of the village and the apprentice blacksmiths who brought the rod, Sundiata struggles to his feet, triumphing over his condition, the iron rod twisting to the shape of a bow in the process. Balla Fasséké celebrates this in the "Hymn to the Bow," which is now a traditional song, performed in the song mode by the griot:

Took up the bow!
Simbon, Master-of-the Bush!

Took up the bow!
Took up the bow!
Ruler of bards and smiths

...

The Wizard has risen! (Johnson 62)

Sundiata now builds his strength, earning honor and credit as a hunter. "The multitude loves and fears strength," the griot explains in praise-proverb mode. "All Niani talked of nothing but Djata [Sundiata]; mothers urged their sons to become hunting companions of Djata and to share his games, as if they wanted their offspring to profit from the nascent glory of the buffalo-woman's son" (Naine 22). The episode comes to a conclusion when the young Sundiata finally redeems his mother's honor by pulling up Sassouma Bérété's baobab tree by the roots and replanting it in front of Sogolon's hut.

Sassouma Bérété realizes that Sundiata's magical powers and his accumulating honor make him a legitimate contender for the throne. She cajoles the weak-willed Dankaran Touman to apply pressure. Thus, when Sundiata is in the bush hunting, the king orders that he be stripped of Balla Fasséké. The insult has its desired effect, and Sundiata and his family enter into exile, traveling from city to city, though pursued by Dankaran Touman's agents, who try to sabotage them. The relationship between Sundiata and his half brother echoes the earlier struggles between the buffalo woman and her brother, the king of Do.

The exiles are forced to travel from kingdom to kingdom. Two episodes are of note. Early on, they find themselves welcomed in the palace of Mansa Konkon, the sorcerer king of Djedeba, where they enjoy several months of hospitality and respite. Agents of Dankaran Touman, however, bribe the king. One day, he challenges Sundiata to a game of wori, a game akin to draughts. "If I win—and I shall win—I kill you," Mansa Konkon declares (Naine 30). Sundiata suspects foul play, but confident of his destiny, knows no fear. In an act of self-possessed bravado, he takes one of the king's swords off the wall and fences in the air. The king begins, chanting the appropriate incantation: "I am unbeatable at this game / I am called the 'exterminator king.'" Sundiata echoes his song with the added ironic refrain, "Formerly guests were sacred.../ But the gold came only yesterday" (Naine 30). Flustered that he has been caught violating the sacred taboo of the guest-host relationship, Mansa Konkon concedes the game, giving Sundiata and his family their lives. Thanking the king for his hospitality, the exiles resume their journey. After many more stops along the way, they find themselves in the city of Mema, in a kingdom on the Niger River ruled by old King Kounkara. Here the now ailing Sogolon finds repose, and Sundiata earns such glory as a great warrior that the king hopes to leave his kingdom to him. Sogolon dies, and Sundiata realizes that he must leave to fulfill his own destiny. King Kounkara, dismayed and angered that Sundiata might leave (which seems to him an act of ingratitude), at first refuses to allow Sogolon to be buried without payment of a fee. Sundiata goes off, returning with a basket full of pottery shards, bird feathers, and other bits of trash. The king's advisor rightly interprets this gesture as symbolic of Mema's fate if the king persists in his refusal. Wisely, he relents, and Sogolon is buried with royal honors, her death closing the second cycle of stories and marking the beginning of Sundiata's triumphant return.

While Sundiata has been in exile, the tyrannical Soumaoro Kanté, king of Sosso, aided by a powerful magic that makes him invincible, has been on the rise, conquering various kingdoms and even compelling tribute from the king of Ghana. Next to Sundiata himself, Soumaoro is the most compelling figure in the epic. He is portrayed as utterly ruthless, wearing clothes made of human skin. In a secret chamber high in a great tower, in the middle of his palace, he safeguards the fetishes that give him magical power, his throne surrounded by a circle of nine jars (or calabashes) that contain the heads of defeated kings. The room is guarded by three owls and a monstrous serpent. There is also a giant balafon, a musical instrument akin to a xylophone, on which Soumaoro celebrates his own praises. Despite this, the struggle between Sundiata and Soumaoro Kanté should not be read in terms of a Manichean struggle between good and evil but as something more complex. In many ways Soumaoro may be regarded a cultural hero. Some versions associate him with the blacksmith caste, a master of fire and an important source of occult powers. Among the Dogons of central Mali and the Bambara, the primal or "celestial" smith is the civilizing hero, come to earth to reveal civilization (Eliade 94). Some historians suggest that Soumaoro was really the first emperor (*mansa*) of Mali and that the *Sundiata* contains elements from a now-lost epic tradition about him, a reminder that the victor writes the history. William Johnson reports that Soumaoro is still worshiped in the town of Kouloukoro (Johnson 8).

Fearful of the danger, King Dankaran Touman sends Nana Triban to Soumaoro as tribute, along with Balla Fasséké as an envoy. One day, when the king of Sosso is away, Balla Fasséké manages to find the secret chamber. Frightened by what he sees, he begins playing the balafon, subduing the serpent and owls and causing the heads to resume their human form. Hearing the music, the king returns to the room. Balla Fasséké manages to save himself by improvising a praise song for him. "All hail, Simbon of the deadly arrow. / I salute you, you who wear clothes of human skin" (Naine 40).

The crisis finally breaks when Soumaoro decides to abduct the wife of his nephew and chief general. Outraged, the nephew appeals to Dankaran Touman, who mobilizes his forces. However, they are quickly defeated by Soumaoro, Dankaran Touman flees, and Niani, the capital of Dankaran Touman's kingdom, is burned to the ground. Sundiata and Sogolon, still alive at this point, learn of the disaster from refugees selling baobab leaves in the marketplace. Upon the death of his mother, Sundiata realizes that his destiny involves the defeat of Soumaoro and the recovery of his kingdom.

The armies led by Sundiata confront the vast hosts of Soumaoro. Despite terrible carnage, Sundiata finds that the king of Sosso is impervious to weapons because of his magic and that he can shape-shift, or appear and disappear at will. "The battle of Neguéboria showed Djata [Sundiata], if he needed to be shown, that to beat the king of Sosso other weapons were necessary" (Niane 52). The key to victory comes from Nana Triban and Balla Fasséké, who have managed to escape Sosso amid the chaos, at last reuniting Sundiata with his half sister and griot. Nana Triban explains how she used her wiles to sexually entice Soumaoro, which allowed her to learn that his magic can be destroyed by an arrow mounted with a cock's spur. Armed with this knowledge, Sundiata is finally able to successfully attack and wound the king of Sosso in the next great battle. Realizing that he has lost his power, Soumaoro retreats behind his army, which dissolves in panic and confusion. Sundiata pursues the fleeing Soumaoro up a mountain, killing his horse with a spear. The old king continues up the slope on foot, disappearing into a cave, never to be seen again. Other versions have him turned into a giant stone, thereafter the spirit of the place. Sundiata's army destroys Sosso, "now a spot where guinea fowl and young partridges come to take their dust baths" (Niane 69).

The epic draws to a conclusion as Sundiata consolidates his authority over the various kingdoms of the Manden, becoming the emperor (or mansa), celebrated by everyone, his empire marked by peace and prosperity. Returning to the Islamic theme, the griot explains that "he followed the very word of God.... Under his sun the upright man was rewarded and the wicked one punished" (Niane 81). Niane's version ends with an evocation of the spiritual greatness of Mali, contrasting a diminished present with the glories of the past. "How many piled-up ruins, how much buried splendour!" (Niane 85).

THEMES

At the end of Niane's version of the *Sundiata*, the griot Mamadou Kouyaté addresses his audience: "Men of today, how small you are beside your ancestors, and small in mind too, for you have trouble in grasping the meaning of my words" (Niane 84). His words contain two themes, the enduring authority of the hero, especially when compared with the "men of today," and the authority of the griot as the vehicle for transmitting legitimacy, the possessor of special knowledge.

In traditional Mande culture, there are two sources of power, a vertical line related to family lineage ("father-lineage-ness"), the older having authority over the younger, and also a horizontal line that cuts across the vertical, with various groups of associations or societies drawn from different family lineages. Some of these are age-specific groups, often involving initiations; others are groups formed to engage in charitable work or religious associations. Of special note are hunters' societies (*donson-ton*), concerned with initiating their members in the special knowledge of nature and the wilderness. Because their knowledge and domain of action center on the bush, the hunters are asocial, standing outside or between communities, granting their initiates a special status. "Many believe that hunters are the people in Mande society most capable of rebalancing chaos at the cosmological level through their superior knowledge of the occult," says William Johnson (qtd. in Austen 14). Not surprisingly, Sogolon is brought to Maghan Kon Fatta by the hunter brothers Oulamba and Oulani, lending legitimacy to the marriage, to indeed the union of the lion and the buffalo. Similarly, it is not surprising that Sassouma Bérété perceives a threat to the legitimacy of her son's claims to the throne because of Sundiata's own achievements as a hunter.

There is, however, another way of achieving power outside the horizontal and vertical lines of authority. This derives from sanctioned competition, struggle, and alliances among half siblings in polygamous families. This is seen, for instance, in the antagonistic relationship between Sundiata and his half brother, Dankaran Touman, and in the loyalty between Sundiata and his half sister, Nana Triban. As in any complex set of family relationships, there is a tension between the desire to change and the desire to preserve the status quo, a delicate balance between advancing one's position in the family and rupturing family order, knowing how far to bend the rules without snapping the social order. By analogy, insofar as the family structure is perceived as an expression of the cosmos as a whole, the would-be hero must engage in dangerous behaviors that have the potential to damage the social order. "Cosmologically," says Johnson, "the act of violating norms is seen to release into the atmosphere vast amounts of occult power" (qtd. in Austen 16). The essence of the true hero in Mande society is the one who knows his destiny and is able to negotiate the delicate balance between order and chaos. "The multitude loves and fears strength," says the griot. The one who can demonstrate strength wins power.

Sundiata's behavior exemplifies these characteristics. The declaration to his mother that he will stand shows a self-awareness of his abilities, and further, in uprooting the baobab tree, he creates a disruption that earns him great power in his community. His swagger and bravado in accepting Mansa Kondon's challenge to a deadly game of wori, or his seeming disrespect of his benefactor the king of Mema, are not reckless gestures, but carefully gauged acts, based on his sense of destiny, his own limits, and the limits of his opponents. In contrast, Soumaoro exemplifies the opposite, losing power not because he is evil, per se, but because he has misjudged his own destiny and the limits of others. He overstepped the line, broke the order, and released chaos when he took his nephew's wife. Similarly, he misjudged the loyalty of Nana Triban when he boasted about the secret to his magic, and ultimately, he misjudged the invincibility of his occult powers. The result is the release of power that destroys him and enhances Sundiata.

SUBSEQUENT INFLUENCE

Historically, the empire begun by Sundiata reached its peak during the reign of Mansa Musa (1312–1337), including the capture of Tombouctou. By the end of the fourteenth century, the Mande empire had ceased to exist, a consequence of divisions and struggles with competing indigenous empires and eventually the pressures of the African slave trade and European colonization. By the eighteenth century, the region was controlled by the Segu (Bambara), who themselves lost control in an 1862 jihad led by al-Hajj 'Umar of the Tukulor tribe. In turn, this empire as well as that of the Mandingo chief Samory (1830–1900) were conquered by French colonial forces, culminating in the formation of the French Sudan in 1898. The year 1959 saw the establishment of the Sudanese Republic, followed in June 1960 by the Mali Federation, an independent sovereign state. This gave way in August 1960 to the Republic of Mali under the one-party dictatorship of Modibo Keita, followed by regional difficulties to the present. (To legitimize his power, Modibo Keita appealed to the hereditary authority of the Sundiata Keita's family name.)

Scholars argue that the *Sundiata* grew out of a synthesis of praise-songs and various Mande narrative traditions, especially hunter epics (*maana*). It differs from these epics, however, in that it is also designated *tariku* (from the Arabic *tarikh*, history). The effect, says historian Ralph A. Austen, is the transformation of the historical Sundiata into a figure both "superhistorical" and "ahistorical," in that "he remains a verifiable human agent from the past and also because the narrative leaps across mundane history to a mythologized dynastic founder as response to the historical experience of alienation from the sources of material power" (Austen 74). Coming to full fruition in the eighteenth century, the epic became a way for the Mande to reassert its cultural identity as well as its legitimacy among Islamic nations, whether in response to the Bambara, Tukulor, and Samory or to the French. "It is this contemplation of a socially complex yet, by the time of its telling, largely imaginary 'national' identity," writes Austen, "that endows the epic with its power and, perhaps, ironically, gives it meaning to audiences far beyond the Manden or even Africa" (Austen 79–80).

It was largely the effort of D. T. Niane's reconstruction, turning one version of the *Sundiata* into written prose (French, 1960, and English, 1965) and giving it a form, that has allowed it to enter the wider mainstream of world literature. In transforming orature to literature, Niane's work approaches the form of a historical novel, often concentrating or paring down some of the verbal elements of the performance to conform to the expectations of modern narrative. (Analogously, modern readers of the *Iliad* tend to skim over the so-called "black ships" section, whose long genealogies are important to the cultural memory of the original peoples but no longer resonate with the modern reader.) The result is that though Niane preserves some of the flavor and rhythm of the original language, he has eliminated much of the verbal art. Perhaps echoing the spirit of the griot to relate the performance to the modern situation, he has tended to read history in terms of the spirit of modern nationalism. That said, it remains an important achievement in the canonization of the *Sundiata*. Other versions that have followed Niane were mentioned earlier in the chapter, including those edited by William Johnson, Gordon Innes, and David C. Conrad, all aiming to follow more closely the formal qualities of the original performances. Camara Laye's *The Guardian of the Word,* on the other hand, draws more explicitly on the resources of the novel. Like Niane, Laye sees the text as commenting on the modern political condition in Africa.

The *Sundiata* in turn has inspired other works, some of special note. Camara Laye's novel *The Radiance of the King* (1954/65) reads elements of the *Sundiata* through Kafka. Similarly, Yambo Ouologuem's *Bound to Violence* (1968/71) and Ahmadou Kourouma's *The Suns of Independence* (1970/81) and *Monnè* (1990) play against the theme of a ruler who uses an appeal to the occult to hold on to power, playing ironically against the epic tradition. In Alex Haley's *Roots* (1976), the name of Kunta Kinte makes deliberate allusion to family names found in the *Sundiata*. Also of interest is Maryse Conde's *Segu* (1984/87), which picks up the history of Mali in the eighteenth century. Elements can also be found in recent African cinema. Director Cheick Oumar Sissoko's *Guimba the Tyrant* (1995), on a variety of motifs, draws especially on the figure of Soumaoro. Particularly fine is Dani Kouyaté's *Keita: The Heritage of the Griot* (1994), which recounts the story of Sundiata up through his triumphant standing on his two feet. It is told within the frame narrative of a modern-day griot's arriving at the home of a boy named Mabo Keita to teach him the meaning of his name. All of this is a reminder to the boy that culture and civilization did not begin with Western colonization. At the end of the film, the griot disappears, and the spirit of a hunter tells the boy that he must seek his griot to complete the story. True to the spirit of the original, Sundiata remains "the man for the morrow" and the "day to follow," the embodiment of a past that promises a future.

SUGGESTED READINGS

Allen, J.W.T., ed. *The Customs of the Swahili People: The* Desturi za Waswahili *of Mtoro bin Mwinyi Bakari*. Berkeley: University of California Press, 1981.

Austen, Ralph A., ed. *In Search of Sunjata: The Mande Oral Epic as History, Literature, and Performance*. Bloomington: Indiana University Press, 1999.

Barlet, Olivier. *African Cinemas: Decolonizing the Gaze*. Trans. Chris Turner. London: Zed Books, 2000.

Beier, Ulli, ed. *Introduction to African Literature: An Anthology of Critical Writing*. London: Longman, 1979.

Belcher, Stephen. *Epic Traditions of Africa*. Bloomington: Indiana University Press, 1999.

Biebuyck, Daniel P. *The Mwindo Epic from the Banyanga*. Berkeley: University of California Press, 1969.

Bird, Charles S., and Martha B. Kendall. "The Mande Hero: Text and Context." *Explorations in African Systems of Thought*. Ed. Ivan Karp and Charles S. Bird. Washington, D.C.: Smithsonian Institution Press, 1980. 13–26.

Bulman, Stephen. "The Buffalo-Woman Tale: Political Imperatives and Narrative Constraints in the Sunjata Epic." *Discourse and Its Disguises: The Interpretation of African Oral Texts*. Ed. Karin Barber and P. F. de Moraes Farias. Birmingham: Centre of West African Studies, University of Birmingham, 1989. 171–188.

Conrad, David C., ed. *Sunjata: A West African Epic of the Mande Peoples*. Indianapolis: Hackett Publishing Company, 2004.

Dorson, Richard M., ed. *African Folklore*. New York: Anchor Books, 1972.

Eliade, Mircea. *The Forge and the Crucible: The Origins and Structures of Alchemy*. Trans. Stephen Corrin. Chicago: University of Chicago Press, 1978.

Gugler, Josef. *African Film: Re-Imagining a Continent*. Bloomington: Indiana University Press, 2003.

Hamdun, Said, and Noël King. *Ibn Battuta in Black Africa*. Princeton: Markus Wiener Publishers, 1994.

Hay, Margaret Jean, ed. *African Novels in the Classroom*. Boulder, CO: Lynne Rienner Publishers, 2000.

Hegel, Georg, and Wilhelm Friedrich. *The Philosophy of History*. Trans. J. Sibree. New York: Dover Publications, 1956.

Heine, Bernd, and Derek Nurse, eds. *African Languages: An Introduction*. Cambridge: Cambridge University Press, 2000.

Innes, Gordon, ed. *Sunjata: The Mandinka Versions*. London: School of Oriental and African Studies, University of London, 1974.

Jansen, Jan. "The Sunjata Epic—The Ultimate Version." *Research in African Literatures* 32.1 (Spring 2001): 14–46.

Johnson, William John, ed. *The Epic of Son-Jara: A West African Tradition*. Bloomington: Indiana University Press, 1992.

Kesteloot, Lilyan, and Amadou Traore. *Da Monzon de Segu: épopée bambara*. Paris: F. Nathan, 1972.

Kourouma, Ahmadou. *The Suns of Independence*. Trans. Adrian Adams. New York: African Publishing Company, 1981.

Kunene, Mazisi. *Emperor Shaka the Great: A Zulu Epic*. London: Heinemann, 1979.

Laye, Camara. *The Guardian of the Word*. Trans. James Kirkup. New York: 1984.

Maneniang', Mubima. *The Lianja Epic*. Nairobi: East African Educational Publishers, 1999.

Mbiti, John S. *African Religions and Philosophy*. 2nd ed. London: Heinemann, 1989.

Mofolo, Thomas. *Chaka*. Trans. Daniel P. Kunene. London: Heinemann, 1981.

Mudimbe, V. Y. *The Invention of Africa: Gnosis, Philosophy and the Order of Knowledge*. Bloomington: Indiana University Press, 1988.

Ngũgĩ wa Thiong'o. *Penpoints, Gunpoints, and Dreams: Towards a Critical Theory of the Arts and the State in Africa*. Oxford: Clarendon Press, 1998.

Niane, D.T. *Sundiata: An Epic of Old Mali*. Trans. G.D. Pickett. Harlow, Essex: Addison Wesley Longman, 1994.

Okabou, Ojobolo. *The Ozidi Saga*. Trans. J.P. Clark-Bekederemo. Washington, D.C.: Howard University Press, 1991.

Okpewho, Isidore. *The Epic in Africa: Toward a Poetics of the Oral Performance*. New York: Columbia University Press, 1979.

Ouologuem, Yambo. *Bound to Violence*. Trans. Ralph Manheim. London: Heinemann, 1971.

Thackway, Melissa. *Africa Shoots Back: Alternative Perspectives in Sub-Saharan Francophone African Film*. Bloomington: Indiana University Press, 2003.

5

Poetry of Li Po

Two things of opposite natures seem to depend
On one another, as a man depends
On a woman, day on night, the imagined
On the real. This is the origin of change.
—Wallace Stevens, "Notes Toward a Supreme Fiction" (392)

Don't think, look!
—Ludwig Wittgenstein, *Philosophical Investigations* (#66)

The Tang dynasty of China (618–907 C.E.) produced some of the finest achievements in Chinese poetry, and among the poets of this period, Li Po (also transliterated Li Bai or Li Bo, and Rihaku in Japanese) is considered among the greatest. In this ranking he is often paired with his friend Tu Fu, as well as the poets Bo Juyi, Wang Wei, and Han-shan. Sometimes known by the title "Banished Immortal," or *zhexian*, an epithet that combines the themes of exile and the ineffable qualities that transcend human limitations, he cultivated an aura of mystery and projected a persona of reckless bravado and quiet spirituality, producing an art that seemed to blend spontaneity with high polish, the poet genius, consuming life and flouting social conventions. At the same time, he is the poet mystic, contemplating the moon, probing the melancholy of departure and absence. He is the radical in the garb of traditional forms. All of this has served to detach him from the specifics of time and place, creating a myth of the poet who belongs nowhere and everywhere. All of this combines to make Li Po the "unattainable" ideal in Chinese poetry, giving expression to the inexpressible, articulating the experience beyond words. It is also what has given him resonance beyond China, even despite the limitations of translation. His aesthetic of absence evoked by images exercised a profound influence on modernist poetry in the West, as did his sense of the correspondence of nature suffused with spiritual significance. In turn the persona of the wandering and unconventional poet mystic spoke to the spiritual and aesthetic yearnings of unconventional writers such as the Beats, making him among the most influential Chinese poets.

HISTORICAL AND BIOGRAPHICAL CONTEXT

With the fall of the Han dynasty (202 B.C.E.–220 B.C.E.), China fragmented into political and social chaos. The north and south were eventually reunited under the Sui (581–618 C.E.), which in turn fell to the Tang (618–906 C.E.), thereby continuing the process of reunification and expansion, witnessing the farthest projections of the Chinese empire and a period of political and social stability that nurtured some of the highest achievements of Chinese civilization and some of its finest contributions to world culture. Li Po lived during the reign of the emperor Hsüan-Tsung, known by the title Ming Huong (the "brilliant Emperor"), a reign that marked the zenith of the Tang, but also the beginning of its decline.

There is much ambiguity around the specifics of Li Po's life, and he himself was always careful in the cultivation of his public persona. The legend of Li Po, Stephen Owen notes, far exceeds the meager record (Owen 117). Much of what we know is derived from and therefore conditioned by his poetry. It is generally agreed that he was born in 701 C.E. in central Asia, in what is now Kyrgyzstan, outside the boundaries of China proper. His family seems to have been merchants or traders, though Li Po liked to suggest that he was kin to the royal Li clan. The family moved to Ch'ang-ming in the Szechuan province of western China, continuing as merchants and as minor officials in the government bureaucracy. Although demonstrating an early talent, Li Po never took the imperial examinations that were the conventional route into the civil service and the key to government preferment. (Tu Fu was to fail the exam, but was able to secure a government job anyway.) Rather, he pursued the role of *hsieh*, variously translated "knight-errant" or "bravo," a sort of itinerant avenger working outside official channels, though sanctioned by Confucianism, also a reminder that the Kung Fu heroes of Chinese popular culture are part of a long-established tradition. "Li Po ran his sword through quite a number of people," his (perhaps credulous) friend Wei Hao claimed (Waley 6). In a move not uncommon among a certain class of soldiers-of-fortune, Li Po retreated to the mountains where he spent several years as a Daoist recluse. In one early poem he describes visiting a Daoist master in the mountains. The tranquil scene is interrupted by the barking of a dog, though the master himself is not to be found: "While bamboo parts blue haze. A stream / hangs in flight beneath emerald peaks. / No one knows where you've gone. Still / for rest, I've found two or three pines" (Hinton 3). From an early stage, Li Po plays on the recurrent paired motif of presence and absence. Similarly, all through his life he pursued an interest in Daoist alchemy and its quest for the golden elixir of immortality. Stephen Owen points out that Li Po was one of the first Chinese poets to draw extensively on the imagery of alchemical lore. Parodying a traditional song and playing on this imagery, Li Po despaired over his failure to find the golden elixir,: "moon-rabbit's immortality balm is empty, / and the timeless *fu-sang* [mulberry] tree kindling" (Hinton 110).

By the year 724 he was married, the father of a son, and living in An-lu in eastern China. From references in his poetry, it is supposed that over the course of his life, he was married four times and had another son and a daughter; for example, there is the poem "Sent to My Two Children in Sha-Ch'iu" (Hinton 61). The apparent death of his first wife and son around 730 set him on the life of a wanderer, enjoying increasing fame for his abilities as a poet and his exploits as a carouser. Not surprisingly, many of his poems are about departure and absence. One late poem is addressed to his absent wife: "This separation hurts, and Yeh-lang [the remote city where he is to be exiled] is beyond sky. / Moonlight fills the house, but news never comes." The moonlight is a plenitude that underlines the emptiness of the room. In a re-current motif of circularity, he adds, "I watch geese disappear north in spring, and now / they're coming south, but no letter from Yü-chang" (Hinton 99).

His fame finally reached the imperial court in its capital Ch'ang-an (Xi'an). Through the good offices of a friend, from whom he earned the famous accolade "banished immortal," Li Po attended the emperor Hsüan-Tsung in 742. The emperor showed his favor, though instead of the coveted government office, gave Li Po a position in the Hanlin Academy as a court poet whose duties involved composing occasional verse, writing declarations, commemorating social occasions, and making inscriptions. His reputation for carousing and outrageous behavior made him a sort of official bad boy in residence for the amusement of the court, with stories of his being able to write poetry even when drunk. "What's taking that wine seller so long?" he asks in one poem, explaining, "Mountain flowers smiling, taunting me, / it's the perfect time to sip some wine" (Hinton 31). Despite his penchant for dissipation, he was capable of composing much fine and sensitive work, marked by a subtle and evocative use of imagery. Among the most famous poems to come out of his stay at court is the moving "Jade-Staircase Grievance":

The dew is white upon the jade steps,
And wets her gauze stocking. The night is far gone.
She turns within, lets fall the crystal curtain,
And gazes up at the autumn moon, shining through.
(Obata with modifications 48)

The poem describes the circumstances of a court lady who has fallen out of favor with her lover. Evoking a mood of melancholy, Li Po imagines the lady sadly waiting in vain for her lover to visit her. The image of dew on the steps correlates to the late hour and long wait. The general atmosphere is momentarily shocked and heightened by the sensation of the stocking foot stepping into the cold dew, an immediate and tangible evocation of the present that intensifies and pulls us into the moment, like lightning on a summer night, or a dog barking on a warm afternoon. In turn, he juxtaposes the images of the solid, "crystalline" and jeweled blinds with the transient autumn moon. This deployment of images invites comparison with the poor lady, a sort of court ornament confronting the transience of her beauty and her life. The poem illustrates many of Li Po's favorite strategies: the mood-shattering sensation that draws our attention to the immediacy of presence, the juxtaposition of opposites, the tone of melancholy absence, and the motif of cycles that mark impermanence or inevitable change.

Li Po's routine eventually wore thin, and he was dismissed from court around 744, resuming his peripatetic lifestyle. At about this time, he met the younger Tu Fu (712–790 c.e.), aptly in a wineshop, and thus began their lifelong friendship. Since then, they have perpetually been linked together, defined as polar opposites: Li Po the genius, the Daoist immortal; Tu Fu, the erudite scholar, the Confucian sage. The mystical poet, ever elusive and fluid, *versus* the ethical poet, truthful and solid. Two playful poems addressed to each other indicate something of how each perceived the other, or at least the other's public persona. In his "Eight Immortals of the Wine Cup," Tu Fu writes, "As for Li Po, give him a jugful, / He will write one hundred poems" (Obata 186). Li Po returns the favor, writing, "it's Tu Fu / under a midday sun sporting his huge farmer's hat." Addressing him directly, he asks, "How is it you've gotten so thin since we parted? / Must be all those poems you've been suffering over" (Hinton 54). In short, from the start it is the image of a drunken Li Po, spontaneously pouring forth, and a laborious and dutiful Tu Fu, sweating over his craftsmanship. Beneath these personae, reality is undoubtedly somewhere in-between. Both Daoist and Confucian doctrine sanction that truly creative spontaneity requires the internalization of a high degree of skill and self-discipline and that craftsmanship without some spark of genius quickly becomes formal and pedantic. The improvisations of a Bach or jazz musician involve both genius and practice.

At this time, China was struck by a succession of natural, political, and military disasters, complicated by the fact that the emperor Hsüan-Tsung, having grown bored with politics, focused his attentions on alchemy and on his consort, Yang Kuei-fei. The poet Bo Juyi (772–846) commemorated this fatal romance in his ballad "The Everlasting Wrong" ("Ch'ang hen ko"), a work of widespread fame and influence throughout China and Japan. The distracted emperor left governance in the hands of his prime minister, Li Lin-fu. To consolidate his own power, Li Lin-fu replaced ethnic Chinese military governors in the provinces with foreign warlords whom he thought he could better control. In December 755, one of these warlords, An Lu-shan (of ethnic Turkish background), seizing the opportunity, swept out of the north and captured Lo-Yang, the northern capital, and declared himself emperor. The following year, he captured and sacked Ch'ang-an, obliging Hsüan-Tsung and his court to retreat. Trying to avoid the onslaught, Li Po and his family fled south. The dating of his poems is difficult to ascertain, but his "War South of the Great Wall," disguised in the form of a folksong set in the Han Dynasty, supposedly sung by a woman lamenting the loss of her husband, expresses his own sense of despair. "It never changes: nothing since ancient times but bleached bones in fields of yellow sand," the narrator laments. "A Ch'in emperor built the Great Wall to seal Mongols out, / and still, in the Han, we're setting beacon fires ablaze." Shifting from a general mood of despair to concrete images of horror, the narrator adds, "wounded horses wailing, crying out toward heaven, / hawks and crows tearing at people, / lifting off to scatter dangling entrails in dying trees" (Hinton 58).

In 757 he became attached to Prince Lin, the emperor's 16th son, who had been sent to stiffen government resistence in the southeast. Lin, however, had his own ambitions, deciding to break with the emperor and establish himself as ruler of an independent southern kingdom. Lin's rebellion was quickly put down. By 758 the An Lu-shan rebellion was under control, and a shaky order was reestablished. Although Li Po seems to have been largely apolitical, he was arrested and charged with treason because of his brief association with Prince Lin. He was first exonerated, then rearrested, and finally sentenced to exile in Yeh-lang, beyond the Wu Mountains and the Three-Gorges, effectively a death sentence beyond the boundaries of China. Lingering at K'uei-chou while traveling west, he was recalled from exile, thereafter resuming his life of wandering.

The Tang Dynasty never fully recovered the stability and splendor of its golden era, turning increasingly inward and finally disintegrating into what was known as the Five Dynasties and Ten Kingdoms (907–960). Similarly, Li Po's old age consisted of a few last years of wandering as a refugee and invalid, his health badly compromised by a combination of hardship and heavy drinking. (His interest in magic elixirs, which often involved mercury, may also have contributed to his decline.) Several of his poems comment wryly on the white-haired old man in the mirror. Ill, he took up residence with his kinsman Li Yang-ping, a government official and a noted calligrapher; anticipating the end, Li Po asked Li Yang to edit his chaotic manuscripts. Li Po died in 762, according to legend, drowning while drunk in a boat, trying to embrace the moon. His grave mount, now part of a temple complex, is in Dangtu, though legends about the wanderings of his restless body continue. Many of his manuscripts had been scattered during his hardships and travels, with the result that the edition Li Yang-ping brought out in 762 contained only several hundred of the several thousand poems that Li Po had allegedly written. Since then, further materials have turned up, some of doubtful authenticity. The Sung Dynasty edition of Kuo Yo-shih (1000) edited by Kuo Yo-Shih, brought the number up to 765 poems, and that edited by Sung Ming-chi (1080), up to 1000. Wang Chi's Ching Dynasty edition (1759) is considered the final one.

CHINESE POETIC TRADITION

It is often said that there is no epic poem in Chinese literature. If by epic we mean long narrative songs celebrating warrior heroes, such as *Beowulf*, the *Iliad*, or the *Mahābhārata*, this is true. (That impulse found its expression in the classic Chinese novel.) But insofar as the epic is also about the center of identity, what it means to belong to a culture, then two works can be named: the *Classic of Songs* (the *Shih Ching*) and the *Songs of the South* (the *Chuci*). The former derives from the peoples of Northern China who lived along the Yellow River, whereas the latter comes from the old southern kingdom of Chu, around the valley and tributaries of the Yangtze River. The *Classic of Songs*, also known as the *Book of Odes* or the *Book of Songs*, is conventionally cited as the beginning of Chinese poetry. Dating around 600 B.C.E., it is a compilation of 305 poems or ballads treating customs; festivals; celebrations of hunting, planting, harvesting, victories, heroes, and legendary ancestors; and themes of courtship, marriage, friendship, eulogy, and their concomitant variations. With three exceptions, authorship of the poems is anonymous, though according to tradition, Confucius compiled the *Classic of Songs*. Whether or not this is true, it is repeatedly cited by Confucius as one of the five classics *(ching)*, the books that composed the core of the educational curriculum, and, in a deeper sense, the Chinese cultural identity. The other classics were the *Book of Documents* (*Shu ching*), the *Book of Changes* (*Yi Jing*), the *Record of Ritual* (*Li ji*), and the *Spring and Autumn Annals* (*Chunqiu*). In its canonical role, the *Classic of Songs* establishes the shape and subject matter for most subsequent Chinese poetry.

The *Songs of the South* was compiled in the second century by Ch'u Tz'u, but attributed to the authorship of Qu Yuan, dating from the fourth century B.C.E.. If the *Classic of Songs* contains the earliest recorded Chinese poems, Qu Yuan, who identifies himself as a disaffected nobleman descended from the gods, represents the first Chinese poet. Fourteen cycles of poems in the anthology are attributed to him, and a distinct authorial voice can be discerned. At the end of a long work titled "On Encountering Troubles" ("Jiu ge"), he even concludes with the perennial complaint of many poets: "Enough! There are no true men in the state: no one understands me" (Hawkes 78). If the *Classic of Songs* has its origins in the customs and rituals of social life, the *Songs of the South*, with its flights through the air, dream sequences, and spirit worlds, points to probable origins in shamanism.

The affiliation of the *Classic of Songs*, and by extension Chinese poetry in general, with Confucianism produces a conception of poetry related to ritual practice. Underlying Confucian doctrine is the goal of achieving a harmony between the inner and the outer, between nature and the individual, and among individuals. This harmony is achieved through the imitation of proper behaviors until they become internalized; by this process of ritualized activity, one disciplines and cultivates oneself. Thus, the composition of poetry (along with the learning of a musical instrument, or a martial art) had several functions. First, it is an integral part of this training and self-discipline, seeking to bring skills in harmony with vision, to become one or unified with the act. Second, the composition of poetry to commemorate various festivals or social occasions becomes part of the ritual gesture to achieve social harmony, much as (to use a simplistic analogy) the "ritual" of sending a birthday card or a thank you note helps to nurture good feelings or harmony. Third, this ritual act evokes a corresponding response, part of a system of mutual obligations that becomes the basis for social and political organization. For Confucius, the larger structure of society and government is the collective expression of individual and family rituals. Given this, it is not surprising that Confucius, living in a time of profound political and social unrest, should favor songs that evoke the ritual behaviors of the personal and of everyday life, rather than songs immortalizing the extraordinary adventures of warriors. His world suffered from too much of the latter. The Chinese aesthetician Liu Hsieh (about 465–522 C.E.) makes a similar point when he writes that "[men] of the highest order aim at the establishment of virtue; men of a lower order seek to immortalize their convictions in words" (Liu 94). Poetry is about acting or transforming, not representing or recording.

As with the case of some birthday-card givers, the act can become perfunctory, an empty, even resented gesture. Similarly, much (bad) poetry can simply become formal, a collection of cliches or formulas mechanically applied.

The ideal goal, however, is to achieve an expressive unity between form and intentions. In a work known as the *Venerated Documents*, we find one of the earliest Chinese statements on the nature of poetry: "Poetry articulates the purposive mind [*thi ngon chi / shi yan zhi*]" (qtd. in Kelley 39). Rather than think of art as representation, the poem exists as an act or an expression. The poem is the extension of the purposive mind, an external expression of the inner emotions. The physical world, combining the specific physical environment with a specific moment in time and history, evokes an emotion. To the cultivated mind, this emotion finds expression in the poem. The result is an integral connection or unity between the specifics of the occasion and the mind.

Underlying this aesthetic is a cosmology derived from Daoism. Whereas Western thought tends to dualism, seeing hierarchies of difference between subject and object, man and nature, individual and society, creator and creation, and internal and external, East Asian thought tends to the non-dualistic, trying to dissolve the differences. Daoism, on the other hand, sees the cosmos in terms of one reality, the union of shifting forces, characterized by the principles *yin* (feminine, passive, earthy, low) and *yang* (masculine, active, celestial, high). The human mind is the union of these principles. "True subjectivity opens up the privatized ego so that the self can enter into fruitful communion with others," writes the contemporary philosopher Tu Wei-Ming (Tu 93). In creating a poem or other work of art, human beings participate in a transforming process. The critic Chung Hung (c. 468–518 c.e.) says it concisely in his *Poetry Gradings* (*Shih-p'in chu*): "Life-breath (*ch'i*) moves the external world, and the external world moves us" (qtd. in Wexted 390).

As with the case of low and high, yin and yang are not absolute entities, but mutually defined by each other, perpetually altering according to their relative contexts. In this way, we have a pattern of clearly defined opposites that are at the same time not differences. In his book *Wen-hsin tiao-lung* (*The Literary Mind and the Carving of Dragons*), the aesthetician Liu Hsieh derives all patterns (*wen*) from the yin–yang dynamic. In turn, by means of synecdoche—the figure of speech in which the part stands for the whole—he links the various opposites. Thus, heaven and earth are signified in a color pattern by black (color of sky) and yellow (the color of earth). Similarly, round shapes signify heaven, and square shapes represent earth; in turn, the sun and moon designate the heaven, and mountains and rivers designate the earth. Finally, because all of these synecdoche for earth and heaven relate to the archetypal yin–yang pattern of low and high, we may by extension relate low/yin with yellow, square, and mountains and rivers, and high/yang with black, round, and the sun and moon. Thus, the portrait of nature articulated in poetry or paintings expresses an intricate web of connections that link back to the basic natural order and our perception of that order. Applying this more specifically to literary patterns (*wen-chang*), Liu Hsieh writes, "Emotion is the warp of literary pattern, linguistic form the woof of ideas." Explaining, he adds, "Only when the warp is straight can the woof be rightly formed, and only when ideas are definite can linguistic form be meaningful. This is the fundamental principle in literary creation" (Liu 176).

All of this pertains to our appreciation of the Tang poets, informing a number of their characteristics. Pauline Yu cites two fundamental assumptions held by the Tang poets that derive from the *Classic of Songs* and the Daoist aesthetic. First, poetic imagery is analogical, building on the "meaning-conveying properties of the images," and "concrete phenomenon could, by virtue of cosmic categorical correspondences, embody and evoke larger significance" (Yu, *Reading* 168). Images of the moon, rivers, and lone pine trees are not just descriptive, but expressive of a larger web of correspondences. Second, the Tang poets held the belief that "the poem as a whole constituted an historical or autobiographical document, drawn from the author's lived experience" (Yu, *Reading* 168).

A brief note on Buddhism is also in order. (See a fuller discussion of Buddhism in chapter 7 on the *Journey to the West*.) Although the later Tang tried to expel Buddhism from China, as part of a general turn inward and rejection of any influence perceived to be foreign, Buddhism is important in any appreciation of the early Tang poetry. (It would not be atypical for a Chinese poet to be Confucian, Daoist, and Buddhist all without any sense of discontinuity.) Buddhism, particularly Ch'an Buddhism (Zen in Japanese), plays a prominent role in the art of Li Po. Ch'an (which means "meditation") developed as a response to Mahayana and Theraveda Buddhism. Central to this doctrine is the notion that there is no *real* difference between *samsara*, the cycles of birth and death in which suffering humans are trapped, and *nirvana*, the extinction of self. The (no)thing-ness of the world signifies its emptiness. This position is summarized by a famous poem by Tun-Huang, the sixth patriarch:

> Bodhi originally has no tree,
> The mirror also has no stand.
> Buddha nature is always clean and pure;
> Where is there room for dust? (Tun-Huang 132)

Everything that exists is empty, a notion that coalesces with the fluid conception of nature in Daoism. Thus, if the cycles of samsara inform the emptiness of being, then the emptiness of nirvana is identical. Here nirvana is not extinction, but a state of bliss, perfect tranquility, and profound wisdom. The essence of enlightenment, then, is a realization of the "suchness," or "thusness" (*tathatā*) of all things and the "sameness" (*samatā*) of all material and psychic states. "Thusness" and "emptiness" are in fact identical, when understood from the perspective of enlightenment. The nature of this insight is thought to be so fundamental as to be beyond conceptualization or even language. "Wisdom, all-knowing and all-penetrating, is deep, inconceivable and ineffable, transcending all concepts and words," writes historian of religion Heinrich Dumoulin (Dumoulin 1.42). The so-called Southern School, also known as "suddenness," as distinct from the "gradualness" of the North, argues that enlightenment comes in a sudden flash of insight, a heightening of our perception of the identity of "thusness" and "emptiness," or what some Zen thinkers called "manifest suchness."

It is readily evident from these remarks how Ch'an Buddhism, blending with Daoism, influences Li Po's aesthetic. First, it points to his frequent use of the motif of cycles, underlying the transience or (no)thing-ness of things. Second, it points to the underlying significance of absence, stillness, or ephemeral things as correlatives to the Buddhist notion of emptiness. The empty is as significant as the full. Third, it relates to the theme of the unexpressible, the notion that the real significance is somehow beyond the limits of language, an awareness that draws us to the impossibility of adequately conceptualizing the world or achieving any completion. In turn it informs the theme of spontaneity, the notion of an action that transcends the limits of reason. Fourth, it helps us understand the sudden and momentary disrupting flashes of experience—the barking dog, the wet foot, the sight of human entrails hanging in trees—that blast us out of habitual thought, heightening our awareness of the moment and the "thusness" of things. Such a perception of "thusness" underlines its "emptiness." In turn, both Li Po and this aesthetic of sudden flashes of the intensified perception of the moment later influence the art of the Japanese poets Bashō and Buson. Much of this is brought together in a famous anecdote in the writings of the Daoist thinker Chuang Tzu, cited by Li Po as well as by a number of Chinese aestheticians. Asked why he never needs to sharpen his butcher knife, Cook Ting explains, "When I started to cut up oxen, what I saw was just a complete ox. After three years, I had learnt not to see the ox as whole. Now I practice with my mind, not with my eyes. I ignore my sense and follow my spirit" (Chuang Tzu 23). Following his spirit, Cook Ting has achieved true spontaneity. The key to this Daoist theme involves a liberation from conceptual thinking, working instead from a pre-rational intuition, perceiving things in terms of their "manifest suchness."

THEMES AND IMAGES

To appreciate the nature of Li Po's aesthetic, it is useful to contrast him with Tu Fu. The critic Paula M. Varsano notes that Li Po's art conceptualizes the world in terms of a plenitude understood not in terms of completion, but in the impossibility of completion, a presence that signifies absence (Varsano 8). Plenitude is conventionally defined by the parallel contrast of *xu* (empty) and *shi* (full). Here *xu* does not signify empty in the sense of void, but something fluid (as opposed to solid and unchanging), elusive, subjective, possible (rather than actual); another way of thinking about this is as the "site" in the sense of the place necessary for being to happen. All of this relates to Li Po's art. By contrast, the *shi* of Tu Fu's art is a plenitude of solidity, actuality, stability, or fixity, the realm of appearance. Compare the following poem by Tu Fu with the one by Li Po sent to his wife, quoted earlier.

> Warning drums have ended all travel.
> A lone goose cries across autumn
> Borderlands. White Dew begins tonight.
> My old village. My scattered brothers—
> And no home to ask Are they alive or dead?
> Letters never arrive. War comes
> And goes—then comes like this again. (Hinton, *Tu Fu* 42)

Superficially the two poems are about the same things: the absent loved one, the lack of letters, the pain of separation. Each also uses similar imagery: the flying goose, the changing season, the moonlight. Yet in Tu Fu, everything is marked by its presence, the fullness of appearance. The scene is filled with sights and sounds, a plenitude of things signifying a tangible here and now. His lone goose is present, making a noise; the dew is present; the moonlight is present; the autumn sky is present. By contrast, Li Po's goose is disappearing into the north, signaling the ever-moving cycles of the seasons. The juxtaposition of the "moonlight that fills the house" with the "news never comes" illuminates the emptiness of the room rather than the full sky. Similarly, the question about the scattered brothers—"Are they alive or dead?"—foregrounds them in the poet's imagination, a question mark that has a (theoretically) definite answer. By contrast, Li Po's characterization of the city Yeh-lang as "beyond the sky," playing on the Daoist imagery that relates horizon and sky to heaven or the beyond, underlines inaccessibility and even unreality. Both poems end on the motif of a cycle. Tu Fu contrasts the failure of letters to arrive with the inevitable and recurrent arrival of war. Reversing the order and the emphasis, Li Po describes the recurrent seasonal going and coming of the geese with the failure of the letter to arrive. Thus, Tu Fu finally underlines the *real* presence of war, whereas Li Po underlines the *real* absence of the letter. Both poems are finely crafted and evocative, but for Li Po, the poem defines a space filled with emptiness *(xu)*, filled by markers that signal the fleeting or unattainable, what invites completion, while acknowledging the impossibility of such a completion.

Pulling all of these considerations together, and cognizant of the limits of space, let us look at three more examples of Li Po's poetry in greater detail. First consider "On the Phoenix Terrace," written sometime during the An Lu-shan rebellion. The title is also sometimes translated "The Phoenix Tower." In his 1915 collection *Cathay*, Ezra Pound translated this poem as "The City of Choan."

> On the phoenix terrace, phoenix at play.
> Phoenix gone; terrace empty; the river alone flows.
> Wu Palace: flowers and weeds bury the dark paths.
> Robes and caps of Chin Dynasty have gone into grave mounds.
> The Three Mountains half-falling beyond the sky,
> White Egret Isle splits the river into two.
> Always, floating clouds cover the sun:
> No sight of Ch'ang an: makes man sad. (Yip modified by Cooksey 203)

The images in each couplet build and elaborate on the images of the previous, rungs on a conceptual ladder that climb to the final statement of mood. The actual Phoenix Terrace (or Tower) itself is north of Nanjing, which was once the capital of the Wu and Chin. According to tradition, these mythical birds appear only in times of peace. Thus, their absence signifies times of unrest. Without stating it directly, Li Po intensifies the point by the parallel imagery of the phoenix *gone*, the terrace *empty*, and the river *alone* (flowing). Ironically, the only thing present, the river, is a conventional image that signifies perceptual change in Daoist terms, or the cycle of birth and death in Buddhist terms. The next two lines relate to the imagery of the first two, from which an implicit political statement may be inferred, though not stated in so many words. Flowers and weeds now cover the path to the palace that had once belonged to the Wu, and burial mounds are all that is left of the power and authority of the Chin. As the phoenix is gone, so are these once thriving kingdoms, the flowers, weeds, and mounds the representation of both the glory that was and the ruins that are left. They are a *something*, a "thusness" that signifies *emptiness* (xu). The next two lines evoke the mutually shifting relationship between the Daoist yin and yang, by a chiasmic crossing of images: the earthly dissolving into air and the solid breaking up the fluid. The Three Mountains seen at a distance seem to merge into the sky, and the Egret Isle divides the river. This evocation of the yin–yang glances back on the earlier lines, underlining the lack of permanence in nature, let alone in human achievement. Everything is subject to change. The last two lines bring everything forward to the moment. The floating clouds covering the sun, the fluid and darkening element obscuring the bright and glorious, invite us to complete the thought with a parallel reading with regard to the capital of the Tang, its physical remoteness from the poet, correlative of its transience, and by extension, the fate of the dynasty. With the political merging into the personal, all of the images come together to evoke the final mood of sadness or sorrow.

Many of Li Po's best poems are about departure and the sadness of saying farewell. Among the most famous has the generic title "Taking Leave of a Friend."

> Green mountains lie across the north wall.
> White water winds the east city.
> Here once we part,
> Lone tumbleweed; ten-thousand miles to travel.
> Floating clouds; a wanderer's mood.
> Setting sun; an old friend's feeling.
> We wave hands, you go from here.
> Neigh, neigh goes the horse at parting. (Yip 180)

The first couplet establishes a parallelism of images and a contrast of themes. The site of the departure is bordered by the mountains (solid) on one side and the water (fluid) on the other. The moment, the site of the poet's experience, is at the conjunction of the yin and yang. This Daoist juxtaposition of mountain and water also resonates with Buddhism. The *Sansuigyo* (*Mountain and Water Sutra*) of the *Shobogenzo* of Dōgen (1200–1253), founder of Sōtō Zen, elaborates the convention and meaning that Li Po is deploying: "Both [mountains and water] abide in place in the Dharma, having realized ultimate virtue. Because they are in the state before the kalpa of emptiness, they are vigorous activity in the present" (Dōgen 1.141). The next line foregrounds the specificity of place ("this place") and time ("once") that are the points of separation, again the motif of a *here* that signifies where we are not. The next four lines build a parallelism in which each image suggests a correspondence or elaboration of the others: On one hand, there are the lone tumbleweed, the floating cloud, and the setting sun, coming together in the image of the waving hand (Ezra Pound translates the gesture "who bow over their clasped hands"), the physical realities of motion and wandering travel. On the other hand, the thousands of miles to travel, the wanderer's thoughts, and the feelings of old friends come together in the psychic reality of the departing friend. The last line returns to the strategy of shock or disruption that we have seen elsewhere. The word translated "neigh" is the onomatopoeic *hsiao,* the sound a horse makes—yet another instance of the flash of sensation like the barking dog or the wet foot, breaking the poet's revery, bringing him back to the reality of the immediate moment. Again it is the awareness of a presence that heightens the sense of loss and emptiness, that underlines the actuality of the friend's receding into the distance.

Drinking is a favorite theme in many of Li Po's poems. Among the most famous and beloved is "Drinking Alone Beneath the Moon."

> From a pot of wine among the flowers
> I drink alone. There is no one with me—
> Till, raising my cup, I ask the bright moon
> To bring me my shadow and make us three.
> Alas, the moon is unable to drink
> And my shadow tags along vacantly;
> But still for a while I have these friends
> To cheer me through the end of spring.
> I sing. The moon wanders back and forth.
> I dance. My shadow tumbles after.
> As long as I know, we are boon companions.
> And then I was drunk, and we lost one another.
> Friends forever, we'll hail each other
> Across the long River of Stars. (Bynner modified by Cooksey 59–60)

The significance of most of the imagery is evident from what has already been said. Li Po builds on the tension between presence and absence, expressed by the fact of the narrator's drinking alone, drawing from a single wine pot. Paula M. Varsano notes the importance of wine and intoxication as an evocative motif in Li Po, expressing a blurring of the boundaries of imagination, memory, and perception, as well as a direct confrontation with experience, the wine's having penetrated or suspended the artificial boundaries of subject and object, the mediation of reason (Varsano 279). When I am sober, and my reason is fully operative, I am cognizant of differences: moon, self, shadow. But if I am intoxicated and the categorizing faculties of reason are suspended, then difference disappears. "And then I was drunk, and we lost one another." Of special note is the Daoist image of the self (the "I" of the poet) as the relationship or site between shifting opposites—the bright light of the moon, the dark form of the shadow. All of these entities exist in a complex relationship of dependancy on each other; movement of the one alters the others. There is a sort of mystical union between the self, shadow, and moon and the larger cycles of nature, signified by the heavens and the "River of Stars" (the Milky Way), itself conceived and represented as something flowing, subject to continual change. I may seem alone, an isolate atom, among the myriad objects of nature ("among the flowers"), but I am really at home among friends, a part of the greater whole. Everything remains familiar, even amid the cycles of change, as the poet, the moon, and the shadow wave to each other across the vastness.

SUBSEQUENT INFLUENCE

"Who dares to mount the altar of Li [Po] and Tu [Fu]?" asks the poet Du Mu (qtd. in Varsano 44). Although some critics in the Song dynasty (960–1279) were dismissive of Li Po, calling his poetry "all flowers and no fruit" (qtd. in Varsano 2), especially when they compared him with Tu Fu, his reputation has never flagged. In part, the ambiguities about his life and origins, his perpetual wandering, and the myth of the "unattainable" have served to detach him from the specifics of any affiliation with class, party, or region, making him a figure belonging to China as a whole. In turn, the shift of Neo-Confucianism from an orientation to the classics, to a more internal (Daoist) conception of sagehood, served to cement his canonical status. Li Po is now such an integral part of the culture that to be familiar with it assumes an intimate familiarity and appreciation of him. Because of this canonical status, he has exercised an influence on every East Asian writer, Vietnamese, Japanese, or Korean, who has come under the cultural influence of China.

The Western awareness of Li Po has been much more recent, limited by China's deliberate closure to the wider world and by the challenges of the Chinese language. To the West he has either been the mystical poet, drunk on wine or the beauty of nature, or the wistful poet of exile, forever saying goodbye, lamenting the absent loved one. The earliest references come from Christian missionaries. The memoirs of the Frenchman Joseph Marie Amiot (published in Paris between 1776 and 1796), contain a brief entry on "Ly-pe, Poête." Another account is offered in Théodore Pavie's 1839 "Le Poète Ly Tai-pe." In 1862 the Marquis d'Hervey Saint-Denys (1823–1892) produced an anthology of Tang poetry in French, working from the Chinese. In 1867 Judith Gautier (1846–1917), daughter of the poet Théophile Gautier, produced another French anthology, Le Livre de Jade, with the help of a Chinese exile named Ting Tun-ling. Pointing to the theme of drunkenness, she likened Li Po to the Persian poet Omar Khayyám. Working from Saint-Denys's French and Hans Heilmann's 1905 German translations, Hans Bethge produced his Die Chinesische Flöte (1907), which became the source and inspiration for Gustav Mahler's oratorio Das Lied von der Erde. The fifth movement of the latter text, "Der Trunkene im Frühling" ("Drunk in Spring"), is based on one of Li Po's poems.

It is more difficult to ascertain Li Po's impact on English-speaking writers. The scholar and linguist H. A. Giles brought out his *Gems of Chinese Literature* in 1884. It was, however, through the efforts of the American expatriate poet, Ezra Pound (1885–1972) that Li Po exercised a profound effect on modernist poetry. Seeking an aesthetic that was purified of the emotional, and often verbose, language of late Victorian poetry, Pound was fascinated by the nature of the Chinese ideogram and was drawn to Li Po's use of expressive images. Working with the notebooks of Ernest Fenollosa (1853–1908), who had been an American diplomat in Japan and a passionate sinophile, Pound developed what he termed Imagism. In 1915 he published *Cathay*, which included 10 versions of poems by Li Po. Among the most famous is his "The River-Merchant's Wife: A Letter," based on Li Po's "Song of Ch'ang-kan." The latter uses a traditional ballad form known as *yüeh-fu*, literally a "music bureau" song, after the poems collected by Han dynasty scholars. Because Fenollosa had worked with Japanese editions, Pound cited Li Po by the Japanese version of his name, Rihaku, as well as the Japanese version of place names, for instance "Chokan" for Chang-kan. "The River-Merchant's Wife" is considered by many as among the best modernist poems in the English language. The success of *Cathay* stimulated Pound's Imagist rival, Amy Lowell (1874–1925), to offer up her own versions, producing *Fir-Flowers Tablets* (1924), which she prepared in collaboration with her Chinese-speaking friend Florence Ayscough. Since then, Li Po has remained an enduring presence in Western literature, enjoying a number of translations (see the Suggested Readings for a sampling of English versions). Much of the appeal is captured in some lines by the American poet and novelist Conrad Aiken (1889–1973):

> Somewhere beyond the Gorge Li Po is gone,
> looking for friendship or an old love's sleeve
> or writing letters to his children, lost,
> and to his children's children, and to us. (Aiken 9)

More recently, Li Po has found sympathy among a variety of poets, especially the Beats or those associated with them, drawn to the notion of the poet as mystic, or the Daoist/Buddhist poet of nature. Of special note is the work of poet Gary Snyder, himself a serious student of the Asian languages and literature in addition to his more recent interest in native American traditions. Li Po's life and poetry have even found their way into historical fiction, such as Simon Elegant's *A Floating Life* (1997). In his poetry, Li Po remains the immortal, his true golden elixir.

SUGGESTED READINGS

Aiken, Conrad. *A Letter from Li Po and Other Poems*. New York: Oxford University Press, 1955.

Birch, Cyril, ed. *Anthology of Chinese Literature: From Early Times to the Fourteenth Century*. New York: Grove Press, 1965.

Bynner, Witter, trans. *The Jade Mountain: A Chinese Anthology*. New York: Vintage Books, 1972.

Chuang Tzu. *The Book of Chuang Tzu*. Trans. Martin Palmer. London: Penguin Books, 1996.

Dōgen. *Shobogenzo*. 4 vols. Trans. Gudo Wafu Nishijima and Chodo Cross. Tokyo: Dogen Sangha, 1996.

Dumoulin, Heinrich. *Zen Buddhism: A History*. 2 vols. Trans. James W. Heisig and Paul Knitter. New York: Macmillan Publishing Company, 1988.

Elegant, Simon. *A Floating Life: The Adventures of Li Po, An Historical Novel*. Hopewell, NJ: Ecco Press, 1997.

Hawkes, David, trans. *The Songs of the South: An Ancient Chinese Anthology of Poems by Qu Yuan and Other Poets*. London: Penguin Books, 1985.

Hinton, David, trans. *The Selected Poems of Li Po*. New York: New Directions, 1996.

———, trans. *The Selected Poems of Tu Fu*. New York: New Directions, 1989.

Kaltenmark, Odile. *Chinese Literature*. Trans. Anne-Marie Geoghegan. New York: Walker and Co., 1964.

Kelley, Liam C. *Beyond the Bronze Pillars: Envoy Poetry and the Sino-Vietnamese Relationship*. Honolulu: University of Hawai'i Press, 2005.

Kenner, Hugh. *The Pound Era*. Berkeley: University of California Press, 1971.

Liscomb, Kathlyn Maureen. "Li Bai: A Hero Among Poets, in the Visual, Dramatic, and Literary Arts of China." *Art Bulletin* 81.3 (September 1999): 354–389.

Liu, Hsieh. *The Literary Mind and the Carving of Dragons*. Trans. Vincent Yu-chung Shih. New York: Columbia University Press, 1959.

Liu, James J. Y. *The Art of Chinese Poetry*. Chicago: University of Chicago Press, 1962.

Liu, Wuji. *An Introduction to Chinese Literature*. Bloomington: Indiana University Press, 1966.

Minford, John, and Joseph S. M. Lau, eds. *From Antiquity to the Tang*. Vol. 1 in *Classical Chinese Literature: An Anthology of Translations*. New York: Columbia University Press, 2000.

Obata, Shigeyoshi, trans. *The Works of Li Po*. New York: Paragon Books, 1965.

Owen, Stephen. *The Great Age of Chinese Poetry: The High T'ang*. New Haven: Yale University Press, 1981.

Pine, Red, trans. *Poems of the Masters: China's Classic Anthology of T'ang and Sung Dynasty Verse*. Copper Canyon Press, 2003.

Pound, Ezra. *Personae: The Shorter Poems*. Ed. Lea Baechler and A. Walton Litz. New York: New Directions, 1990.

Schafer, Edward H. *The Golden Peaches of Samarkand: A Study of T'ang Exotics*. Berkeley: University of California Press, 1963.

Stevens, Wallace. *The Collected Poems*. New York: Vintage, 1982.

Tu, Wei-Ming. *Confucian Thought: Selfhood as Creative Transformation*. Albany: State University of New York Press, 1985.

Tun-Huang. *The Platform Sutra of the Sixth Patriarch*. Trans. Philip B. Yampolsky. New York: Columbia University Press, 1967.

Varsano, Paula M. *Tracking the Banished Immortal: The Poetry of Li Bo and Its Critical Reception*. Honolulu: University of Hawai'i Press, 2003.

Waley, Arthur. *The Poetry and Career of Li Po: 701–762 A.D.* London: George Allen and Unwin, 1950.

———, trans. *The Book of Songs: The Ancient Chinese Classic of Poetry*. New York: Grove Press, 1960.

Watson, Burton. *Chinese Lyricism: Shih Poetry from the Second to the Twelfth Century*. New York: Columbia University Press, 1971.

Wexted, John Timothy. "Chinese Influences on the *Kokinshū* Prefaces." In *Kokinshū: A Collection of Poems Ancient and Modern*. Trans. Laurel Rasplica Rodd and Mary Catherine Henkenius. Princeton: Princeton University Press, 1984. 387–400.

Wong, Siu-kit. *The Genius of Li Po, A.D. 701–762*. Hong Kong: University of Hong Kong, 1974.

Yip, Wai-lim, ed and trans. *Chinese Poetry: An Anthology of Major Modes of Genres*. Durham: Duke University Press, 1997.

Yu, Pauline. *The Reading of Imagery in the Chinese Poetic Tradition*. Princeton: Princeton University Press, 1987.

Yu, Pauline, Peter Bol, Stephen Owen, and Willard Peterson. *Ways with Words: Writing about Reading Texts from Early China*. Berkeley: University of California Press, 2000.

6

Murasaki Shikibu
The Tale of Genji
(c. 1000 C.E.)

Everything "begins," then, with citation, in the creases of a certain veil, a certain mirrorlike screen.

—Jacques Derrida (*Dissemination* 316)

His body continued burning for twelve hundred years, after which his body came to an end.

—*The Lotus Sutra* (*Three* 305)

The Tale of Genji (*Genji Monogatari*) is the greatest work in Japanese literature and is commonly regarded as the first novel in world literature, standing as an undisputed masterpiece. Its author, Murasaki Shikibu, a woman who flourished between 973 and 1013 C.E. in the court of Heian Japan (795–1185 C.E.), stands in relation to Japanese literature as Cervantes does to Spanish literature, Dante to Italian, and Shakespeare to English. Her novel stretches over three generations, tracing the life of Genji, the Shining Lord (*Hikaru*), his enduring love for Lady Murasaki (not to be confused with the author), and the transcendence of their reputation, expressed in the lives of Genji's stolid son Yūgiri and his hapless son Kaoru and grandson Niou. It chronicles a world of refined and elegant sensibilities and an aristocratic ideal that for many Japanese still evokes a sense of nostalgia. Yet within this idealization, Murasaki has aspired to a realism that captures the moral ambiguities and psychological complexities of human interactions, avoiding the fantastic elements common in her literary antecedents: the Shining One, despite his sophistication and accomplishments, is by no means a saint. The quality of his character is not so much moral goodness as profound self-awareness and self-understanding. Unlike his peers and descendants, Genji knows himself. But Murasaki's achievement is multilayered. Not only does she tell an engaging story, but additionally, her narrative offers a subtle and subversive look at the political and gender assumptions that construct her world. She also paints a sympathetic Buddhist allegory on the illusion of appearances and the transience of human life and human accomplishments. Given its narrative and thematic richness, it is not surprising that the *Tale of Genji* enjoys wide popularity, even after a thousand years.

GENJI AND THE NOVEL

It is a critical commonplace to describe the *Tale of Genji* as the first novel in world literature, or at least the first psychological novel. Such designations, however, require qualification. *Tale of Genji* did not spring out of a vacuum, but exists in a complex relationship with its language, with the sociolinguistic implications of its written expression, and with its literary and generic antecedents. The development of a written form of the Japanese language, coupled with the cultural relationship with China, played an important role in the development of Japanese literature. From the eighth century, Japanese authors adapted the Chinese system of writing. However, because Chinese is generally monosyllabic and Japanese polysyllabic, such a form of writing was awkward and cumbersome, requiring a long string of Chinese ideograms to express one Japanese word. Eventually, the Japanese began to develop a system that treated the Chinese characters as symbols representing sounds rather than words, evolving into the two-*kana* syllabary of *hiragana* and *katakana*. Because the Chinese language still carried a cachet of high culture and learning, men were expected to use it in official documents. Women, on the other hand, were supposed to write in Japanese, using *hiragana*, also known as *onnade*, "woman's hand." Easier to write and closer to the native spoken Japanese, the hiragana script was well suited for composition, becoming a natural vehicle for literature. In turn it made it easier to represent in writing the sociolinguistic features of women in the Heian court. This is often marked in writing by the tendency toward tenselessness, the practice of implicit subject positions, the avoidance of pronomials, and the use of titles, nicknames, and "honorific language" rather than actual names, making it easy to deploy a creative ambiguity and to shift the relationship between the speaker, auditor, and referent (Okada 173–174). Speaking of women's culture in the Heian court, critic H. Richard Okada writes, "In those 'rooms of their own,' women wrote for each other and for posterity in highly literate and mutually critical and competitive contexts. They were enabled, through their linguistic medium and their politico-cultural space to speak for themselves and for their men, the latter often existing to be 'read' and 'written' by women, in a 'feminine hand'" (Okada 163). It is exactly this sociolinguistic practice that permitted the development of the traditional Japanese genres in literature. Although the categories are not absolute, it is relevant to briefly consider five: Japanese poetry (*waka*) and poetry anthologies, the diary (*nikki*), the essay (*zuihitsu*), the tale (*setsuwa*), and prose narrative (*monogatori*).

Traditionally, the Japanese equated literature with poetry. Central to the Japanese conception of poetry is that it should express the poet's heart, focusing on an aesthetics of truthfulness and sincerity. "Japanese poetry takes root in the soil of one's heart and blossoms forth in the forest of words" (Rodd 379), declares Ki no Yoshimochi (c. 884–946 C.E.), the chief editor of the imperial anthology *Kokinshū* (c. 905 C.E.). The goal is to express the aesthetic state known as *mono no aware*, or simply *aware*, an intuitive, yet cultured ability to grasp the experience of the world, its movement, possibilities, and limits— what some translate as "ah-ness" (Rimer 143). It involves a concentrated and highly allusive art from which meaning is implied rather than explicitly stated.

The *waka* is the classic verse form in Japanese poetry, a poem constructed out of 31 syllables distributed in lines of 5, 7, 5, 7, and 7 syllables. (Later poetic forms including *tanka*, *renga*, and *haiku* develop from modification of this form.) Many of these brief lyrics were collected in anthologies (*chokusenshū*). In turn these anthologies often represented not just compilations of poems, but something carefully selected and arranged to produce a larger effect. Like the novel, these anthologies must be read in terms of the collective impact of the whole. The earliest, and perhaps the greatest, is the *The Collection of Ten Thousand Leaves* (Man'yōshū), compiled in the late Nara or early Heian periods, which contains a mixture of Japanese and Chinese forms. Also of importance is the *Collection of Waka, Old and New* (Kokinshū), compiled by imperial decree. These and other anthologies served to codify poetic diction and to establish a canon of poetic references that formed the shared culture of literate men and women. Murasaki's references to places such as Suma, Ise, or Uji would immediately evoke poetic links and associations among her readers. In turn, the *waka* and the anthologies inform other literary forms as well. It was a common practice to make a point indirectly, by quoting, paraphrasing, or even just alluding to a well-known *waka*. Thus, throughout the *Tale of Genji*, the characters cite lines of verse to express their feelings or to imply something discreetly without actually saying it. Indeed, each chapter heading refers to a passage of verse that appears in it. As such, the quoted poetry is not an ornament, but an important key to the tone and theme of the chapter. It has also been suggested that the diary (*nikki*) and the *monogatari* grew out of the practice of providing a narrative frame to account for the circumstances that gave rise to the particular *waka*.

The *nikki* or literary diary is an old genre in Japanese literature. Rather than representing a daily record of activities, these works tended to recreate events from the author's life and were meant for public consumption. According to convention, men wrote in Chinese, often providing a public record of official visits, rituals, and court records, whereas women used the "feminine" *hiragana* to address more personal matters. At the same time, many men would also write under the guise of the "feminine hand," drawn to its versatility. One of the finest of these early diaries, the *Kagerō Nikki* (*The Gossamer Years*), was written by a man. Murasaki herself kept a diary that has come down to us. Composed in the first person, the diaries often shifted back and forth between actual events and fictional elaborations, a sort of fictionalized autobiography. Thus, critics distinguish the "False I," especially in the case of men writing in the "feminine" style. Not infrequently, such diaries overlap with the tale. In turn, the diary would later influence the development of the confessional "I-Novels" in early modern Japanese fiction. Also under the category of diary are travel diaries (*kiko*), among the most famous being Matsuo Bashō's *The Narrow Road through the Provinces* (*Oku no Hosomichi*), published in 1702, a combination of haiku and prose narrative.

The essay (*zuihitsu*, literally "following the brush") is another traditional genre. Here the essay represents more a compilation of thoughts on a topic than a fully developed thesis. J. Thomas Rimer draws parallels with Pascal's *Pensée*. Unlike the *nikki*, the narrative "I" is assumed to be the author. Among the most famous *zuihitsu* is Sei Shōnagon's *Pillow Book* (*Makura no Sōshi*). A contemporary of Murasaki, Shōnagon was a lady-in-waiting in the Michinaga household. She appears in *Genji* as the nurse of the young Murasaki. The actual Murasaki recalled tartly in her diary that "Sei Shōnagon...was dreadfully conceited," explaining that "she thought herself so clever, and littered her writings with Chinese characters" (Shikibu 131). Despite this assessment, posterity generally considers Sei Shōnagon the better prose stylist, though her overall achievement does not match *The Tale of Genji*.

The distinctions between *setsuwa* and *monogatari* are not rigorous. Both represent narratives. Written in prose, the *setsuwa* are short, often didactic in nature, drawing on legend, folklore, or Buddhist writings and often playing on the fantastic. Though traditionally titled a *monogatari*, the earliest extant *setsuwa* is the ninth-century *The Tale of the Bamboo Cutter* (*Taketori Monogatari*). Murasaki called it "the ancestor of all tales" (Tyler 325). The story centers on a mysterious young woman who turns out to be a celestial being from the moon, discovered in a stalk of bamboo by an old bamboo cutter. She is known as the "Shining Princess" (*Tale of Bamboo* 17), an epithet that anticipates Murasaki's "Shining One." She is courted by five handsome noblemen whom she puts off with a series of impossible quests. The *monogatari*, literally "telling of things," mixes literary genre, combining prose and poetry. It often overlaps with the *nikki*, though differs in that the subject matter is not the "I" that one would expect in a diary. One of the most important sources for *The Tale of Genji* is the tenth-century *Tales of Ise* (*Ise Monogatari*), comprising 125 loosely unified episodes that chronicle the adventures of its hero, Narihira. Its influence on Murasaki cannot be overemphasized, both formally and thematically. Like Genji, Nahihira is a courtier of high rank, exemplifying the ideals of the Heian gentleman, handsome, elegant, sensitive, aesthetically gifted, and an audacious lover. Among his loves, like Genji, is the high priestess of the Shrine of Ise. In turn, although there are many implausible elements in both *The Tale of Genji* and *Tales of Ise*, both aspire to a realistic treatment of their characters, eschewing the explicit fantasy found in *The Tale of the Bamboo Cutter*.

Several times in the *Tale of Genji*, Murasaki describes what she is doing as an author. Early on, she addresses her audience (or reader):

> I have written of them [Genji's trials and tribulations] now only because certain lords and ladies criticized my story for resembling fiction, wishing to know why even those who knew Genji best should have thought him perfect, just because he was an Emperor's son. No doubt I must now beg everyone's indulgence for my effrontery in painting so wicked a portrait of him. (Tyler 80)

In this apostrophe, Murasaki distinguishes what she is doing from "fiction," by the claim that she portrays Genji as he is, rather than presenting an idealized portrait that passes over his flaws. She indirectly reiterates this point much later. One wet day, finding his current love, Tamakayura, engrossed in copying out various tales, Genji teasingly complains, "There you are caught up in fables, taking them quite seriously and writing away without a thought for your tangled hair in this stiflingly warm rain!" (Tyler 461). He goes on to admit that among the "lies," there are some "plausibly touching scenes, convincingly told," even some of the "magnificently contrived wonders" (Tyler 461). They are, he continues, the product of someone's "persuasively glib imagination" (Tyler 461). Tamakayura replies acidly that he should know, implying that he is adept at telling glib lies. Stung by this rejoinder, Genji apologizes, suggesting that tales are true insofar as they describe the workings of human nature and that unlike history, they contain "truly rewarding particulars" (Tyler 461). "The telling begins when all those things the teller longs to have pass on to future generations...overflow the teller's heart" (Tyler 461). The point is not the communication of information, but the expression of passions or the evocation of comprehension or understanding.

Genji's aesthetics are reminiscent of those applied to *waka*, which also aspires to express the passions of the heart. Musing on the matter, however, his aesthetic takes a moral and religious turn. He compares what goes on in stories to the Buddhist concept of *hōben* (translated "expedient means," "skillful means," or "tactfulness"). "Although one may distinguish between the deep and the shallow, it is wrong always to dismiss what one finds in tales as false. There is talk of 'expedient means' also in the teachings that the Buddha in his great goodness left us," Genji reflects, adding, "the gap between enlightenment and the passions is, after all, no wider than the gap that in tales sets off the good from the bad" (Tyler 461–462). The moral good of a story is equivalent to the Buddhist concept of enlightenment. There is some irony in this comparison of literature with Buddhist teachings, given that Buddhists considered most literature frivolous, if not actually harmful. Indeed, several twelfth- and thirteenth-century Buddhist tracts imagine Murasaki suffering in hell for her literary efforts (Bowring 82).

Genji (and we may presume Murasaki) invites us to read narrative in terms of the Buddhist concept of "expedient means," important to later developments in Mahayana Buddhism. It was elaborated extensively in the second chapter of the *Lotus Sutra*, a work that Murasaki makes frequent reference to throughout the *Tale*. Central to its doctrine is that because of the illusory nature of appearance, "only a buddha together with a buddha can fathom the Reality of All Existence" (*Three* 52). All knowledge is at best provisional. Comprehension goes beyond the limits of rational argument. Thus the Buddha or a Bodhisattva must rely on indirect means: "the meaning of the laws which the buddhas expound as opportunity serves is difficult to understand.... I expound the laws by numberless tactful ways [expedient means] and with various reasonings and parabolic expressions" (*Three* 59). In each case the results are temporary, part of a perpetual process of revaluation by which religious expression is understood in terms of "provisional articulation and eventual dismantling" (Pye 161), in which appearance dissipates, and the literal becomes figurative. For Genji, the tales that Tamakayura enjoys can be treated as an expedient means that might lead to some flash of understanding or enlightenment, but should never be held as representing anything real. In the end, all things will disappear, though some trace of understanding may remain.

MURASAKI AND THE CULTURAL CONTEXTS

The *Tale of Genji* opens with an ambiguous disclaimer: "In a certain reign (whose can it have been?) someone of no very great rank, among all His

Majesty's Consorts and Intimates, enjoyed exceptional favor" (Tyler 3). To underline the political ramifications of such favoritism, Murasaki reminds her audience of the dreadful fate of Yang Kuei-fei, consort of the Chinese emperor Hsüan-Tsung (see chapter 5 about Li Po). The Tang poet Bo Juyi (Po Chü-i) commemorated this fatal romance in his popular ballad *The Everlasting Wrong* (*Ch'ang hen ko*), to which Murasaki makes several references. In a double gesture, Murasaki seemingly lifts her narrative out of any historical context, while firmly grounding it into the sexual politics of her world. To understand what she is doing, and the more subversive dimensions of the *Tale*, it is important to examine the power structure in Heian Japan.

Although Japanese culture paid lip service to a Confucian bureaucracy and its virtues, power flowed from family affiliation, passed along the female line. For this reason, the ruling class practiced polygamy with an assortment of wives, consorts, and concubines. This ideology was reinforced by Shintoism ("the way of the gods, or *kami*"), which based social identity on a combination of ancestor and spirit worship; more specifically Shintoism established a cult of the emperor that traced his line back to the sun goddess Amaterasu. Although the emperor was the spiritual center of society, real authority resided with various regents and officials linked by clan loyalty. In the historical period when Murasaki lived and wrote, the Fujiwara clan dominated. The head of the clan, Fujiwara no Michinaga (966–1027), exercised de facto rule over Japan through his family links to the emperors, based on a complex network of ties, including the claim that he was the brother-in-law of two prior emperors, uncle to one, and uncle and father-in-law to another, and eventually the grandfather to two more. In 999 he had arranged that his 11-year-old daughter, Shōshi, become consort to the emperor Ichijō. With the death of the first empress, Teishi, in 1000, the sister of his nephew and political rival, Michinaga consolidated his authority. Shōshi's production of a son in 1008, who would in turn become an emperor, assured Michinaga's future power. A *Tale of Flowering Fortunes* (*Eiga monogatari*), written around 1092, offers a fictional account of the fortunes of the Fujiwara, and especially Michinaga. In such circumstances, it is evident why women played a subtle, but crucial role in politics or why a distracted emperor, such as Hsüan-Tsung or the emperor of that "certain reign," might short-circuit the carefully constructed network. A woman in the court remained private only if she remained childless. Having children was profoundly politicizing, thrusting the mother into the pubic maelstrom. It also glosses the significance of the character Murasaki's remaining childless. Genji wishes to preserve the object of his desire as an ideal. There is a sense that the author Murasaki had an appreciation of the precariousness of political stability. Indeed, the Heian collapsed in a civil war between the Taira (Heike) and the Minamoto (Genji) clans, culminating in the rise of a military class under the shogunate of Minamoto no Yoritomo. (The civil war was later recounted in the *Heike Monogatari*, embodying the martial ideal of the samurai warrior, and second only to the *Tale of Genji* in its influence on the Japanese psyche.)

What little we actually know about Murasaki Shikibu is based primarily on her diary, a series of autobiographical poems, and a few court records. Her dates are conventionally given as from 973 to sometime after 1013, the last time her name appeared on an official registry. We do not even know her real name. Following the practice of *hiragana*, she is known only through her title and nickname. Shikibu is an honorific based on her father's office, meaning "Bureau of Ceremonial," and Murasaki, which means "purple" or "violet," is a nicknamed applied to her as the creator of Lady Murasaki in the *Tale of Genji*. In her diary, she records a courtier poking his head into her room, asking, "Would our little Murasaki be in attendance by any chance?" To this she replied, that because Genji was not present, Murasaki could not be present either, a put-down that implied that the courtier was a far cry from the elegant gentleman (Shikibu 91).

Murasaki was the daughter of Fujiwara no Tametoki, a gentleman of good birth, but of a minor branch of the ruling clan. As a result, he was a member of the often fluid *zuryō* class of mid-level officials. (Analogously, the surname Genji signifies not merely Murasaki's hero, but also members of the Minamoto clan and the designation of princes who had been reduced to an ambiguous middle status between royalty and commoner, ineligible to become an emperor.) Her mother seems to have died when Murasaki was still a child. She grew up in her father's house, where she was educated along with her brother. "When my brother...was a young boy learning the Chinese classics," she records in her diary, "I was in the habit of listening to him and I became unusually proficient at understanding those passages which he found too difficult to grasp" (Shikibu 139). She adds in a comment that speaks of the condition of women in her world, "Father, a most learned man, was always regretting the fact: 'Just my luck!' he would say. 'What a pity she was not born a man'" (Shikibu 139).

In 996 Murasaki accompanied her father to a post as provincial governor of Echizen in western Japan. Part of this seems to have been in order to avoid marrying Fujiwara no Nobutaka, a second cousin about the age of her father, who already had several wives and a son Murasaki's age. Later changing her mind, she married Nobutaka in 998. Exchanged poems seem to suggest that despite her original reservations, the marriage was happy. A daughter, Kenshi (also known as Daini no Sanmi), was born in 999. Nobutaka, however, died in an epidemic, in 1001. Following the poetic conventions, she evokes her grief indirectly in a poem probably addressed to a stepdaughter. In an expression of *aware*, she embodies her feelings of loss in the image of the back of the departing figure and the writings ("traces") of the departed father.

In the evening mist
The mandarin duck swims
Out of sight;
Is the child then led astray
Gazing at her father's traces? (Shikibu 230)

She seems to have begun work on the *Tale of Genji* early in her widow-
hood. About 1005, she entered the court as a lady-in-waiting, her literary and
linguistic accomplishments gaining her employment by Michinaga as tutor
to his daughter, Shōshi. Some scholars argue that Michinaga is the prototype
for Prince Genji, and some have suggested that Murasaki became a mistress,
though this seems a fanciful interpretation of the evidence. In her capacity
as lady-in-waiting, she tells of reading the works of Po Chü-i in secret to the
empress. She also speaks of immersing herself in the Buddhist sutras. In the
brilliant circle of women around Shōshi, the *Tale of Genji* developed, where it
was read, transcribed, copied, and circulated. Scrutinizing many of the authorial asides, the scholar and critic Tamazami Takuyua has argued that the *Tale
of Genji* developed out of oral performance, the practice of Murasaki's telling
stories. Murasaki records in her diary, dating sometime around 1008, that
Michinaga "found a copy of the Tale that I had had brought from home for
safe-keeping. It seems that he gave the whole thing to his second daughter"
(Shikibu 95). "I no longer had the fair copy in my possession and was sure
that the version she had would hurt my reputation," she worried (Shikibu 95).
How complete this manuscript was is a matter of conjecture. One way or the
other, a diary entry by Lady Sarashina referring to a period around 1021 indicates the existence of a substantial written version. The definitive text was
collated by the poet Fujiwara Teika (1162–1251), which remains the basis for
the standard 54-chapter version that comes down to us.

We know little about Murasaki's last years. Her diary portrays her as retiring
and pious, strongly devoted to the Buddha Amida (Amitābha in Sanskrit),
central to the sect of Pure Land (Jōdo) Buddhism, which holds that those
who were not yet ready for the final salvation of nirvana may at least achieve
refuge by being reborn into the Paradise of Amida. She was critical of osten-
tatious displays of learning, whether in herself or others. Her last poems show
an increasing sadness over the loss of friends and the indifference of nature.
In an exchange of poems and letters over the death of a friend, she wonders
about the futility of such poems and letters:

Who will read it?
Who will live forever
In this world?

A letter left behind
In her undying memory. (Shikibu 255)

Despite her misgivings, the *Tale of Genji* has proven to be a letter that is still read, and her memory is still alive.

PLOT AND CHARACTER DEVELOPMENT

In the version that comes down to us, the *Tale of Genji* contains 54 chapters. There is some controversy over the order of composition as well as the authorship of some of them. A number of scholars argue that the first chapter was added later by way of introduction, and others that the style of chapters 42 through 44 indicates a different authorship. There is also some question about the authorship of the final "Uji" chapters. Nevertheless, there is an overall organic unity, the story stretching over a period of 75 years and embracing three generations, beginning with the birth of Genji and concluding with the musings of his 28-year-old son, Kaoru. Although there are a number of ways to organize or divide the *Tale*, many take as their starting point the assertion by critic Ikeda Kikan that the *Tale* falls into three parts: Genji's glory and youth (chapters 1–33), his conflict and death (chapters 34–41), and the transcendence of his death (chapters 42–54) (Miner, *Princeton* 204). With hundreds of characters and dozens of intersecting plotlines, we can consider only the barest outline.

The first and longest part of the *Tale* (chapters 1–33) traces the life of Genji from his conception to the age of 39. In circumspect manner, we are told that the Kiritsubo Emperor was so passionately in love with one of the ladies of the court that it was attributed to a relationship from some earlier incarnation. Because this relationship potentially threatens the lines of succession, especially after a boy is born, the court is hostile to the lady, leading to her repeated humiliation, despair, and early death, when the boy is only three. Because of the boy's almost otherworldly beauty and accomplishments, the emperor keeps him near as a reminder of his lover. To protect him, however, the emperor makes him a commoner (Genji status, described earlier), so that he will not be in competition for the succession, a move that both liberates him and casts him into a floating existence. Eventually, the emperor takes a new consort, Fujitsabo, because of her strong resemblance to his old love. Genji also becomes fascinated by her when he is told of her resemblance to the mother he cannot remember. Fujitsabo becomes the first instance of a recurrent motif of substitutions or surrogates that runs throughout the *Tale*, what critic Haruo Shiane characterizes as "repetition and difference" (Shirane 151). Later, Genji is struck by the resemblance between

Murasaki and Fujitsabo, her aunt. Similarly, Kaoru sees the image of his love Ōigimi in her half sister Ukifune. Throughout, the object of love is always something absent, the present and immediate focus of affection merely an expedient means. This pattern also shapes much of the action, in which later episodes echo earlier ones, often providing a retrospective revaluation of the earlier. Thematically crucial, however, is the significance revealed by the difference within the repetition. Thus, for instance, Kaoru (whose name means "fragrant captain") becomes a sort of lesser Genji, having his father's sensitivities, but lacking his self-understanding or decisiveness. Similarly, Genji's grandson, Niou (whose name means "perfumed highness"), has his grandfather's beauty and abandon, but lacks his sensitivity. In the end, living up to their names, both prove to be insubstantial repetitions of Genji, merely pleasant traces of what is now gone.

In the opening of the second chapter, the narrator announces, "Shining Genji: the name was imposing, but not so its bearer's many deplorable lapses" (Tyler 21). This is another of the central themes of the *Tale*, related to the Buddhist doctrine that the world of appearance is illusory, nourishing false hopes and desires that cause suffering and unhappiness. Conflating with the motif of repetition and difference, the surrogate is often somehow less than the original, somehow increasingly removed from the truth. By all appearances, Genji, now 17, is a young man of talent, grace, and refinement, but with a weakness for women, pursuing numerous affairs, casual and passionate. Ironically, the only woman he has no feelings for is his wife, Aoi, the result of an arranged marriage to assure family connections. Aoi's brother, Tō no Chūjō, brash and insensitive, is Genji's friend and rival throughout. (Their characters and rivalries are echoed later in Kaoru and Niou.) While Genji is pursuing a relationship with Lady Rokujō, the widow of a crown prince, he becomes enamored of a mysterious young woman known as Yūgao (meaning "Evening Flower" or "Twilight Beautiful"). While they spend a night together in a deserted and dilapidated mansion, Genji dreams of a beautiful woman seated by his pillow, only to be awakened by the awareness "of a heavy menacing presence" (Tyler 67). Summoning his servants, Genji is horrified to find that Yūgao is dead, the victim of some hostile spirit. It is eventually established that she died when possessed by the wildly jealous spirit of Lady Rokujō. This spirit will also prove fatal to Aoi and later will threaten Mirasaki. This is Genji's first close confrontation with death and the loss of someone he loves. Yūgao's death marks the opening of many later developments. Indeed, part of Murasaki Shikibu's narrative strategy is to introduce characters or situations whose significance will become apparent only as the text unfolds. Obsessed by his passion for this lost lady, Genji travels to the mountain retreat where she is to be cremated, so that he might have one last look. While there he notices the coast of Akashi in the distance, anticipating his later romance with the Akashi Lady. He also first sees Murasaki, at the time a girl about 10. It will also later develop that Yūgao had a daughter by Tō no Chūjō who is at this time about three. This is Tamakayura, who will become yet another of Genji's infatuations, a substitute for her dead mother. Genji also becomes attracted to Lady Rokujō's daughter, Akikonomu, the high priestess of Ise and later a consort to the Reizei emperor.

The death of Yūgao has two immediate consequences. First, Genji begins to toy with the idea of adopting Murasaki so that he might form her into his female ideal. He soon puts this plan into motion with the aid of the girl's nurse, Shōnagon, in effect kidnaping Murasaki and setting her up in a wing of his mansion. Yūgao's death also increases his resolve to get closer to his step-mother, Fujitsubo. Murasaki indicates with deliberately circumspect ambiguity that the relationship takes a sexual turn. "To Her Highness the memory of that last, most unfortunate incident was a source of enduring suffering" (Tyler 97). To their mutual distress, Fujitsubo becomes pregnant by Genji, though no one, not even the emperor, Genji's father, seems to suspect the affair. Indeed, the son that is born will eventually become the Reizei Emperor, upon the retirement of the Kiritsubo Emperor's "first" son, the Suzaku Emperor (Genji's half brother). Again, we see repetition and difference, manifest in a substitution and a discrepancy between appearance and reality that also carries a subversive subtext: the matrilineal inheritance of the emperors is not always what it seems.

When Genji is about 22, Aoi dies in childbirth, though spirit possession is suspected. Only when she is lost does he begin to appreciate her. Their son, Yūgiri, survives. Lacking his father's charm, Yūgiri will find his life plagued by trying unsuccessfully to live up to his father's shining reputation. Genji also moves to formalize and consummate his relationship with Murasaki, who is now about 15 or 16. Because of her more lowly birth, he cannot make her his chief wife, but although he has a series of affairs over the years, she remains the primary love of his life. Genji's ambiguous status in court, coupled with his reckless behavior, brings down the wrath of the Suzaku Emperor's mother, who is worried about Genji's intentions in relation to her son. When Genji's friends and family members are passed over for royal preferment, he decides to atone for his behavior by going into a self-imposed exile in Suma, near the Akashi coast. Here he meets and falls in love with a reluctant young woman, the Akashi Lady. The relationship is pushed by her father, a retired official who though he has taken Buddhist vows, still hopes to pursue his worldly ambitions through his daughter's liaison. Later, this episode will be echoed in yet another instance of repetition and difference, when the father of Ōigimi, living in Uji, encourages her (unsuccessfully) to marry Kaoru.

When Genji finally returns to court in triumph, he learns that the Akashi Lady is pregnant. She gives birth, and Genji adopts their daughter, letting Murasaki act as surrogate mother. "She would playfully cuddle her and give her her own pretty breast to suck. The sight was well worth seeing" (Tyler 352). This child, known as the Akashi Princess, eventually marries a later emperor, becoming the mother of Niou. Ironically, Murasaki and Genji never have children together. Their relationship becomes a sort of closed ideal that is never repeated. (By way of contrast, Yūgiri, Genji's son by Aoi, goes on to father 12 children.)

In the last of the first part, Genji's fortunes reach their pinnacle. The Reizei Emperor, guessing his real paternity and acknowledging his filial duty, honors Genji with the rank and privileges equivalent to a retired emperor. Genji also receives a bequest of land on the death of Lady Rokujō, to atone for the behavior of her troubled spirit. On this land, he builds a palace complex and pleasure garden named Rokujō-in in her honor. In its four wings, he houses his accumulated ladies, each wing a quadrant of the compass and possessing a seasonal garden symbolic of the lady. South-West/Autumn contains Akikonomu, the former Ise priestess, orphaned daughter of Lady Rokujō. North-West/Winter houses the Akashi Lady; South-East/Spring has Murasaki and the Akashi Princess; and North-East/Summer is home to a minor figure known as Orange Blossom and Tamakayura, the orphaned daughter of Yōgao (Evening Flower). It is important to note that each of the ladies had been orphaned or abandoned, in either case, a status that had left her floating in a social limbo. Genji is playing the role of their protector.

The second part of the *Tale* (chapters 34–41) picks up Genji's life at age 41 and traces his decline through the age of 52. Japanese tradition suggested that 40 was the ideal age. "What shall it avail a man to drag out till he becomes decrepit and unsightly," asks Yoshida Kenko (1283–1352) in his famous *Essays in Idleness*. "Long life brings many shames. At most before his fortieth year is full it is seemly for a man to die" (Kenko 5). The retired Suzaku Emperor, feeling that his end is near, wishes to take Buddhist orders. He is worried, however, about his daughter, known as the Third Princess, age 13 or 14. He wants Genji to marry the girl to assure her position in society. Genji is reluctant, but finally accedes to his brother-in-law's entreaties. The girl is flighty and shallow, and despite Genji's assurances, Murasaki becomes jealous; her health breaks down, and he moves her out of Rokujō-in to be closer to the palace. While Genji is away, the Third Princess is pursued by Kashiwagi, the 23-year-old son of Genji's old friend and rival Tō no Chūjō, and becomes pregnant by him. Accidently discovering a hidden letter, Genji learns of the affair. Not blind to the many ironies of the situation, he is philosophical. "He had only himself to blame if at times he felt lost and lonely," Genji muses about himself, "but he was proud enough to see no reason why such a man as himself should not have what he desired" (Tyler 622). Later confronting the Third Princess, he says, "Perhaps in your eyes I am merely a tiresome and contemptible old man; either thought is cruel and bitter. Do at least contain yourself while His Eminence [her father the Suzaku Emperor] is still alive" (Tyler 665). The Princess gives birth to a son, Kaoru, whom everyone supposes to be Genji's son. Repetition and difference have now taken an ironic twist. Genji secretly fathered the Reizei Emperor, and now Kashiwagi has secretly fathered Genji's supposed son. Genji once pursued Tō no Chūjō's daughter, Tamakayura, and now Chūjō's son pursues Genji's wife. "This world is dross. It is nothing," Genji concludes, taking a Buddhist stance (Tyler 666). Part 2 ends by recording the decline and death of Murasaki at the age of 43. She wishes to take Buddhist orders, to become a nun, but Genji refuses to let her go, preferring to keep her near him to the end. The chapter describing her death is titled "Minori," the Japanese translation of the Sanskrit "Dharma," which signifies law or truth in Buddhist thought, putting her death into the context of the Buddhist doctrine that there is no permanence in the world, even of the ideal.

The third part of the *Tale* (chapters 42–54), often known as the Uji chapters because of their setting, picks up the narrative some eight years later, announcing that Genji is dead, his absence paradoxically a constant presence. "His light was gone, and none among his many descendants could compare to what he had been" (Tyler 785). The story now centers on Kaoru and Niou, Genji's hapless son and grandson, and the action shifts to rural Uji. Kaoru, who has a spiritual side, has traveled there to consult with a retired prince known for his learning in religious matters. There Kaoru meets the old man's two daughters, falling in love with Ōigimi, the oldest. Despite the urging of her father, Ōigimi keeps putting Kaoru off, deferring him toward her younger sister. In turn, Kaoru is indecisive, unable to commit himself until the elder sister Ōigimi becomes ill and dies. This repetition of the Yūgao story differs, however, in that Kaoru does not achieve any wisdom. Instead, he turns his affections to the young sister, who in turn directs him toward a half sister named Ukifune, who bears a remarkable resemblance to Ōigimi. Ukifune, whose name means "boat upon the waters," finds herself courted by both Kaoru and Niou, spiritually attracted to the one, but sexually fascinated by the other. Eventually distraught by her dilemma, she attempts suicide, throwing herself in the Uji River. At first the young men suppose she is dead, but eventually, Kaoru learns that she survived, having been found by the Prelate of Yokawa, who has provided her with a refuge. In the end, confusing his obsession with love, Karou renews his pursuit, perplexed when Ukifune rebuffs his entreaties. He is confounded by the inconclusiveness of the affair, unable to understand either himself or Ukifune. "After full deliberation, [he] consigned her to invisibility" (Tyler 1120). Like the image in the title of the last chapter, "The Floating Bridge of Dreams" (*"yume no ukihashi"*), the diminished world of Genji dissipates and disappears in the shimmer of the water.

SUBSEQUENT INFLUENCE

Even at an early stage, Murasaki's novel found enthusiastic readers. "I was burning with impatience and curiosity, and in my prayers I used to say, 'Let me see the entire *Tale of Genji* from beginning to end!'" recalled the Lady Sarashina in her diary (Morris, *As* 46). In the twelfth and thirteenth centuries, as mentioned previously, Buddhist polemicists criticized both Murasaki and the *Tale*. In a thirteenth-century Nō play, the *Ima monogatari*, a "formless spectre" appears in a dream: "I am Murasaki Shikibu.... For my assemblage of that multitude of untruths, and for leading people's hearts astray, I have been cast into hell" (qtd. in Bowring 82). Such attacks, of course, testify to the *Tale*'s popularity. The production in 1675 of the first wood block printed version in the Tokugawa period (1600–1868) played an important role in *Genji*'s wider transmission and popularity. All of this was facilitated by a rising class of wealthy commoners, interested in emulating the refinements of the past. Ihara Saikaku (1642–1693) explored this world of nouveaux riche in his *Life of an Amorous Man* (1682), a parody of the *Tale*. The bourgeoning popular Kabuki and Bunraku (puppet) theaters also mined the *Tale* for stories and characters. It was well into the Meiji period (1868–1912), however, before the *Tale* began to take on a canonical status. The year 1890 saw the first edition printed with movable type, soon followed by three competing editions, along with concomitant reading guides and commentaries. Much of this interest may be understood in terms of a response to westernization. There is a double thrust to this. Part of it is an exploration and reaffirmation of the Japanese national character, and part of it is the construction and assertion of a Japanese cultural identity that could compete with the West. Thus, many concurred with the critic Tsubouchi Shōyō in his 1885 manifesto *The Essence of the Novel*, which argued that the *Tale* was consonant with the great works of nineteenth-century English fiction (Rimer 200). Yosano Akiko published the first modern Japanese translation (1912–1913). Thereafter, many Japanese authors produced modern translations of *Genji* as a form of literary and cultural discipline, including Enchi Fumiko and Tanabe Seiko. Tanizaki Junichirō completed three (1939–1941, 1951–1954, and 1965).

The *Tale of Genji* has proven to be an important source for stories, characters, and themes in Japanese literature. Scholars have documented over 10,000 direct references to the *Tale* in Japanese books (Mikals-Adachi 115).

Familiarity with the *Tale*, its characters, and its themes is therefore crucial to any serious appreciation of modern Japanese literature. It is possible here to mention only a handful of modern instances. Genji's grandsons were favorite models for later writers. Karou proved an important prototype for the sensitive yet weak young men found in Natsume Sōseki's 1914 *Kokoro* or Dazai Osamu's 1947 *The Setting Sun*. Similarly, the confident, but insensitive Niou informs Shuichi in Kawabata Yasunari's *The Sound of the Mountain* (1949–1954). Kawabata, the first Japanese writer to win the Nobel Prize for Literature (1968), plays extensively with the themes and motifs from the *Tale*. Of special note is his 1952 *A Thousand Cranes*, which centers on a man attracted to the mistress of his dead father and then, upon her death, to her daughter, the motif of repetition and difference. *Snow Country* (1937), echoing Genji's relationship with the Akashi Lady, is about Shuichi, an aesthete from Tokyo and connoisseur of Western ballet, who pursues a provincial geisha at a remote spa. By contrast, Enchi Fumiko's *Masks* (1958) returns to the women's perspective of the original, examining the idea of living spirits as a means of self-expression, playing on Rokujo's possession of Aoi and Yūgao. Also of interest is her *Tale of False Fortunes* (1965), which looks at the world of Murasaki with an ironic take on the *Eiga Monogatari*. Tanizaki Junichirō's short story "The Bridge of Dreams," from his *Seven Japanese Tales*, alludes directly to the last chapter of the *Tale*. *The Makiokia Sister* (1943–1948) represents his own version of the *Tale*, especially the Uji chapters. As with those chapters in the *Tale*, Tanizaki treats the parallel themes of self-deception, loss, and evanescence. In *The Temple of the Golden Pavilion* (1956), as in many of his novels, Mishima Yukio takes this a step further, probing a desire for a purity and lost beauty that led to nihilism. Similarly, the themes, characters, and sweep of his tetralogy *The Sea of Fertility* (1968–1971) show an even stronger affinity.

Not surprisingly, the romantic elements of Murasaki's tale, especially from the earlier chapters, have contributed to a number of Japanese movies. Two that are readily available are of significance. Director Gisaburo Sugii, noted for his anime treatment of Jenji Miyazwa's *Night of the Galactic Railroad* (1985), also made a fine feature-length animated version of *The Tale of Genji* (1987). In 2001 Tonko Hoikawa directed the live-action *Genji: A Thousand-Year Love* (*Sennen no ko—hikaru Genji monogatari*), a multilayered version that recounts both the story of Murasaki Shikibu and her creation in parallel narratives. In an added twist, Genji is played by a woman, the actress Yuki Amami.

In the West, knowledge of the *Tale of Genji* was initially limited to a few specialists in Asian languages, who largely dismissed it as too remote to be widely interesting. In 1882 a Japanese attaché in London, Suematsu Kenchō, imbued with the Meiji program of Japanese cultural identity, published an English translation of the first 17 chapters. He even translated the characters' names; Murasaki is called Violet, making her a good Victorian matron.

It was, however, the complete and literate translation by the British Sinologist Arthur Waley, published in six installments between 1925 and 1933, that truly introduced Murasaki and the *Tale of Genji* to a wide reading public and stimulated the production of translations in other Western languages. Reviewing the first installment for *Vogue* (1925), Virginia Woolf wrote, "All comparisons between Murasaki and the great Western writers serve but to bring out her perfection and their force" (Woolf 268). At the same time, she finds that this perfection and refinement dilute the power and the vigor that she believes is the requisite for great literature: "Some element of horror, of terror, or sordidity [sic], some root of experience has been removed from the Eastern world" (Woolf 267). Woolf's assessment is hampered by two factors. First, with only the first installment of Waley, she had the perspective of only the first nine chapters, lacking the necessary sense of the whole. Second, Waley's translation tended to straighten and eliminate the ambiguities of Murasaki's language, submerging the subtle political tensions. Although Waley's achievement and influence cannot be overstated, he had some limitations, making the editorial decision not to include the poetry and casting the text in the tone of a fairy tale. His version has largely been superseded by the English translations of Edward G. Seidenstickler (1976) and Royall Tyler (2001).

It is common among Western critics, following the leads of Waley and Donald Keene, to read Murasaki against Proust's *À la recherche du temps perdu*, comparing the rarefied social rituals of a cultured aristocracy, as well as the play of loss and memory. (Madame LaFayette's 1678 *La Princesse de Clèves* and Guillermo Cabrera-Infante's 1979 *La Habana para un Infante Difunto* [*Infante's Inferno*] also offer rich comparisons.) Murasaki, however, is the inverse of Proust. Memory and art do not redeem the past, but underline the sense of loss, the strong awareness of evanescence, the illusory nature of worldly achievements. Similarly, French writer Marguerite Yourcenar, playing on the eight-year hiatus in the narrative between chapters 41 and 42, makes Genji a repentant Don Juan in her short story "The Last Love of Prince Genji," included in her collection *Oriental Tales* (1938). Ultimately, the *Tale of Genji* rightly stands on its own, a masterpiece of world literature. As Genji tells Tamakazura, "Come, let us make our story one like no other and give it to all the world!" (Tyler 462). His words have proven prophetic.

SUGGESTED READINGS

Bargen, Doris G. "The Search for Things Past in the *Genji Monogatari*." *Harvard Journal of Asiatic Studies* 51.1 (June 1991): 199–232.

Brazell, Karen, trans. *The Confessions of Lady Nijō*. Stanford: Stanford University Press, 1973.

Bowring, Richard. *Murasaki Shikibu: The Tale of Genji*. Cambridge: Cambridge University Press, 2004.

Cabrera-Infante, Guillermo. *Infante's Inferno*. Trans. Suzanne Jill Levine. New York: Avon Books, 1984.

Caddeau, Patrick W. *Appraising Genji: Literary Criticism and Cultural Anxiety in the Age of the Last Samurai*. Albany: State University of New York Press, 2006.

Chan, Wing-tsit. "The Lotus Sutra." *Approaches to the Asian Classics*. Ed. William de Bary and Irene Bloom. New York: Columbia University Press, 1990. 220–231.

Dazai, Osamu. *The Setting Sun*. Trans. Donald Keene. New York: New Directions, 1956.

Derrida, Jacques. *Dissemination*. Trans. Barbara Johnson. Chicago: University of Chicago Press, 1981.

Enchi, Fumiko. *Masks*. Trans. Juliet Winters Carpenter. New York: Vintage Books, 1983.

———. *A Tale of False Fortunes*. Trans. Roger K. Thomas. Honolulu: University of Hawai'i Press, 2000.

Field, Norma. *The Splendor of Longing in the Tale of Genji*. Princeton: Princeton University Press, 1987.

Hirota, Akiko. "*The Tale of Genji*: From Heian Classic to Heisei Comic." *Journal of Popular Culture* 31.2 (Fall 1997): 29–68.

Ihara Saikaku. *The Life of an Amorous Man*. Trans. Kengi Hamada. Rutland, VT: Tuttle Publishing, 1964.

Kamens, Edward, ed. *Approaches to Teaching Murasaki Shikibu's The Tale of Genji*. New York: Modern Language Association, 1993.

Kato, Shuichi. *Form, Style, Tradition: Reflections on Japanese Art and Society*. Trans. John Bester. Tokyo: Kodansha International, 1971.

———. *A History of Japanese Literature*. 3 vols. Trans. Don Sanderson. Tokyo: Kodansha International, 1993.

Kawabata, Yasunari. *Snow Country*. Trans. Edward G. Seidensticker. New York: Vintage, 1996.

———. *Thousand Cranes*. Trans. Edward G. Seidensticker. New York: Knopf, 1986.

Keene, Donald. *Japanese Literature: An Introduction for Western Readers*. New York: Grove Press, 1955.

———. *Seeds in the Heart: Japanese Literature from Earliest Times to the Late Sixteenth Century*. Vol. 1. of *A History of Japanese Literature*. New York: Columbia University Press, 1999.

———, trans. *The Tale of the Bamboo Cutter*. Tokyo: Kodansha International, 1998.

Kenko, Yoshida. *Essays in Idleness*. Trans. G. B. Sansom. New York: Cosimo Classics, 2005.

Kōjin, Karatani. *Origins of Modern Japanese Literature*. Trans. Brett de Bary. Durham: Duke University Press, 1993.

McCullough, Helen Craig, trans. *The Tale of the Heike*. Stanford: Stanford University Press, 1988.

———, trans. *Tales of Ise: Lyrical Episodes from 10th Century Japan*. Stanford: Standford University Press, 1968.

McCullough, William H., and Helen Craig McCullough, trans. *A Tale of Flowering Fortunes: Annals of Japanese Aristocratic Life in the Heian Period*. 2 vols. Stanford: Stanford University Press, 1980.

Mikals-Adachi, Eileen B. "Echoes of the Past: *The Tale of Genji* and Modern Japanese Literature." *South Asian Review* 19.16 (December 1995): 115–121.

Miner, Earl, Hiroko Odagiri, and Robert E. Morrell. *The Princeton Companion to Classical Japanese Literature*. Princeton: Princeton University Press, 1985.

Miner, Earl. "Some Thematic and Structural Features of the *Genji Monogatari*." *Monumenta Nipponica* 24.1/2 (1969): 1–19.

Mishima, Yukio. *The Decay of the Angel*. Trans. Edward G. Seidensticker. New York: Vintage International, 1990.

———. *Runaway Horses*. Trans. Michael Gallagher. New York: Vintage International, 1990.

———. *Spring Snow*. Trans. Michael Gallagher. New York: Vintage International, 1990.

———. *The Temple of Dawn*. Trans. E. Dale Saunders and Cecilia Segawa Seigle. New York: Vintage International, 1990.

Morris, Ivan, trans. *As I Crossed A Bridge of Dreams: Recollections of a Woman in Eleventh-Century Japan*. New York: Penguin Books, 1975.

———, trans. *The Pillow Book of Sei Shōnagon*. New York: Columbia University Press, 1991.

———. *The World of the Shining Prince: Court Life in Ancient Japan*. London: Penguin Books, 1969.

Murase, Miyeko. *Iconography of The Tale of Genji: Genji Monogatari Ekotoba*. New York: Weatherhill, 1983.

Okada, H. Richard. *Figures of Resistance: Language, Poetry, and Narrating in The Tale of Genji and Other Mid-Heian Texts*. Durham: Duke University Press, 1991.

Okudaira, Hideo. *Emaki: Picture Scrolls*. Trans. Fred Dunbar. Osaka: Hoikusha, 1963.

One Thousand Poems from the Manyōshū: The Complete Nippon Gakujutsu Shikokai Translation. Mineola, NY: Dover Publications, 2005.

Pekarik, Andrew, ed. *Unifune: Love in The Tale of Genji*. New York: Columbia University Press, 1982.

Puette, William J. *A Reader's Guide: The Tale of Genji*. Boston: Tuttle Publishing, 1992.

Pye, Michael. *Skilful Means: A Concept in Mahayana Buddhism*. 2nd ed. London: Routledge, 2003.

Rimer, J. Thomas. *Modern Japanese Fiction and Its Traditions: An Introduction*. Princeton: Princeton University Press, 1978.

Rodd, Laurel Rasplica, and Mary Catherine Henkenius, trans. *Kokinshū: A Collection of Poems Ancient and Modern*. Princeton: Princeton University Press, 1996.

Rowley, G. G. "Literary Canon and National Identity: *The Tale of Genji* in Meiji Japan." *Japan Forum* 9.1 (1997): 1–15.

Shikibu, Murasaki. *Murasaki Shikibu: Her Diary and Poetic Memoirs*. Trans. Richard Bowring. Princeton: Princeton University Press, 1982.

Shirane, Haruo. *The Bridge of Dreams: A Poetics of "The Tale of Genji."* Stanford: Stanford University Press, 1987.

Tanizaki, Jun'ichirō. *In Praise of Shadows.* Trans. Thomas J. Harper and Edward G. Seidensticker. New Haven: Leete's Island Books, 1977.

———. *The Makioka Sisters.* Trans. Edward G. Seidensticker. New York: Grosset and Dunlap, 1957.

———. *Seven Japanese Tales.* Trans. Howard Hibbett. New York: Vintage Books, 1996.

Three Fold Lotus Sutra. Trans. Bunnō Katō, Yoshirō Tamura, and Kōjorō Miyasaka. New York: Weatherhill, 1975.

Tyler, Royall, trans. *The Tale of Genji.* By Murasaki Shikibu. New York: Viking, 2001.

Wallace, John R. "Tarrying with the Negative: Aesthetic Vision in Murasaki and Mishima." *Monumenta Nipponica* 52.2 (Summer 1997): 181–99.

Woolf, Virginia. *The Essays of Virginia Woolf.* Vol. 4. Ed. Andrew McNeillie. London: Hogarth Press, 1994.

Yourcenar, Marguerite. *Oriental Tales.* Trans. Alberto Manguel. New York: Farrar Straus Giroux, 1985.

7

Wu Ch'êng-ên
The Journey to the West
(1592)

The deluded person wishes to be born in the East or West, [for the enlightened person] any land is just the same. If only the mind has no impurity, the Western Land is not far.

—*The Platform Sutra of the Sixth Patriarch* (157)

Its movements can't be blocked by mountains, rivers, or rock walls. Its unstoppable powers penetrate the Mountain of Five Skandhas and cross the River of Samsara.

—Bodhidharma, "Bloodstream Sermon" (21)

The classic Ming dynasty novel *The Journey to the West* (*Hsi-yu Chi*), published in 1592 and conventionally attributed to Wu Ch'êng-ên, stands as one of "the four extraordinary books (*ssu ta ch'i-shu*)" (Plaks ix) of traditional Chinese fiction. The other three are the *San-kuo-chih yen-i* (*The Romance of the Three Kingdoms*), the *Shui-hu chuan* (*The Water Margins* or *All Men Are Brothers*), and the *Chin P'ing Mei* (which has been translated as *Golden Lotus*). These four combine with two eighteenth-century novels, *Ju-lin wai-shih* (*The Scholars*) and, most famous of all, the *Hung-lou meng* (*The Dream of the Red Chamber*, whose first 80 chapters are also known independently as *The Story of a Stone*), to form what modern scholars term the "six classic novels (*Ku-tien hsiao-shuo*)." Each of these books represents the culmination of a process of recension, in which antecedent versions and other sources were synthesized into one coherent narrative form, making the latter the authoritative version, the one that defines all later treatments. As a result, these books became the models for subsequent Chinese fiction, at least down to the early twentieth century when writers such as Lu Xun (1881–1936) sought alternatives. This might be compared with Thomas Malory's *Le Morte D'Arthur* (c. 1469, 1485), the most authoritative account of King Arthur in English, which built on earlier versions—for example, *Alliterative Morte Arthure* (1360), the *Stanzaic* version (c. 1400), the history of Geoffrey of Monmouth (c. 1136), and the Welsh *The Mabinogion* (c. 1200), a compendium with roots in Celtic folklore.

Ostensibly, the core of *The Journey to the West* centers on an account of the legendary transmission of Mahayana Buddhism to China ("The Greater Vehicle"), chronicling the actual historical pilgrimage of the Chinese monk Xuanzang (Tripitaka) as he followed the westward course of the Silk Road to India in pursuit of Buddhist scriptures. Over time, this history accumulated layers of fantastic adventures, accounts of exotic locations, Buddhist demonology, traditional folklore, and most significantly, a group of four guardian-disciples: a dragon-horse; a cannibalistic ogre known as Sha Ho-shang or the "Sand Monk" (Sandy in Arthur Waley's translation); a half-human, half-pig known as Pa-Chieh (Pigsy in Waley); and most famous of all, Sun Wu-k'ung, the Stone Monkey (or Monkey King), also known by the epithet "Great Sage, Equal to Heaven." In the course of the journey, they encounter a host of exotic figures, including the Jade Emperor of Heaven; Kuan-yin, Bodhisattva of Compassion; the infamous White Boned Lady (or Cadaver Demon); Red Boy; Bull Demon; and Princess Iron Fan, all of whom have become an integral part of Chinese popular culture.

Although the *Journey* brings together a variety of antecedent folk traditions, including perhaps material about Hanumān, the Monkey king of the Indian epic *Rāmāyana* who leads an army of monkeys to help the hero Rāma rescue his wife Sītā from the demon king Rāvana, and tales from the *Jātaka*, a collection of traditional stories about the Buddha's former lives, it is more than merely a string of stories. The resulting 100-chapter narrative forms a coherent whole, dramatizing an elaborate allegory about the Buddhist conception of the soul and enlightenment, coupled with the Confucian preoccupation with self-definition in relation to its social context. "The concentric circles that define the self in terms of family, community, country, and the world are undoubtedly social groups," writes the modern Chinese philosopher Tu Wei-Ming on the nature of humanity in Confucianism. "But, in the Confucian perspective, they are also realms of selfhood that symbolize the authentic human possibility for ethicoreligious growth" (Tu 57–58). In other words, the *Journey* can be understood as a profound meditation on the nature and transformation of the self.

MAHAYANA BUDDHISM

Buddhism is one of the great salvation religions to emerge from the Axial Age (about 800 B.C.E.–200 B.C.E.), along with Daoism, Confucianism, Hinduism, Rabbinic Judaism, Christianity, and Islam. Its founder, known as Gotama Siddhattha (or Siddhartha), and known also by the title Sakyamuni ("sage born of the Śākya tribe") and later as the Buddha (from the Sanskrit *budh*, "to awaken" or "perceive"—that is, the enlightened one) was born in Northern India and flourished from 624 to 544 B.C.E. Early surviving accounts of his life indicate that though he lived in luxury and privilege, he realized that both rich and poor were subject to old age, disease, and death, leading to a sense of "annoyance, shame and disgust" (qtd. in Nakamura 20). Later accounts embroider these meditations into the Legend of the Four Gates, in which Gotama saw first an old man, then a diseased man, then a corpse, and finally a hermit. *The Journey to the West* plays on this legend in the episode of Cart-Slow (chapters 44–46), in which the pilgrims are challenged to a contest by some Daoist magicians to guess the contents of a series of boxes, a contest that Monkey wins by secretly transforming the objects. First, a red robe and lacquered dish are changed to old broken crockery, after which a ripe peach is reduced to a peach pit, and finally a boy dressed as a Daoist acolyte is transformed into a Buddhist monk. The broken crockery suggests old age or disease; the peach pit (the skull of the peach, so to speak), death; and the monk, the hermit. (Through a long line of transmission, the Four Gates also informs Portia's contest of the gold, silver, and lead caskets in Shakespeare's *Merchant of Venice* as well as numerous fairy tales.)

Renouncing his life of luxury, Gotama pursues a life of rigorous asceticism. In the legendary materials, he struggles against the temptations of various demons, finally achieving enlightenment under the aśvattha (bohhi or bo) tree. Contemplating Dependent Origination, the causal web that interconnects everything, the Buddha arrives at the Four Noble Truths: that all conscious beings suffer; that the suffering comes from craving and attachment to things, which traps us to the wheel of endless reincarnation; that liberation comes from renunciation or non-attachment; and that renunciation is achieved through the Eight-Fold Path, which involves cultivating right views, intentions, speech, conduct, livelihood, effort, mindfulness, and concentration. Because self (the "I" and the "mine") is the indisputable condition for suffering, the key to salvation lies in non-self, in achieving a state of liberation called *nirvana*. The word derives from the Sanskrit *nir*, "out," and *va*, "to blow." Through shared Indo-European roots, *va* is also related to English words such as *vent* and *weather*). Metaphorically speaking, if life can be thought of as the flame of an oil lamp, and rebirth as one oil lamp lighting the next and so on, then nirvana means the blowing out of the flame. The path to enlightenment preached by the Buddha was practical in nature, rejecting any dogmatic notion of set formula or ritual for achieving liberation. After the Buddha, however, schools began to form and competing doctrines started to solidify.

The two most prominent types of Buddhism are Hinayana (the so-called lesser vehicle, a derogatory term given by the Mahayana), which developed between 400 and 250 B.C.E. and which is still prominent as Theravada Buddhism ("Old Wisdom School") in Thailand, Laos, Cambodia, and Sri Lanka, and Mahayana (the "greater vehicle"), which developed between 0 and 500 C.E. and which is still prominent in Nepal, China, Vietnam, and Japan. Hinayana contends that enlightenment is limited to those who renounce the household, putting emphasis on brotherhood (*samgha*) and the formation of monastic orders. Closely related to this is the cult of *arhats* (*arakan* in Japanese, *luohan* in Chinese), a body of saints or sages who have achieved enlightenment. Many of these were historical figures, later embellished by legend and folklore and now prominent in Buddhist iconography, each with various representative features. In turn, nirvana is understood as extinction. Mahayana, in contrast, advocates universal salvation. The figure of the arhat is pushed to the background by the bodhisattva, a savior figure who postpones nirvana to help others achieve Buddhahood. The pilgrims of *The Journey* are constantly aided by Kuan-yin, Bodhisattva of Compassion. In turn nirvana is conceived not as extinction, but as a state of bliss, perfect tranquility, and profound wisdom. This is understood in terms of *sūnyatā* or emptiness, not in the sense of void or vacuum, but in the dissolving of the subject–object dualism by which the self defines itself in relation to everything other than itself. In the words of the *Heart Sutra,* one of the foundational works of Mahayana Buddhism and frequently chanted by Tripitaka, "in emptiness there is no form, no sensation, no perception, no memory and no consciousness" (Pine, *Heart* 96). What is left is the radical "suchness" of things, without the mediation of any conceptual framework. "Bodhisattvas take refuge in *Prajñaparamita* ['wisdom-gone-beyond,' that is, transcendental wisdom]: and live without walls of the mind" (Pine, *Heart* 130, 133).

PLOT AND CHARACTER DEVELOPMENT

Observing the conventions of what Andrew H. Plaks terms the "literati novel" (Plaks 3–52), the *Journey* is divided into 100 chapters, the first 12 of which are prologue, tracing the origins of the various pilgrims and the circumstances of the pilgrimage. The journey proper begins with chapter 13, the pilgrims finally reaching India in chapter 98, and returning to China in chapters 99 and 100. The pilgrimage itself is divided into a series of largely autonomous episodes. In chapter 99, the pilgrims are told that they were destined to endure 81 trials and so must suffer one more, having endured only 80. There are not so many, but the narrative forms a series of discrete units two to five chapters in length.

As with many traditional stories, the prologue begins in the beginning with the creation of the Stone Monkey, Sun Wu-K'ung, out of the elements. Once upon a time, the young Monkey discovers a cave behind a waterfall, when he accepts a dare to jump into the water. There he establishes a kingdom for monkeys thereafter called the Water-Curtain Cave of Fruit-Flower Mountain. Spiritual crisis shatters this idyll, when Monkey, like the Buddha, begins to contemplate his mortality. Bursting into tears one day during a feast, he moans that he and all of the monkeys will be subject to the sovereignty of Yama, King of the Underworld, and that the prospect of death renders their lives vain and meaningless. To this a sage ape replies, "If the Great King is so farsighted, it may well indicate the sprouting of his religious inclination." To satisfy this religious inclination, Monkey first seeks the Daoist Patriarch Subodhi, who trains him in magic. Returning, he discovers that an ogre has expelled the monkeys from the Fruit and Flower Cave. Monkey arms himself with a magical steel wand that was originally a support holding up the sky in the palace of the Dragon King of the South Sea and that may be contracted to the size of a pin or expanded to that of a pillar. So armed, Monkey liberates his cave from the ogre, seeking power and raising havoc along the way. To deal with the complaints, the Jade Emperor of Heaven, in good Confucian fashion, proposes to dispose of this threat by co-opting it in order to reestablish harmony. Thus, Monkey is offered a minor post in the celestial bureaucracy—*Pi-ma-wên* (literally "horse leech"). Indeed, the vain Monkey is obsessed with accumulated titles, supposing that they signify his greatness. After a series of misadventures, disrupting the Peach Festival and stealing magic elixir, all precipitated by Monkey's greed and gluttony, he flees heaven, again causes havoc, is again reconciled, and yet again runs amok, repeatedly and single-handedly defeating heavenly hosts of celestial warriors. This time the Daoists intervene, and Monkey is captured by Lao Tzu, the legendary founder of Daoism, who proposes to dissolve him in an alchemical crucible, the Brazier of Eight Trigrams. (Much of Daoist practice focused on alchemy and magic.) The long cooking serves only to give Monkey red eyes, and he again escapes captivity and further ravages the Jade Heaven.

Read in terms of Buddhist allegory, Monkey is the embodiment of will, caught in a perpetual cycle of desires that drive *samsara*. Indeed, he is often identified by the epithet "Mind Monkey," a false willfulness. In a self-reflexive moment tearing the fabric of pure existence, he has become aware of mortality and immortality, the first flickering of religious enlightenment. His first attempts to solve the problem, however, take him in the opposite direction, making him suppose that his salvation is in material power and titles, a reification of illusions of the world and an intensification of desire. As the political allegory reveals, all of these are fragile facades. Similarly, neither the Confucian attempt to rectify harmony nor the Daoist attempt to control the elements with magic offers a solution to the Monkey problem.

Here the Buddha enters the scene. Holding out his hand, he challenges Monkey to a wager. If Monkey can somersault off of the Buddha's right hand, the Buddha will ask the Jade Emperor to join with him in the Western paradise and cede the Celestial Palace to Monkey. If not, Monkey will do penance. Thinking this an easy bet, Monkey leaps up and stands in the center of the Buddha's outstretched palm, which is described as the size of a lotus leaf. Taking off like a rocket, Monkey streaks through space until he sees "five flesh-pink pillars." Supposing that he has reached the edge of the universe, he marks his triumph first by signing his name to the middle pillar, then by urinating on the first pillar. Returning to the Buddha to demand his prize, he is chagrined to learn that he has never left the Buddha's palm, that the five pillars were in reality the fingers of the Buddha's right hand, a fact confirmed by the signature on the middle finger and the pungent odor of monkey urine between his thumb and index finger. Monkey tries to escape, but the Buddha flips over his hand and throws the distraught Monkey out of the Western Heavenly Gate. "The five fingers were transformed into the Five Phases of metal, wood, water, fire, and earth. They became, in fact, five connected mountains, named Five-Phases Mountain [Wu Hsing Shan], which pinned him down with just enough pressure to keep him there" (1.174).

In the remaining chapters of the prologue (8–12), the story of the monk Tripitaka is recounted, and the official occasion for the pilgrimage is established. It is explained that the T'ang Emperor of China must atone for a past sin by sending an expedition to India in order to seek out new Buddhist scriptures, the old scriptures having somehow gone out of date. (Implicit in this is the competition between Theravada and Mahayana branches of Buddhism.) All of these events are in fact orchestrated by the Buddha, acting through Kuan-yin, Bodhisattva of Compassion. Tripitaka, known throughout the novel as the master, is appointed to the task, and Kuan-yin arranges for the release of Monkey to accompany him as a disciple-guardian. Glad to be free, he is still rambunctious and willful and must be subdued by Tripitaka with the aid of a magic fillet that expands or contracts on Monkey's head. In chapters 12–23, Monkey and Tripitaka gather three more disciple-guardians, first Pa-Chieh (Pigsey), a being who is half-human and half-pig, amiable, gluttonous, and lazy. He is followed by the fierce red-bearded cannibal Sha Ho-shang, (the Sand Monk, because he inhabited the sand dunes), decked in a necklace of human skulls. The fifth pilgrim is the dragon-horse. When Tripitaka's own horse is swallowed by a dragon, Monkey compels the dragon to take on the form of a horse in order to carry the master.

The five pilgrims now get under way. Andrew Plaks outlines the basic recurrent formula for the typical episode (207–208). Each begins with the pilgrims on the road in a state of contentment. They encounter an obstacle or other upset. This leads to discontent and bickering, followed by the appearance of a demon. The demon snatches away Tripitaka and one or more of the disciples. Monkey now seeks the lair of the demon with his magic powers or the aid of someone else. Initially, he is repelled in his efforts, but he eventually breaks the spell of the demon with the help of some secret power or a Buddhist savior. The demon is subdued, its true identity revealed, and the pilgrims are liberated from illusion and able to resume their journey, closing a circle and starting the process over again. This formula underlines the themes of Buddhist enlightenment. Our sufferings, according to Buddhist doctrine, derive from false consciousness, leading to false attachments, the source of evil. In one of the many passages of verse interspersed throughout the text, the narrator says,

> The Mind is the Buddha and the Buddha is Mind;
> Both Mind and Buddha are important things.
> If you perceive there's neither Mind nor Thing,
> Yours is the *dharmakāya* ["sheath of reality," or
> the reality of all beings] of True Mind. (Wu 1.297)

Or, in the words of the *Platform Sutra of the Sixth Patriarch*, one of the central documents of Ch'an Buddhism, "If people think of all the evil things, then they will practice evil" (*Platform* 141). Correspondingly, "If you are awakened to correct views, the wisdom of *prajñā* [intuitive wisdom] will wipe away ignorance and delusion, and you will save yourselves" (*Platform* 143–144). The demons that plague the five pilgrims are the product of the pilgrims' false consciousness, and their liberation comes from attaining the correct view of things.

It is impossible in a brief space to outline more than a handful of the adventures, but some have achieved canonical status in the popular imagination and are worth lingering over. In chapters 27–31, the pilgrims encounter the White Boned Lady or Cadaver Demon while searching for food. Hoping to regain her youth by eating the pure body of Tripitaka (part of the alchemical doctrine of Daoism), the demon tries to maneuver to his side by approaching the group disguised as an 18-year-old girl, carrying bowls of rice and fried noodles. Monkey suspects something is wrong and kills the girl with his club, much to the horror and disgust of Tripitaka, even though they discover that the rice in the bowl has turned into maggots, and the noodles, toads. The demon's spirit, having escaped the corpse before Monkey's blow, now appears as an old woman, supposedly the girl's mother. This time Monkey kills the old woman, but again the demon spirit escapes. When he finally appears in the body of an old man, Monkey is successful in killing both body and spirit, leaving only a pile of white bone. Tripitaka fails to comprehend what has happened and is so infuriated when Monkey suggests that his interest in the girl might have been sexual that he exiles him. Monkey is distraught that he will not be able to repay the debt for his liberation. Echoing Confucian doctrine, he laments, "I knowing kindness without repaying am no princely man [to have observed the moral ideal of a Confucian gentleman (*junzi*)]" (2.24). When Tripitaka refuses to look at him, Monkey transforms himself into four, surrounding the master on all sides so that he must acknowledge his presence. The whole episode underscores the deeper theme of distinguishing true appearances from false and being blinded by desires. Reflecting later, Monkey sighs, "the T'ang monk [Tripitaka] is wholly ignorant of who is worthy and who is foolish" (2.36).

In chapters 37–39, Tripitaka and his disciples are approached by the watery ghost king of the Black Cock Realm, who implores them to rescue his son and wife from a demon who has stolen his identity and taken his place. The story, as a number of readers note, is a sort of Chinese *Hamlet*. The demon this time turns out to be the lion associated with the arhat Mañjusrī. In chapters 44–46, the pilgrims discover that the Buddhists have been enslaved by the slow-witted ruler of the Cart-Slow Kingdom, acting under the advice of three Daoist sages. After an elaborate series of contests, involving Monkey's being decapitated, disemboweled, and boiled in oil, all without permanent effect, the sages are revealed to be a tiger, deer, and goat in disguise. In the end, Monkey declares to the king, "You should realize that the true way is the gate of Zen. Hereafter you should never believe in false doctrines." Having asserted the primacy of Buddhism, he adds, "I hope that you will honor the unity of the Three Religions: revere the monks [Buddhists], revere also the Daoists, and take care to nurture the talented [Confucians]" (2.354).

Chapters 48 and 49 mark the transition out of China across the "Heaven-Reaching River of eight hundred miles" (2.401). Finding the river frozen, the pilgrims start out over the ice. It breaks, however, and the sinking Tripitika is seized and imprisoned by a river dragon. With the aid of Kuan-yin, Monkey effects a rescue, subduing the dragon, who turns out to be a goldfish with magical powers. The pilgrims are finally helped across the river on the back of a giant turtle, on the promise that they will ask the Buddha to help the turtle cast off his shell and become human. The image of the five pilgrims on the back of the great turtle forms a rich and complex emblem. The figure of the turtle with its domed back was a recurrent symbol of the cosmos in China, a figure central to ancient Chinese culture and myth. The shell was often used for oracle bone divination, and from the grid-work pattern on the back of the turtle's carapace comes the recurrent motif of five in ancient cosmology—for example, the five elements (fire, water, wood, earth, and metal) and the five cardinal points (Zenith, East, West, North, South). This in turn corresponds to the five pilgrims and other Buddhist themes—the five *Jinas* or *Tathagathas* (the Great Buddhas of Wisdom), the five *skandas* or "aggregates" that make up the psycho-physical organism (form, sensation, apperception, volition, and consciousness), and the five steps to salvation (Frédéric 124–127).

Once across the river, difficulties still remain, as Tripitaka's virtue is repeatedly tested by a succession of demonesses. Chapters 59–61 describe Monkey's famous encounter with Princess Iron-Fan (also known as Raksasi or Female Demon) and her consort Bull Demon King (sometimes known as Buffalo King). The pilgrims are stopped by an erupting volcano. Monkey seeks out Iron-Fan, who possesses a magic palm fan. One wave of the fan will extinguish a fire, a second will produce a torrential wind that blows anything in its path to great distances, and a third will produce rain. Unfortunately for Monkey, Princess Iron-Fan happens to be the mother of Red Boy, one of Monkey's earlier adversaries (chapters 40–42). Because of Monkey's prior dealings with Red Boy, Princess Iron Fan is not sympathetic to his plight, tries to cut off his head, and then sends him thousands of miles away with a wave of the magic fan. Monkey returns and, disguised as a tea bubble, enters her stomach from where he compels her to lend him the fan. Monkey returns to the fiery mountain, but is chagrined to learn that Iron Fan has tricked him with a bait-and-switch scam. Taking his cue from Iron Fan's deception, he returns disguised as Bull Demon, tricking the fan from her. In turn, the real Bull Demon disguised as Pigsey counter-tricks Monkey. Finally joined by the real Pigsey, Monkey fights with Bull Demon, a battle in which they engage in an escalating series of transformations. Bull first becomes a small bird. Monkey replies by becoming a hawk. Bull then becomes a snake, and Monkey a stork. When Bull becomes a fox, Monkey appears as a tiger. Finally, Bull Demon takes on the shape of a giant bull. As the Bull Demon is about to be subdued, Iron Fan finally relents and gives Monkey the fan to release her husband. Having learned that he cannot trust the truth of appearances, Monkey is finally successful in extinguishing the flames of the fiery mountain, bringing rain and the rebirth of life to the parched land.

Chapter 98 marks the group's arrival at the Spirit Mountain and the Thunderclap Monastery of the Western Heaven where the Buddha resides. To get there, the pilgrims must cross a river in a bottomless boat, during which Tripitaka witnesses his own body float away from his spirit, signifying his deliverance from mortal flesh and bone. Finally reaching his goal, he is presented with three baskets of scriptures (the name Tripitaka derives from the Sanskrit for "three baskets"—cognate through Indo-European roots to *tri-*, signifying three). The return to China is dispatched in brief and uneventful terms, save for when the pilgrims must again return across the great river, again on the back of the great turtle, who asks about his request. Correctly guessing that Tripitaka forgot to ask the Buddha about transcending his shell to become a human, the annoyed turtle submerges, casting the pilgrims and the boxes of scripture into the water. Once they have scrambled to the shore, they are suddenly struck by a torrential storm, the 81st trial that they must suffer to complete their destiny. A number of the scriptures are damaged, a reminder that the vehicle (the scriptures themselves) is itself imperfect and impermanent, not the real goal of the journey, but merely the means: crossing a river, one abandons the raft. Chastened, the pilgrims enjoy a triumphant return to China, bringing the journey to the West full circle.

THEMES

The *Journey to the West* can be read on a number of levels, political and religious. One level focuses on social and political satire, reflecting the fact that Wu Ch'êng-ên or any member of the literati would probably have been a part of the elaborate imperial bureaucracy and civil service. Under ideal conditions, an office was based on merit, determined by a series of progressive civil service exams predicated on a command of the Confucian classics. This bureaucracy, which even included an office of poetry, administered every aspect of the empire. The various parallel universes of the Jade Heaven, the realms of spirits, and even Monkey's own Water-Curtain Cave of Fruit-Flower Mountain are structured with such bureaucratic hierarchies, each with its privileges, perquisites, and petty officiousness. Monkey's realm is administered by a Confucian bureaucracy of apes whose multicolored rumps correspond to the colors of the buttons worn on the caps of the Confucian civil servants to signify rank. At one point he is taken prisoner by the agents of Yama, the god of death. Bluffing, Monkey demands to see the official records in which his life and death are recorded. The flustered clerks comply, and Monkey takes up a brush and proceeds to cancel his death as well as the deaths of his friends. In turn, the heavenly hierarchy reduplicates the earthly hierarchy, so Monkey's adventures in the Jade Heaven offer a political commentary on the state of things in the China of the Ming Dynasty. Bureaucrats, who can be bullied or bribed, are shown to be stupid and corrupt, and even the Divine Jade Emperor is portrayed as ineffectual and incompetent. Indeed, this political theme is so persistent that a 1965 feature-length animated version of *Havoc in Heaven*, directed by Wan Laiming, was initially banned in China because the Jade Emperor was thought to resemble Mao Tze-tung too closely.

Monkey's revolt in heaven can be read as a primer on staging a real political uprising. Indeed, some 46 years after the publication of the *Journey*, the 276-year-old Ming Dynasty collapsed as a result of the Xing (Manchu) invasion.

Of the various levels, the religious allegory is the most elaborate and multilayered. Monkey's contest with the Buddha is indicative of the complexity of the whole novel. The episode culminating at the five pillars allegorizes the notion that the truth of the Buddha extends to the edge of the universe. Like his hand, nothing can go beyond Buddhism. "The Mind is the Buddha and the Buddha is Mind." In turn Monkey's dual human and animal natures are signified by the two ways he marks his territory: one with written characters denoting his titles, and the other with urine. Both are identified with each other, and each is dismissed. Whether a human animal or an animal human, he is trapped in his focus on the status of space or the belief that his symbols correspond to realities. In turn, the five fingers of the Buddha's hand as well as the five peaks of Five-Phases Mountain relate to a series of correspondences that link them with the five elements and five pilgrims (Monkey–Fire, Tripitika–Water, Pigsy–Wood, Sandy–Earth, and the Dragon-horse–Metal) and most significantly, the *skandas* or "five aggregates."

In an added layer, the episode with the Buddha's hand significantly plays with Buddhist imagery. The descriptions of the Buddha's hand movements draw on the iconography of *mudras* (or *yin*)—the symbolic hand gestures used in Buddhist sculpture and painting to represent divine forces and manifestations. Monkey first crouches on the open palm of the Buddha, an image that resembles the *mudra* of the "wish-granting jewel"—*hoshu-in* (Frédéric 49). He then somersaults from that position until he reaches the five flesh-pink pillars, which turn out to be the right hand of the Buddha, raised up, palm facing outward, fingers upright. This gesture suggests the *Abhaya Mudra* (or *Shiwuwei Yin*), typical in Buddhist sculpture and symbolizing protection, benevolence, peace, and the dispersal of fear (Frédéric 40). Finally, when the Monkey realizes that he has made an error, the Buddha closes his fingers on him and turns his hand palm down in order to throw Monkey to the earth. Two *mudras* are possible. The formation of a closed fist, *musti mudra* (*Jinggang Yin*), symbolizes firmness of spirit. *Ongyo-in* (*Yinxing Yin*) is a magic *mudra*, and the gesture features the extended right hand, palm downward, while the left hand forms a fist, which is held before the breast. The combined gesture is used to exorcize demons (Frédéric 49–50). The movement of hand gestures parallels Monkey's spiritual encounter with the Buddha. In making his wager, he is in the wish-granting position. He then confronts the Buddha's aspect of benevolence and peace (*Abhaya Mudra*). When Monkey fails to understand this, he encounters the firmness of the Buddha and is exorcized from the Celestial Palace and is thus trapped under the five fingers.

One of the characteristics of the Chinese literati novels is the play with numerology and the use of chapter numbers to indicate significant transitions. For example, in the *Journey*, chapters 9, 49, and 99 contain the thematically significant motif of crossing water. Chapter 9 describes how the infant Tripitaka's father was drowned by brigands and how the baby was saved by his mother floating him away on a raft (he is therefore often known by the epithet Water-Float). Chapter 49, the halfway point of both the novel and the journey, marks an important transition when the pilgrims cross the great river on the back of the giant turtle, as does chapter 99, when they recross the river on the back of the turtle on the return trip, though with a less triumphant outcome.

The river and boat or raft symbolism is central to Mahayana Buddhism. Throughout the classical texts of Buddhism, the river, or crossing the river, is a metaphor of having escaped the cycles of birth and death. "Few among men are they who cross to the further shore," declares the *Dhammapada*. "The others merely run up and down the bank on this side" (Rahula 128). The *Platform Sutra*, for instance, cites the Sanskrit term *pāramitā*, meaning "other-shore-reached" (*Platform* 147). Similarly, the *Diamond Sutra* describes *dharma* (signifying either virtue or scripture in Buddhism) as a raft. The river signifies *samsara*, the impermanence of reality, the eternal cycles of birth and death. At a deeper level, the river is a metaphor for the self, understood not as a being, but as a becoming, not as some fixed entity or thing, but as an ever-shifting relationship between. That is, self is nothing. Similarly the scriptures and virtues are the raft or boat, the *greater* vehicle, that conducts us across the river to salvation. Tripitaka's recurrent association with water and transportation marks the self's struggle with self-transcendence.

The theme of the five skandas is of special importance to the *Journey*. Central to Mahayana Buddhist doctrine, personhood or the self is understood not as a fixed entity, but as a shifting relation among five components that constitute the mind: form, sensation, apperception, volition (or predisposition), and consciousness. In this way it conceives the emptiness or no-*thing*-ness of the self. Often compared with the bubbles in foam, the components are separate yet cannot be separated, forming a transient whole. Their momentary interactions create the illusion of reality, and from that mirage, our various attachments and suffering derive. Corresponding to the five aggregates, the bickering and often disharmonious five pilgrims together form a sort of whole, a problematic everyman struggling for salvation. By themselves, each embodies a variety of human weaknesses. Tripitaka, for instance, may be deeply pious, but is often querulous, cowardly, and indecisive, easily swayed by bad advice, especially from the foolish Pa-Chieh. Monkey may be brave and energetic, but is also vain, impatient, reckless, and willful. When they are out of harmony and become *self*-conscious of themselves and each other, demons emerge to plague them. When they are working in harmony with each other, working to counterbalance the weaknesses of the others, forgetting themselves, they are happy. In broad terms, then, *The Journey to the West* is about the maturity of the self, its struggle to understand its proper nature, to liberate itself from illusions and false attachments, and to thereby achieve enlightenment.

SUBSEQUENT INFLUENCE

Among the earliest responses to the *Journey* is Tung Yüeh's seventeenth-century novel *Hsi-yu pu* (*Supplement to Journey to the West*, available in English as *The Tower of Myriad Mirrors*). At the same time, Monkey's westward adventures have moved east, finding wide expression in Asia and the Pacific Rim, including in painting, sculpture, comic books, cartoon animation, live-action movies, television, and puppetry. A number of Monkey's adventures have entered the repertoire of the Beijing Opera, featuring elaborate acrobatic feats. Even Mao Tse-tung evoked Monkey, calling on him to clear the dust with his "mammoth club": "Today we cheer the Great Sage / for the demon mist rises again" (Mao 105). Later opponents of the so-called Gang of Four branded Mao's widow, Jiang Quing, with the epithet "White Boned Demon." From China, *The Journey to the West* has traveled south to Vietnam and east to Korea and Japan. Yukio Mishima's novel *The Temple of Dawn* (1970), for instance, alludes significantly to Monkey, and those familiar with *The Journey* will recognize several sly references in Masayuki Suo's widely popular 1996/1997 movie *Shall We Dance?* It has also found expression in several live-action television series, such as *Suiyûki* (1978–1980). As Xuanzang's adventures followed the Silk Road, so Monkey's transmission followed the path of Asian immigration to the Far East—that is to say, the United States, Canada, and beyond, becoming the basis of many stories and allusions, contributing to such contemporary works as Maxine Hong Kingston's *Tripmaster Monkey*, Patricia Chao's *The Monkey King* (1998), Frank Chin's *Gunga Din Highway*, and Timothy Mo's *Monkey King Sour Sweet* (1980), as well as Gerald Vizenor's cross-cultural hero Griever from *An American Monkey King in China*. One might also consider Fred Ho's Afro-Asian multimedia musical, *Journey Beyond the West* (1996). There have also been a variety of graphic novel or *manga* versions, from Taiwanese cartoonist Tsai Chih Chung's (Cai Zhi Zhong) whimsical postmodern take to Terada Katsuya's 1995 porno-violent manga adaptation, resembling something from the nightmares of H. R. Giger.

Monkey and the stories of the *Journey* were a natural for animation. The Wan brothers, Wan Laiming (1899–1997), his twin brother Wan Guchan (1899–1995), Wan Chaochen (1906–1992), and Wan Dihuan (b. 1907), created the first Chinese animation, inspired by Max Fleischer's *Out of the Ink Well* in the early 1920s. Their concern was to create a Chinese response that reflected the "national character [*minzu fengge*]." Further inspired by Walt Disney's groundbreaking *Snow White and the Seven Dwarfs* (1937), Wan Laiming and Wan Guchan produced the first feature-length animation in China, the 1941 *Tieshan Gongzhu* (*Princess Iron Fan*), based on chapters 59–61 of the *Journey*. Responding to the Japanese occupation of Shanghai, Bull Demon looks like a Samurai warrior riding a tank-like dinosaur. In 1958 Wan Guchan created the short *Zhu Baizhe* [Pigsey] *Eats the Watermelon*, using innovative paper cutout animation. Finally, most agree that the masterpiece of the Shanghai Animation Studio is the feature-length film *Sun wukong dano tiangong* (*Monkey King Disturbs the Celestial Palace*), also known as *Havoc in Heaven*, based on chapters 3–5 of the *Journey*, the episode also known as "The Monkey King Disturbs the Celestial Palace [*Sun wukong dano tiangong*]." It was directed by Wan Laiming and appeared in two parts, the first in 1961 and the second in 1964 (Bendazzi 182–183; Lent 8–12).

Monkey is also an important cultural icon in Japan. A number of film versions have come out of Japan, including a live-action serialized version (*Saiyuki*, 1978–1980, directed by Yusuke Watanabe) and several animated versions, including the recent *Monkey Magic* (1998), an anime series directed by Tameo Kohanawa and produced by Bandai Entertainment in conjunction with Canadian television, and the anime series *Saiyuki*, based on the manga version of Minckuri Kazuya. Ironically, it was through a Japanese appropriation and transformation that an animated version of the Monkey King traveled east to reach the West in 1961, several years before *Havoc in Heaven*. *Alakazam the Great*, made in Japan in 1960 as *Saiyuki* and then rewritten, edited, and dubbed for an American audience, appeared in 1961, featuring the vocal talent of Frankie Avalon as Alakazam (Monkey) and Jonathan Winters in the Pigsey role.

In the children's book *The Making of Monkey King* (1998), Monkey's early adventures are retold by Robert Kraus and Debby Chen. The book is illustrated with a series of charming and witty paintings by Wenhai Ma. In one of these, Monkey is shown at the cave of the Daoist patriarch, Subodhi, where he has gone to learn magic. In the scene, Subodhi is shown inscribing Monkey's new name, "Sun Wukong," on a scroll, a sort of initiation ceremony. Many disciples are surrounding Monkey and Subodhi, witnessing and applauding this ritual of passage and identity. Under close scrutiny, one begins to recognize many of the faces in this crowd. Quite distinct are those of Shakespeare, Tolstoy, Goethe, and Rabindranath Tagore, to name a few among many. In Ma's astute reading, Monkey has rightly been acknowledged among the ranks of world literature.

SUGGESTED READINGS

Allan, Sarah. *The Shape of the Turtle: Myth, Art, and Cosmos in Early China*. Albany: State University of New York Press, 1991.

Alley, Rewi. *Opera de Pekin*. Beijing: Editions du Nouveau Monde, 1984.

Bechert, Heinz, and Richard Gombrich, eds. *The World of Buddhism: Buddhist Monks and Nuns in Society and Culture*. London: Thames and Hudson, 1984.

Bendazzi, Giannalberto. *Cartoons: One Hundred Years of Cinema Animation*. Trans. Anna Taraboletti-Segre. Bloomington: Indiana University Press, 1999.

Blofeld, John. *Bodhisattva of Compassion: The Mystical Tradition of Kuan Yin*. Boston: Shambhala, 1978.

Bohhidharma. *The Zen Teachings of Bodhidharma*. Trans. Red Pine. San Francisco: North Point Press, 1987.

Conze, Edward. *Buddhism: Its Essence and Development*. New York: Harper and Row, 1959.

Cooksey, Thomas L. "Hero of the Margin: The Trickster as Deterritorialized Animal." *Thalia: Studies in Literary Humor* 18.1–2 (1998): 50–61.

Cowell, E. B., ed. *The Jataka, or Stories of the Buddha's Former Births*. 6 vols. Delhi: Motilal Banarsidass Publishers, 1990.

Farquhar, Mary Ann. "Monks and Monkey: A Study of 'National Style' in Chinese Animation." *Animation Journal* (Spring 1993): 4–27.

Frédéric, Louis. *Buddhism: Flammarion Iconographic Guides*. Trans. Nissim Marshall. Paris: Flammarion, 1995.

Gao, R. L. *Adventures of Monkey King*. Monterey: Victory Press, 1989.

Hsia, C. T. *The Classic Chinese Novel: A Critical Introduction*. New York: Columbia University Press, 1968.

Hynes, William J., and William G. Doty, eds. *Mythical Trickster Figures: Contours, Contexts, and Criticisms*. Tuscaloosa: University of Alabama Press, 1993.

Jiang, Ji-Li. *The Magical Monkey King: Mischief in Heaven*. New York: HarperCollins, 2002.

Kraus, Robert, and Debby Chen. *The Making of Monkey King*. Union City: Pan Asian Publications, 1998.

Lent, John, ed. *Animation in Asia and the Pacific*. Bloomington: Indiana University Press, 2001.

Mao Tze-tung. *The Poems of Mao Tze-tung*. Trans. Willis Barnstone. New York: Harper and Row, 1972.

Nakamura, Hajime. *Gotama Buddha*. Los Angeles-Tokyo: Buddhist Books International, 1977.

Paz, Octavio. *The Monkey Grammarian*. Trans. Helen Lane. New York: Arcade Publishing: Little, Brown and Company, 1990.

Pine, Red, trans. *The Diamond Sutra: Text and Commentaries*. Washington, D.C.: Counterpoint, 2001.

————, trans. *The Heart Sutra*. Washington, D.C.: Shoemaker and Hoard, 2004.

Plaks, Andrew H. *The Four Masterworks of the Ming Novel: Ssu ta Ch'i-shu*. Princeton: Princeton University Press, 1987.

Quiquemelle, Marie-Claire. "The Wan Brothers and Sixty Years of Animated Film in China." *Perspectives on Chinese Cinema*. Ed. Chris Berry. 2nd ed. London: BFI, 1991. 175–186.

Rahula, Walpola. *What the Buddha Taught*. New York: Grove Press, 1974.

Saussy, Haun. *The Problem of a Chinese Aesthetics*. Stanford: Stanford University Press, 1993.

Schuon, Frithjof. *Treasures of Buddhism*. Bloomington: World Wisdom Books, 1993.

Tu, Wei-Ming. *Confucian Thought: Selfhood as Creative Transformation*. Albany: State University of New York Press, 1985.

Tung, Yüeh. *The Tower of Myriad Mirrors: A Supplement to* Journey to the West. Trans. Shuen-fu Lin and Larry Schulz. Berkeley: Asian Humanities Press, 1988.

Wang, Jing. *The Story of Stone: Intertextuality, Ancient Chinese Stone Lore, and the Stone Symbolism of Dream of the Red Chamber, Water Margin, and the Journey to the West*. Durham: Duke University Press, 1992.

Wichmann, Elizabeth. *Listening to Theatre: The Aural Dimension of Beijing Opera*. Honolulu: University of Hawai'i Press, 1991.

Wriggins, Sally Hovey. *Xuanzang: A Buddhist Pilgrimage on the Silk Road*. Boulder: Westview Press, 1996.

Wright, Arthur F. *Buddhism in Chinese History*. Stanford: Stanford University Press, 1959.

Wu Ch'êng-ên. *The Journey to the West*. Trans. Anthony C. Yu. 4 vols. Chicago: Chicago University Press, 1977.

————. *Monkey*. Trans. Arthur Waley. London: Penguin Books, 1961.

Yampolsky, Philip B., trans. *The Platform Sutra of the Sixth Patriarch*. New York: Columbia University Press, 1967.

Young, Ed. *Monkey King*. New York: HarperCollins, 2001.

BREVARD COMMUNITY COLLEGE
MELBOURNE CAMPUS LIBRARY
3865 N. WICKHAM ROAD
MELBOURNE, FL 32935

8

Farīd al-Dīn 'Attār
The Conference of Birds
(1177?)

A call came from the Essence of the All:
"Leave soul and body, transitory one!
You, O My goal and purpose, enter now
And see My Essence face to face, My friend!"
In awe, he lost his speech and lost himself—
Muhammad did not know Muhammad here,
Saw not himself—he saw the Soul of Souls,
The Face of Him who made the universe!

—*Ilāhi-nāma* of Farīd al-Dīn 'Attār (qtd. in Schimmel, *And* 167–168)

We have been taught the speech of Birds, and on us has been bestowed (a little) of all things.

—Qur'an (Surah 27:16)

The Conference of Birds (*Mantiq al-tayr*—literally "the Language of the Birds") by the twelfth-century Persian poet Farīd al-Dīn 'Attār is a masterpiece of narrative art and a classic of Islamic-Sufi spirituality. The title derives from the Qur'an (Surah 27:16). The epic itself (*masnavi*) recounts the arduous pilgrimage of 30 birds led by the hoopoe, seeking their legendary king, the Simorgh, a giant bird with magical powers. On a deeper level, the narrative presents an allegory of the soul's quest for unity with God, a mystical experience in the extinction of the self. In the Persian tradition, *The Conference of Birds* stands among the definitive works of Sufi mysticism, with the *Hadiqatu'l-Haqiqat* (*The Walled Garden of Truth*) of Hakim Sana'i of Ghazna and the *Masnavi-e-Ma'navi* of Jalāl al-Din Rumi. At the same time, it stands as exemplary in a rich body of Middle Eastern and Central Asian storytelling, taking its place in a complex web of stories and influences, including the Sanskrit *Pañcatantra*, the *Kathāsaritsāgara* of Somadeva (literally "The Ocean of the Sea of Stories"), the Arabic *Kalīla vu Dimna*, and most famous *The Thousand and One Nights*.

BIOGRAPHICAL AND CULTURAL CONTEXTS

Farīd al-Dīn Abū Hāmid Muhammad 'Attār was born in a village near Nishapur (modern Neyshābūr), a city in northeastern Iran, about a hundred miles from the borders of Turkmenistan and Afghanistan. The sources are inconsistent, the dates given for his birth ranging from 1119 to 1157. According to convention, he signed his works either Farīd or 'Attār, 'Attār signifying his title or profession, "druggist" or "apothecary," and derived from *'attār*, indicating a dealer in *'itr* (as in the English attar of roses), an essential oil used in the manufacture of perfumes and medicines. In this capacity he would have kept a shop *(dār ū-khāna)*, dispensing medicines, perfume, and spices, as well as perhaps performing some medical procedures. One early account has him claiming that he composed two of his *mathnavīs* while taking pulses and attending to the needs of five hundred patients a day ('Attār, *Ilāhi-nāma* xx). According to tradition he received his early education at a theological school in the city of Mashhad, a site of pilgrimage in northeastern Iran. 'Attār's subsequent travels took him to Egypt, Damascus, Mecca, Turkestan, and India before he finally settled in his hometown, devoting the rest of his long life to his apothecary practice and his writing. One anecdote, doubtful though gratifying, claims that the 10-year-old Jalāl al-Din Rumi was introduced to the elderly 'Attār, the latter giving him a copy of his *Asrārnāma* (*The Book of Secrets*) and predicting that the boy would grow up to be a great poet. Throughout his life, 'Attār's writings show a strong interest in the radical dimensions of Sufi mysticism, especially expressed in the lives and ideas of the sufi mystics al-Hallaj and Bestami. As with his birth date, the exact date of his death is problematic. The conventional date is 1221, sometime during or just after the Mongol sack of Nishapur (part of a larger invasion begun by Genghis Khan that pushed into the Russian steppes and Hungary and culminated in the fall of Bagdad and the destruction of the 'Abbasid caliphate in 1258). According to one apocryphal tale, the decapitated 'Attār picked up his severed head and composed the *Bisarnama* (*The Book of the Headless One*), a poem sometimes attributed to him. Depending on the reckoning of his birth date, he would have been in his nineties. A shrine, which still remains a place for pilgrimage, was erected over his tomb in the fifteenth century.

Unlike many poets, East or West, ʿAttār claimed never to have sought the patronage of a king or to have written poems praising wealthy men in the hope of a reward. "My heart is disgusted by the obsolete and the patrons," he wrote in his *Musībatnāma* (*The Book of Misfortunes*). "For me wisdom is forever sufficient as a patron. For my head and my soul this high striving is sufficient" (qtd. in Ritter 161). Like the poet Hakim Sanaʾi (d. 1150) before him, he found an alternative to patronage by composing and performing religious and didactic poetry for groups of preachers and religious scholars. Of the 65 titles attributed to him (some accounts claim 114), the focus is religious, didactic, and mystical. Of the titles that are extant and readily available in translation, three are of special note. In addition to *The Conference of Birds*, there is the epic the *Ilāhi-nāma* (*The Book of God*) and the prose work *Tadhkirat al-Auliya* (*Memorial of the Saints*). The *Ilāhi-nāma* consists of a series of dialogues between a king and each of his six princely sons and is concerned with piety and the relationship between worldly goals and religious ideals. The king asks each his highest wish, which he will in turn grant. The first asks to marry the daughter of the king of fairies, an aspiration for sensuality. The second wishes for magical powers. The third wishes for the magical drinking-cup of Jamshid the legendary Persian king; anyone looking into the cup will be able to see the secrets of the world. The fourth wishes for the water of life, that he might enjoy longevity. The fifth wishes for the ring of King Solomon, which will give him mastery of humans, spirits, and the language of animals. Finally, the sixth son desires the art of making gold. In each case the wise king tries to dissuade his sons, showing the ephemeral nature of their desired boons. To make his point, he illustrates his arguments with a series of stories or tales, a strategy similar to that used in *The Conference*. *Memorial of the Saints* is a collection of stories about the great Sufi masters. Much of our knowledge of the influential Abū Yazid Bestamī and the Sufi martyr al-Hallaj (among many others) derives from ʿAttār's account.

ISLAM AND SUFISM

Several concepts from Islamic and more specifically Sufi mysticism have direct import on our appreciation of *The Conference of Birds*. The Islamic world is not monolithic, but embraces many ethnic, national, and linguistic groups, reflecting wide cultural diversity. Nevertheless, within this diversity, all members of the Islamic community (*ummah*) identify with several unifying factors. The first and most important is the Qur'an, understood by all Muslims as the Word of God (*Allah*), transmitted through the Prophet Muhammad. This is amplified by the *Sunnah*, accounts of the deeds of the Prophet, as well as the *Hadīth*, accounts of the saying of the Prophet. Together these three works shape Islamic Law (Sharī 'ah), which specifies social institutions and ritual practices, including daily prayers, pilgrimage to Mecca, and alms to the poor. In this God is understood in terms of divine Oneness and human existence, which is transient, entirely dependent on the will of God. Human action has no effect, and no intercession is possible. "It is Allah Who gives you life, then gives you death," says the Qur'an. "He will gather you together for the Day of Judgment about which there is no doubt" (Surah 45:26). Nothing is greater than God, who may punish the just and reward the wicked if he so wills. The point here is not that God is harsh, arbitrary, or capricious, but that he possesses absolute freedom, an absoluteness that extends beyond any limits. If God were bound by a principle of justice or a rational order, then that principle or order would be greater than God. Thus, all pious men hover between the fear of God's punishment and hope for his forgiveness. Such a conception of the human condition is deeply felt in 'Attār's writing. "All the religious motifs are raised to the ultimate degree," writes the scholar Hellmut Ritter (72), expressed with "incredible poignancy." 'Attār's epics are suffused with a subtle mood of sorrow related to the yearning for God and knowledge, the awareness of an unquenchable desire.

As it is practiced, orthodox Islam is juridical in nature, focused on selfless obedience, justification by means of a profession of faith, and the observance of the laws. Nevertheless, the profound belief in the inaccessibility of God by reason, the unfathomableness of God's will, leads to an element of uncertainty and anxiety in the thoughtful, and it is this anxiety, coupled with love for God, that creates an opening for mysticism, the yearning to see behind the "seventy thousand veils" (al-Ghazālī 44) to comprehend the ground of being in God and the self.

Islamic mysticism takes its starting point from a passage in the Qur'an: "The parable of His Light is as if there were a Niche and within it a Lamp: the Lamp enclosed in Glass: the glass as it were a brilliant star: lit from a blessed Tree, an Olive, neither of the East or the West, whose Oil is well-nigh Luminous, though fire scarce touched it: Light upon Light!" (Surah 24:35). God is the ultimate light whose lumination creates being. Correspondingly, human perception is limited and reflected. To this the Hadīth adds, "If he withdraws it (the veil), the splendor of His countenance would consume His creation so far as His sight reaches" (Sahih Muslim 1.136). Against the light of God, the individual is extinguished. Glossing these passages in The Niche of Lights (Mishkat al-anwar), the great Islamic theologian and jurist Abū Hamid al-Ghazālī (1058–1111) posits a double vision, expressed in terms of the "Face of God." "Viewed in terms of the face of itself, it [the individual being] is nonexistent; but viewed in terms of the face of God, it exists. Hence, nothing exists but God and his face" (al-Ghazālī 17). The finite being next to the infinite God is nothing. Like a shadow, finite being receives its meaning only from the light (of God). For al-Ghazālī and the Islamic mystics, those who have achieved gnostic insight and who have comprehended that there is only one reality, that difference is an illusion. "No room remains in them for the remembrance of any other than God, nor the remembrance of themselves" (al-Ghazālī 17). In other words, the mystical experience means the extinction of the self, or "'extinction from extinction,' since the possessor of the state is extinct from himself and from his own extinction" (al-Ghazālī 18).

The theme of self-extinction is common to many mystical traditions. In Western thought, the Spanish poet and mystic San Juan de la Cruz (1542–1591) comes immediately to mind. It is also prominent in the Sufi tradition of Islam. The Sufi saint Bestamī spoke of casting the self off like a snake casting off its skin in order to achieve unity with God. "He [God] annihilated me from my own being, and made me to be everlasting through His own everlastingness," Bestamī says in 'Attār's *Memorial of the Saints* (106). More controversially, the mystic al-Hallaj went so far as to declare, "I am the Divinity [*anā' l-Haqq*]" (qtd in Ritter 608), an assertion that earned him martyrdom at the hands of the Orthodox Muslims, who took his comments to be blasphemous. It is also prominent among Sufi poets, frequently expressed metaphorically in terms of erotic desire, often of a homoerotic nature, the ecstatic, and drunkenness. This is particularly the case in the work of Jalāl al-Din Rumi (1207–1273) and Hafiz of Shiraz (about 1320/26–1384/90). The theme of self-extinction is also central to 'Attār's *Conference of Birds*.

Islamic mystical traditions find their fullest expression in Sufism, with its focus on ascetic practices, brotherhoods or orders, and the quest for the "inner way" or path (*tarīqah*). Much of this included long retreats under the guidance of a teacher and the use of music and ecstatic dancing in the practice of worship. The name probably derives from the Arabic word *suf*, signifying wool and alluding to the simple woolen mantle worn by Sufi devotées. Although Sufism can be found in all branches of Islam, it is more often identified with Shī'ism than Sunnism, its focus on personal experience and the irrational, theosophical gnosis often at odds with the more legalistic tendencies of the latter. Further, its concern for personal experience informs a conception of sainthood (those who seek or have achieved some unity with God) and puts it in a complex and sometimes rival relationship with the concept and authority of the prophets, as in the case of the martyr al-Hallaj. Much in Sufi doctrine also hints at interactions with Neo-Platonism in the West and Vedanta Hinduism in the East.

Several themes and motifs are of relevance to our appreciation of *The Conference*. First, there is the notion of a brotherhood (a Sufi order) under the guidance of a teacher. Correspondingly, we have the birds under the wise tutelage of the hoopoe, as well as the whole didactic impulse behind storytelling. Second, there is the recurrent motif of the path or mystical quest. Third, there is the motif of the hybrid, in the Sufi context that humans are not pure, but a mixture of contrary moral states and impulses, one moment good and the next wicked. "The awareness of sin and inner uncertainty pass into a sense of inner, religious-ethical rift, which 'Attār describes as hybridity, a vacillation between faith and unbelief, between good and bad behavior" (Ritter 143). In *The Conference*, he often compares the self to a disobedient and mangy dog. "The Self's squint-eyed and cannot guide you well, / Part dog, part parasite, part infidel" ('Attār, *Conference* 96). For this very reason, the path involves renunciation, ultimately that of the self. It is expressed through various Sufi writings by the play with the opposing motifs of annihilation and survival, the irrational and rational, intoxication and sobriety, insanity and sanity, absence and presence, and unity and difference. Fourth, the itinerary of Sufi enlightenment is marked by various "stations," or temporary resting places *(maqāmāt)*. These are a succession of religious attitudes, outlooks on God and the world that shape our behavior and through which the mystic passes on the path. *The Conference* represents these stations in terms of the seven valleys that the birds must pass on their journey to the Simorgh: the Valleys of Quest, of Love, of Insight, of Detachment, of Unity, of Bewilderment, and finally of Poverty and Nothingness. The notion of stages on a mystical path derives from the spiritual autobiography of al-Ghazālī, *Deliverance from Error* (*al-Munqidh min al Dalal*).

SOURCES

The exact date of the composition of *The Conference of Birds* is a matter of conjecture, but two manuscripts claim that it was completed in 1177. The Persia (modern Iran) of 'Attār was culturally and ethnically diverse, including Persians, Kurds, Turks, Greeks, Tartars, and Arabs. On the caravan routes that connected the Mediterranean world with China, Istanbul with Delhi, and India with East Africa, its culture contained a rich mixture of Zoroastrianism, Islam, Hinduism, Buddhism, Judisim, and Christianity. All of these elements find their way into 'Attār's work. We can trace three layers of source materials at play in *The Conference of Birds*. The most obvious relates to the storytelling traditions of the Middle East and South Asia. The second relates to Persian literary conventions, and the third to Islam, especially the narrative tradition related to the *Isrd'*, the account of the prophet Muhammad's Night-Journey, and the Mi'raj, his ascent through the seven heavens to the divine throne, both central documents in Sufi mystical doctrine.

The Conference of Birds deploys a rich variety of stories drawn from Asian and Middle Eastern narrative traditions. Among the most important sources is the *Pañçatantra* (dating around 300 C.E.), a compendium of animal tales much in the mode of Aesop. It was translated from Sanskrit to Pahlavi (old Persian) around 579 C.E. as *The Fables of Bidpai*, and from this into Arabic around 750 C.E. as *The Tales of Kalila and Dimna*. (Kalila and Dimna are two jackals who serve as ministers and advisors to the lion.) The Persian version of this also found its way into the West, becoming an important source for Boccaccio, Chaucer, and later Le Fontaine. Another important repository of stories is the Sanskrit *Kathāsaritsāgara*, the "Ocean of the Sea of Stories," attributed to the Kashmiri Brahmin, Somadeva, and dating around 1070 C.E. Its 18 books is a vast collection of stories organized by a skeleton-frame narrative. In turn many of the individual tales contain separate stories or even stories within these stories. They range over tales of kings and intrigue, magic and trickery, animals and assorted monsters, vampires and ghouls, maidens and lovers, beggars and thieves. Unlike some of its sources, including the *Pañçatantra* and the *Jātaka* tales, fables about the previous, often animal incarnations of the Buddha, the *Kathāsaritsāgara* is concerned more with entertainment than with moral instruction. Among its most famous sections are the "Vetalapanchavinsati" ("Twenty-Five Tales of a Vampire"—Sir Richard Burton, famous for his translation of *The Thousand and One Nights*, published a version of this under the title *Vikram and the Vampire*) and the "Sukasaptati" ("The Seventy Tales of the Parrot"). From these various collections 'Attār draws both the basic idea of an extended frame narrative and many of the tales that he will modify to fill in the frame. Unlike the *Kathāsaritsāgara*, which often swamps the narrative frame in the wash of stories within stories, there is more a sense of unity between the frame and the component stories in *The Conference*, the parts serving the didactic and thematic function of the whole.

The Conference of Birds is composed in rhyming couplets known as mathnavi. It is a form used in Persian heroic narrative poetry, most notably the great epic *Shahnameh* (*The Book of Kings*) by the poet Ferdowsi, but also in romantic narratives, such as Nizami's tragic *Layla and Majnun*. Both of these works, if not necessarily direct sources for 'Attār, lean heavily on the same traditional material and motifs available to him. For instance, the Simorgh appears in the *Shahnameh*, as the foster parent of Zāl (much as the she-wolf reared Romulus and Remus in Roman legend), father of Rostam the great hero. The *Shahnameh* includes a long account of Alexander the Great (known as Sekandar or, in other sources, Iskandar), who is used by 'Attār to exemplify the futility of ambition. The love story of Layla and Majnun ("the distracted one" or "madman") derives from Bedouin legend, but was a favorite throughout Arabic, Persian, and Turkish literature (and perhaps exercised some influence on the European courtly love tradition), finding its finest version in Nizami. Majnun is entranced and passionately in love with Layla, but is prevented from marrying her by her father, who forces Layla to marry another. Distraught, Majnun becomes a wildman in the forest, communing with animals. His intoxicated, if unrequited, love became a favorite metaphor for the Sufi's passion for God. The immediate inspiration for applying the mathnavi to didactic and mystical purposes derives from the poet Hakim Sana'i, whose *The Walled Garden of Truth* (*Hadiqiatu'l—Haqiqat*) was an important influence on later Persian poets.

The central model for Sufi mysticism and the underlying shape of *The Conference* comes from the accounts of the Night-Journey (*Isrd'*) and the Heavenly Ascent (*Mi'raj*) of the prophet Muhammad. The Qur'an writes, "Glory to (Allah), Who took His Servant for a Journey by night from the Sacred Mosque to the Farthest Mosque" (Surah 17:1), that is from Mecca to the Temple Mount in Jerusalem. The *Hadīth* and Ibn Ishaq's *Life of Muhammad* greatly elaborate these lines, explaining how the Prophet rode a magical beast known as al-Buraq (meaning "lightning"), "who would place his hoof at a distance equal to the range of vision" (*Sahih Muslim* 1.121). From Jerusalem he ascended through the seven heavens, encountering various prophets and patriarchs, including Adam, Jesus, Abraham, and Moses. He also saw the place where the wicked are punished. The episode became a favorite subject for poets and artists, and some scholars conjecture that Dante might have found inspiration for the *Divine Comedy* in Latin versions of the Mi'raj that were in circulation. The Mi'raj, also often linked with the image of the Lote-tree, "beyond which none may pass (Surah 53:14), becomes the paradigm of mystical quest, combining the motifs of ascent toward the ultimate limits of human comprehension. 'Attār recounts it directly in his *Ilāhi-nāma* and implicitly in *The Conference*.

PLOT, STRUCTURE, AND CHARACTER DEVELOPMENT

Consideration of the plot of the *Conference* must focus on two levels: one relates to the overarching frame narrative, and the other to the individual stories that are contained in the frame. The frame takes its basic premise from the *Risālat al-tayr* (*The Message of the Birds*) of al-Ghazālī, an anecdote about a group of birds who seek a king in the legendary Simorgh. After many hardships and the loss of many of the birds along the way, they are finally admitted into the presence of the king, who explains that those who died are not lost, that the journey and everything that happens is the will of God. Al-Ghazālī glosses his brief story with the comment, "The invitation now follows to do the same as the birds, to undertake purification, to pray, to recollect God" (qtd. in Ritter 9). 'Attār preserves this basic frame, but both vastly deepens and expands it, to dramatize the stages of mystical enlightenment. This in turn follows the various stages of the pilgrimage, echoing the halting-stages of Sufi enlightenment, and the final vision, a unity with the divine. To underline this theme of mystical unity, 'Attār puns on the name Simorgh and the Persian *sī murgh* ("thirty birds"). In other words, the 30 birds discover that they *are* the Simorgh; they are one with God.

'Attār begins by saluting the major types of birds, correlating each with its patron saint. The first is the hoopoe, the bird of King Solomon. The hoopoe is a real type of bird, related to the kingfisher and about the size of a dove, and its cinnamon color, striped wings, and large crown-like crest give it a regal look and explain its preeminence in myth and folklore. In Arabic folklore, King Solomon supposedly communicated with the Queen of Sheba (Belqis) by means of a talking hoopoe. For this reason, the bird is often associated with Solomon and wisdom. Next comes the finch, associated with Moses, and then the parrot, the bird of Abraham. The narrator next welcomes the partridge, linked with Seleh (a prophet), and the falcon, linked with the prophet Muhammad, followed by the francolin, an Asian partridge, associated with Jesus. Next comes the nightingale, whose singing affiliates it with David; and then the peacock, associated with Adam; the pheasant, with Joseph; the pigeon, with Jonah; and the turtle-dove, with Khezr (guardian of the waters of immortality, a mythical green man figure). Finally, there appear the hawk, associated with the lawgiver Zulgharnin, a great lawgiver; and the goldfinch, the bird of God.

Coming together to confer, the birds of the world decide that they need a king. The hoopoe explains that their king is the Simorgh, but that they must endure a long journey and many hardships to reach him. Announcing the central theme, he declares,

> Escape your self-hood's vicious tyranny
> Whoever can evade the Self transcends
> This world and as a lover he ascends. ('Attār, *Conference* 33)

Echoing various Sufi doctrines and motifs that underline Attār's allegory, the route to the king is an ascent that involves self-extinction like that of the lover's passion.

Many of the birds are morally hybrid in nature and, though they aspire to good, are also weak-willed, making excuses, each according to its character. Indeed, much of the brilliance of 'Attār's artistry is the aptness of his matching each bird with a class of human character flaws. The nightingale would like to go, but is weak and demonstrates that if he were not to stay where he is, there would be no one to sing to lovers. The parrot declares that he is interested only in finding the stream of immortality. The peacock explains that the Simorgh is beyond his understanding, that he prefers a more immediate guide to paradise. The duck, an ascetic, believes he can preserve his purity only by staying in the water. Next, the partridge says he is interested only in jewels, so for him the Simorgh offers nothing of value. Then the homa (a mythical hawk-like bird whose shadow supposedly falls on future kings) is too concerned with his royal prerogatives. The hawk indicates he is too busy hunting with kings, and the heron prefers the solitary shoreline where he can enjoy his sorrows. The owl dismisses the story of the Simorgh as childish, preferring to haunt ruins looking for buried treasure. Finally the finch wishes to be excused because she is too small and weak.

Employing a strategy similar to that of the king in 'Attār's *Ilāhī-nāma*, the hoopoe replies to each of these excuses, telling one or more stories or anecdotes, underlining the vanity and illusion that marks each excuse. In replying to the nightingale, for instance, the hoopoe tells of a dervish who falls passionately in love with a princess who casually happened to smile at him once. Obsessed, he makes such a nuisance of himself that the princess's servants plot to kill him. Pitying the dervish, the princess warns him, explaining that the smile meant nothing, that she will never love him. Two themes emerge, one being that the dervish's misery is self-inflicted, derived from the illusion that the princess loved him. In a not-so-subtle way, he has been blinded by his own vanity. Second, on a deeper level, the dervish learns of the individual's nothingness next to the absoluteness and the arbitrariness of God. It is false consciousness to suppose that one enjoys the special blessing of God.

The remaining birds decide to make the journey, electing the hoopoe as their leader. Indicating the nature of the quest, the hoopoe says that love is the true guide. "A lover," he explains, "is one in whom all thoughts of Self have died; / Those who renounce the Self deserve that name" ('Attār, *Conference* 56). To illustrate, he unfolds the tale of the sheikh Sam'an, the longest single story in *The Conference*.

An old man, the sheikh Sam'an is one of the eminent keepers of Mecca, with some four hundred pupils. One night he dreams of Rome. Perplexed by this dream, he travels to Rome, where he sees a beautiful Christian girl. Falling passionately in love, he decides to stay in Rome to be near the girl and explains this to his shocked disciples, who have accompanied him. Content to wait for the girl to reciprocate his love, Sam'an detaches himself from any ambition. He finally renounces Islam and takes her religion, trying to absorb his identity into hers. To his great confusion and despair, however, she continues to demure, making him wait. He is finally reduced to abject poverty, forced to become the girl's swineherd. In a sort of reverse symmetry, the sheikh's disciples, bewildered by his behavior, return to Mecca. There, however, their shame at their own behavior detaches them from their bewilderment. Dreaming that the old sheikh will reemerge, they return to Rome. The sheikh goes through a process of purification, returns to Islam, and sets out for Mecca. At this point, the Roman girl dreams of the sheikh, feels her own conversion to Islam, and then perishes in her love for him: "her flesh / Yielded the sweet soul from its weakening mesh. / She was a drop returned to Truth's great sea" ('Attār, *Conference* 75).

Critic and translator Dick Davis sees this story as paradigmatic of the whole, a sort of roadmap for the mystical path and a recurrent pattern. In his passion for the Roman girl, the old sheikh passes through a series of psychological stages that anticipate the seven valleys that the birds will encounter (quest, love, insight, detachment, unity, bewilderment, poverty and nothingness). Thus, first his dream sends him on his *quest* to understand its meaning. He then falls in *love* with the Roman girl. This leads to *insight* in his discussion with his disciples. As he waits for the girl to respond to him, he becomes *detached* from his ambition and old life. Seeking a sort of *unity* with the girl, he becomes a Christian in order to be one with her. The girl's further insistence that he wait forces the old sheikh into a state of confused *bewilderment*. Finally reduced to the role of swineherd, he reaches a state of *poverty*, becoming *nothing* to himself and disciples. The self of sheikh Sam'an has been extinguished. Mystical extinction is not literal extinction, and the self slowly reemerges after its experience. The story therefore outlines both the stages of Sufi mysticism and the path and final experience of the birds, when their selves as 30 birds are reduced to nothing, consumed in the sight of the Simorgh, only to eventually reemerge, like the Roman girl now tracing the sheikh's path.

The hoopoe's long story disconcerts the birds, who again express their doubts and ask the hoopoe for more advice, outlining and illustrating 10 negative attributes that might block their progress. These include cowardice, sinfulness, indecision, self, pride, miserliness, ostentation, love of wrong things, fear of death, and bad luck. The hoopoe replies with 10 positive attributes, each corresponding as the counter to the negative. Instead of cowardice, one should emphasize submission; instead of sinfulness, purity; instead of indecision, aspiration; instead of self, loyalty (to others); instead of pride, audacity; instead of miserliness, living only for God; instead of ostentation, contentment; instead of love of wrong things, overcoming fear; instead of fear of death, hope for reward; and instead of bad luck, accepting grace.

The hoopoe tells numerous stories to illustrate the various moral lessons, some fully developed tales, some essentially brief jokes, and others allusions to well-known narratives. Consider two that illustrate audacity. Trying to escape icy sleet, a naked madman takes refuge in a ruined hut. When a tile falls and hits him on the head, the exasperated madman yells at the sky, "Enough! / Why can't you clobber me with better stuff!" ('Attār, *Conference* 142). In another, a poor man borrows an ass from a rich neighbor. The ass wanders off and is killed by wolves. The rich man brings a suit against the poor one for the lost ass. When asked who should pay the damages, the judge replies that it is the one who let the wolves roam free (which is to say, God). In each case, everything is recognized as the will of God, good or ill. Because one has no ultimate control over one's fate, there is no point in nursing injured pride. Rather, one should reply with audacity, a dual gesture that recognizes the omnipotence of God while also expressing one's anger.

After hearing many other stories to illustrate the path, the birds at long last begin the arduous journey, which 'Attār only briefly sketches:

> Some paused bewildered and then turned aside
> To gaze at marvels as if stupefied;
> Some looked for pleasure's path and soon confessed
> They saw no purpose in the pilgrims' quest;
> Not one in every thousand souls arrived—
> In every hundred thousand one survived. ('Attār, *Conference* 214)

Of those that started the quest, only 30 finally arrive at their goal, broken and exhausted. 'Attār structures their encounter with the Simorgh in terms that echo the pattern of sheikh Sam'an's experience. They are approached by a herald who tells them that the king's glory is beyond their comprehension, that they should return where they came from. The birds reply with the story of a moth who was told that he was too frail to enter the flame of a candle. The moth replied, "Simply to reach it is my humble aim" ('Attār, *Conference* 217). In this they express their love of the Simorgh. The herald relents and lets the birds into the palace, but shows them a page from the book of fate in which is recorded every detail of their lives, deeds, and sins, including everything that has occurred on their trip. The effect of this insight into the nature of fate chastens and shames them, thereby detaching them from their sense of control over their destiny. They recall the story of the chagrin experienced by the brothers of Joseph when confronted with the account of their sins (Genesis 45). The 30 birds are finally allowed to face the Simorgh (which, again, means "thirty birds").

> There in the Simorgh's radiant face they saw
> Themselves, the Simorgh of the world—with awe
> They were the Simorgh and the journey's end. ('Attār, *Conference* 219)

So confronted with this unity—that they are the Simorgh—the birds are first bewildered and dismayed and then crumble into nothingness. Their final mystical insight is that their very selves must be extinguished, that outside the lumination (or the voice in this case) of the Simorgh there is nothing.

> The substance of their being was undone,
> And they were lost like shade before the sun;
> Neither the pilgrims nor their guide remained.
> The Simorgh ceased to speak, and silence reigned.
> ('Attār, *Conference* 220)

As with Sam'an, however, extinction of the self is not the end. After a hundred thousand centuries, the birds reemerge from nothingness.

> This Nothingness, this Life, are states no tongue
> At any time has adequately sung—
> Those who can speak still wander far away
> From that dark truth they struggle to convey,
> And by analogies they try to show
> The forms men's partial knowledge cannot know.
> ('Attār, *Conference* 221)

In the end 'Attār is left with the impossible task of describing what is beyond language, reminding us that poetry is at best an analogy and that storytelling is about expressing and evoking, not telling and representing.

The narrator concludes by recounting one last tale, repeating yet again the same pattern. Once upon a time, a great king falls passionately and obsessively in love with a beautiful youth, the son of his trusted minister of state. One night, while the king is drunk, the young man seeks the company of a young woman. They are discovered, and the king in a fit of rage and jealousy orders the youth to be executed. The wise minister gets wind of this and arranges that a convicted murderer be substituted. Detached from the youth, the king is at first satisfied, but then begins to grieve, internalizing him in his dreams. When the minister is convinced that the king has truly repented, he arranges for his son to appear dressed in white. Thus reunited, the king is first bewildered in his happiness and then closes on a note of silence, a correlative of nothingness: "They knew that state of which no man can speak; / This pearl cannot be pierced" ('Attār, *Conference* 229).

In addition to the birds, the various individual stories feature a variety of stock character types. Many of the kings who appear in the stories are represented as moody and capricious, often quick to punish perceived slights. By contrast, fools, beggars, madmen, or others at the bottom of the social ladder are made to appear wise, setting the things of the world into proper perspective. Many stories pair a beggar with a king or other high potentate. Typically, the beggar fails to show the king the regard he thinks his station demands. The beggar then responds in some way that underlines the limits of earthly power. In one such story, the king commands the impudent beggar to flee beyond the range of the king's power. The next morning, the king finds the beggar sitting in a nearby cemetery. When asked why he did not go farther, the beggar explains that he has obeyed the king's injunction, given that his power cannot stretch beyond the grave. In another story, a rich merchant builds a fine house and gives an elaborate entertainment "to gratify his busy self-esteem" ('Attār, *Conference* 107). A begging fool in the area refuses to drink to the merchant's health, claiming, "I'm / So busy that I really haven't time" ('Attār, *Conference* 107). The merchant in his vanity does not recognize that this reply mocks his own pretense of busyness. The theme is further elaborated with the added story of a diligent spider who is greatly impressed with his own cunning in designing an effective web until a housewife casually knocks it away with her broom.

A number of the stories feature saints, patriarchs, prophets, or even God as characters. In one, Jesus drinks water from a jug, only to find it bitter and brackish. He is surprised because when he earlier drank the same water from the stream, it was sweet. The jug suddenly speaks, explaining that its clay was once the clay of a mortal man, and that no matter how the jug has been baked and reshaped, the bitterness that derives from our material being cannot be dispelled. The material is inherently inferior to the spiritual. Only by turning away from the material to the spiritual path, the jug implores, can one hope to have salvation. In another story, a saintly fool encounters the prophet Muhammad, who says that he sees in the fool great tranquility. The fool expresses incredulity because he is plagued with gnats, bed bugs, and fleas. Spiritual tranquility is not about bodily comfort.

THEMES

We have already explicated the major themes of *The Conference of Birds* in describing its relationship with Sufi mysticism. At this stage it is sufficient to reiterate three points. First, whereas works such as the *Ilāhi-nāma* are concerned with the general theme of Islamic piety and with turning toward religious ideas by learning to confront and detach one's self from the falseness of worldly values, *The Conference* is concerned with developing the mystical that develops out of the love and yearning for God.

The second point, growing out of the first, describes the self-consuming nature of this process. The goal is to merge with the divinity of pure being, a process that culminates in the extinction of the self. The true lover of God, for 'Attār, must seek a disposition that seeks to die in God. Appealing to philosopher Martin Heidegger's theme that our being is "being-toward-death," Hellmut Ritter says of 'Attār that "by extending the concept of extinction to cosmic immersion of all things in the primordial realm of Being and to physical death, this death in a new sense also becomes accepted into existence as something meaningful" (Ritter 655–656). Death or the end of individual existence is neither a termination to be approached with dread nor a bridge to the face of God. Rather, to die is to disappear like a drop of water into the ocean, simultaneously vanished and preserved as part of the whole.

Finally, in a profound sense, *The Conference* is about the limitations of the text. Just as self must be transcended, so ultimately must the text as the last mediation that stands in the way of extinction. 'Attār's ultimate theme is the truth of silence, the awareness of the poverty and nothingness of language to articulate love and insight. "I have described the Way," he writes. "Now, you must act—there is no more to say" (229 'Attār, *Conference*).

SUBSEQUENT INFLUENCE

'Attār and *The Conference of Birds* have enjoyed a long and popular reputation. A host of later poets took inspiration, almost immediately and most famously Jalal Al-Din Rumi, the greatest of the Sufi poets. In assessing this influence, Jorge Luis Borges's comments on *The Thousand and One Nights* are not inappropriate: "It is a book so vast that it is not necessary to have read it" (Borges 57). 'Attār's writings have achieved a status that makes them such an integral part of the fabric of cultural assumptions that it is not necessary to make specific attributions. His immediate successor is Rumi, who according to tradition began his own mathnavi at the behest of his disciples, who wanted him to compose a work in the spirit of *The Conference of Birds*. Several times in his work, Rumi acknowledges his debt to 'Attār and the earlier poet Hakim Sana'i. Speaking for many later poets, he wrote, "'Attār was the spirit and Sana'i its two eyes" (qtd. in Schimmel, *Triumphal* 37).

It is tempting to speculate that Geoffrey Chaucer's *Parliament of Fowls* (around 1382) owes something to 'Attār, especially in the central premise of a conference among the birds and the birds representing various human types. At this stage, however, it is impossible to establish any clear line of influence, either direct or indirect.

In modern literature, *The Conference* was adapted into dramatic form and produced by Jean-Claude Carrière and Peter Brook, most noted for their monumental production of the Indian epic *The Mahābhārata*. Novelist Salman Rushdie draws explicitly from *The Conference*, including a giant hoopoe named Butt, as well as the whole range of Middle Eastern and South Asian narrative, in his novel *Haroun and the Sea of Stories*. "Perhaps you know, Disconnector Thief," a Water Genie tells the novel's young hero, "that in the old stories the Hoopoe is the bird that leads all other birds through many dangerous places to their ultimate goal" (Rushdie 64). Tahar Ben Jelloun's 1994 novel *L'Homme rompu*, available in translation as *Corruption* (1995), plays subtly on the seven stages to trace the transformation of its narrator/hero, relating the Sufi concept of nothingness with that of Sartrian Existentialism. "Like the Sufi mystics, I am 'renouncing.' I am flying. I disappear. I am no long a part of this harsh and mediocre world" (Ben Jelloun 133). Also of interest are the novels *Arabian Nights and Days* and *The Harafish* of the Egyptian writer and Nobel Laureate Naguib Mahfouz. More recently, visual artist Shirin Neshat collaborated with singer Sussan Deyhim and others to produce a multimedia interpretation known as the *Logic of the Birds* (2002).

Much modern literature draws motifs from *The Conference*. Sagegh Hedayat's 1937 masterpiece *The Blind Owl* (*Boof-e Koor*) is often regarded as the first modern novel in Iranian literature. Although its deranged and obsessed narrator owes as much to Poe's raven (via Baudelaire) as to 'Attār's hoopoe, the owl 'Attār portrays in *The Conference*, who prefers to live "away from men, in wild, deserted ground," saying that "these ruins are [his] melancholy pleasure" (48), sets the tone and atmosphere for Hedayat. (Filmmaker Raul Ruiz's 1987 movie version, *La Chouette aveugle*, makes the links even more explicit.) On a lighter note, Iranian writer Houshang Golshiri's stories such as "Green as a Parrot, Black as a Crow" and "A Storyteller's Story" are deeply suffused with the narrative traditions that include 'Attār. In the end, we may conclude with Rumi: "Without a kindred spirit there to hear / The storyteller's voice must disappear" (Rumi 6). After more than eight hundred years, 'Attār and *The Conference of Birds* still enjoy many kindred spirits.

SUGGESTED READINGS

Arberry, A. J. *Classical Persian Literature*. London: George Allen and Unwin, 1958.

'Attār, Farīd al-Dīn. *The Conference of the Birds*. Trans. Dick Davis. New York: Penguin Books, 1984.

———. *The Ilāhī-Nāma, or Book of God*. Trans. John Andrew Boyle. Manchester: Manchester University Press, 1976.

———. *Muslim Saints and Mystics: Episodes from the Tadbkirat al-Auliya'*. Trans. A. J. Arberry. London: Arkana, 1990.

———. *The Speech of the Birds: Concerning Migration to the Real, the Mantiqu't-Tair*. Trans. Peter Avery. Cambridge, UK: Islamic Text Society, 1998.

Ben Jelloun, Tahar. *Corruption*. Trans. Carol Volk. New York: The New Press, 1995.

Borges, Jorge Luis. *Seven Nights*. Trans. Eliot Weinberger. New York: New Directions, 1984.

Carrière, Jean-Claude, and Peter Brook. *The Conference of the Birds*. Woodstock, IL: The Dramatic Publishing Company, 1982.

Davis, Dick. "The Journey as Paradigm: Literal and Metaphorical Travel in 'Attār's *Mantiq al-Tayr*." *Edebiyat: The Journal of Middle Eastern Literatures* 4.2 (1993): 173–183.

Ferdowsi, Abolqasen. *Shahameh: The Persian Book of Kings*. Trans. Dick Davis. New York: Viking, 2006.

Fischer, Michael M. J. *Mute Dreams, Blind Owls, and Dispersed Knowledges: Persian Poesis in the Transnational Circuitry*. Durham: Duke University Press, 2004.

al-Ghazālī, Abū Hamid. *Deliverance from Error (al-Munqidh min al Dalal) and Other Relevant Works*. Trans. Richard Joseph McCarthy. Louisville, KY: Fons Vitae, 1980.

———. *The Niche of Lights (Miskhkat al-anwar)*. Trans. David Buchman. Provo, UT: Brigham Young University Press, 1998.

Gerhardt, Mia Irene. *The Art of Story Telling: A Literary Study of the Thousand and One Nights*. Leiden: E. J. Brill, 1963.

Golshiri, Houshang. *Black Parrot, Green Crow: A Collection of Short Fiction*. Ed. Heshmat Moayyad. Washington, D.C.: Mage Publishing, 2003.

Grunebaum, Gustave E. Von. *Medieval Islam: A Study in Cultural Orientation*. 2nd ed. Chicago: University of Chicago Press, 1953.

Hafiz. *The Divan-i-Hafix*. Trans. H. Wilberforce Clarke. Bethesda, MD: Ibex, 1997.

———. Hafiz of Shiraz: *Thirty Poems, an Introduction to the Sufi Master*. Trans. Peter Avery. New York: Other Press, 2003.

Hedayat, Sadegh. *The Blind Owl*. Trans. D. P. Costello. New York: Grove Weidenfeld, 1989.

Ibn Hazm, 'Ali ibn Ahmad. *The Ring of the Dove: A Treatise on the Art and Practice of Arab Love*. Trans. A. J. Arberry. London: Luzac, 1994.

Ibn Ishaq, Muhammad. *The Life of Muhammad (Sirat Rasul Allah)*. Trans. Alfred Guillaume. Karachi: Oxford University Press, 1967.

Irwin, Robert. *The Arabian Nights: A Companion*. London: I. B. Tauris and Company, 2005.

Keshavarz, Fatemeh. *Reading Mystical Lyric: The Case of Jalāl al-Dīn Rumi*. Columbia: University of South Carolina Press, 1998.

Leaman, Oliver. *Islamic Aesthetics: An Introduction*. Notre Dame, IN: University of Notre Dame Press, 2004.

Levy, Reuben. *An Introduction to Persian Literature*. New York: Columbia University Press, 1969.

Lewis, Franklin D. *Rumi: Past and Present, East and West*. Oxford: Oxford University Press, 2000.

Lewisohn, Leonard, and Christopher Shackle, eds. *Attar and the Persian Sufi Tradition: The Art of Spiritual Flight*. London: I. B. Tauris Publishers, 2006.

Mahfouz, Naguib. *The Harafish*. Trans. Catherine Cobham. New York: Anchor Books, 1994.

Nasr, Seyyed Hossein. *The Heart of Islam: Enduring Values for Humanity*. New York: HarperCollins, 2002.

Nizami. *The Story of Layla and Majnun*. Trans. and ed. Rudolf Gelpke. New Lebanon, NY: Omega Publications, 1997.

Pañcatantra: The Book of India's Folk Wisdom. Trans. Patrick Olivelle. Oxford: Oxford University Press, 1997.

The Qur'an. Trans. Abdullah Yusuf Ali. Elmhurst, NY: Tahrike Tarsile Qur'an, Inc, 2001.

Ritter, Hellmut. *The Ocean of the Soul: Men, the World and God in the Stories of Farīd al-Dīn 'Attār*. Trans. John O'Kane. Leiden: Brill, 2003.

Rumi, Jalal Al-Din. *The Masnavi: Book One*. Trans. Jawid Mojaddedi. Oxford: Oxford University Press, 2004.

Rushdie, Salman. *Haroun and the Sea of Stories: A Novel*. New York: Penguin Books, 1990.

Sahim Muslim: Al-Jami-Us-Sahih. Trans. Abdul Hamid Siddiqi. 4 vols. New Delhi: Kitabbhavan, 204.

Schimmel, Annemarie. *And Muhammad Is His Messenger: The Veneration of the Prophet in Islamic Piety*. Chapel Hill: University of North Carolina Press, 1985.

———. *The Triumphal Sun: A Study of the Works of Jalālouddin Rumi*. Albany: State University of New York Press, 1993.

Schuon, Frithjof. *Understanding Islam*. Bloomington, ID: World Wisdom, 2002.

Séguy, Marie-Rose. *The Miraculous Journey of Mahomet: Mirāj Nāmeh*. Trans. Richard Pevear. New York: George Braziller, 1977.

Sharma, Sunil. "The Sufi-Poet-Lover as Martyr: 'Attār and Hāfiz in Persian Poetic Traditions." In *Martyrdom in Literature: Visions of Death and Meaningful Suffering in Europe and the Middle East from Antiquity to Modernity*. Ed. Friederike Pannewick. Wiesbaden: Reichert Verlag, 2004. 237–243.

Somadeva. *Tales from the Kathāsaritsāgara*. Trans. Arshia Sattar. London: Penguin Books, 1994.

Stetkevych, Saroslav. *Muhammad and the Golden Bough: Reconstructing Arabian Myth*. Bloomington: Indiana University Press, 1996.

Trimingham, J. Spencer. *The Sufi Orders in Islam*. Oxford: Oxford University Press, 1998.

Wood, Ramsay. *Tales of Kalila and Dimna: Classic Fables from India*. Rochester, VT: Inner Traditions International, 1986.

9

Nguyen-Du Thanh-hien
The Tale of Kieu
(1813–1820)

If my heart is a traitor's and I have plotted to harm you, father, may I turn to fine dust when I die. But if I have been ever loyal and shown filial piety, and have been deceived by a man, then when I die may I turn into a precious pearl, beyond compare even with the snow for purity.

—a Vietnamese folktale (qtd. in Durand and Nguyen 5)

Nguyen Du's *Tale of Kieu* (*Truyên Kieu*), also known as *Kim-Vân-Kieu*, after its main characters, is the national poem of Vietnam and the only epic poem in world literature whose main hero is a woman. Unlike the epic heroes of the *Iliad* and the *Odyssey*, the *Mahābhārata* and the *Rāmāyana*, or the *Sundiata* and the *Shahnameh*, Kieu is not a warrior, but one who suffers and endures the ravages of betrayal, humiliation, and war, preserving her grace and dignity and sustaining the integrity of her character. Because of this, she resonates with the Vietnamese people who have suffered centuries of war and colonization; she is a beloved figure who embodies a sense of national identity. Reflecting on the significance of the *Tale of Kieu*, filmmaker Trinh T. Minh-ha says, "It is the national love poem of Vietnam whose story every Vietnamese remembers, whether they are in Vietnam or spread around the globe in the Vietnamese communities of the diaspora." She adds, "It's remarkable that a people identifies the destiny of their country with the fate of a woman" (*Cinema Interval* 195). In trying to explain this, she suggests three factors. First, Kieu personifies love. Second, and related to the first, her turn to prostitution in order to help her family and to survive echoes tensions similar to those that mark Vietnam's history of domination by various oppressive regimes, foreign and domestic. But third and most significantly, the story is told in verse whose poetry and rhythms are drawn from the folk traditions. Thus, although Nguyen Du reworks a Chinese literati novel, deploying a sophisticated knowledge of the Chinese classics, the heart of his story is Vietnamese, echoing the legends and songs of Vietnamese popular culture. For most Vietnamese critics, the *Tale of Kieu* is the embodiment of the national spirit (*quoc hon*), the myth of the motherland.

HISTORICAL AND BIOGRAPHICAL CONTEXT

With archaeological evidence that points to a Bronze Age civilization dating back to 2000–1000 B.C.E., Vietnam has endured a long and often difficult history, marked by a recurrent pattern of clan rivalry and dynastic struggle, repeated colonial subjugation, and popular rebellion. The earliest surviving historical records, dating between 111 B.C.E. and 43 C.E., describe Chinese colonization, the first of three periods of Chinese domination. A popular uprising led by Trung Trac, the daughter of a local chieftain, or *wang* (39–43 C.E.), was eventually put down by Chinese duplicity, followed by the execution of Trung Trac and her sister Trung Nhi. Both have assumed the status of national heroes. Struggle against the Ming dynasty led to independence under Lê Loi and the founding of the Lê dynasty (1427–1788). Much as in feudal Japan, the emperors were largely figureheads, power residing between the competing Trinh clans of the north and the Nguyen clans of the south and administered by a Confucian bureaucracy. This period was a high point in the cultural development of Vietnam, especially in literature. It also saw the arrival of European explorers, merchants, and missionaries. The illusory stability of the Lê empire nurtured rampant corruption. Although always sympathetic to the lost dynasty, Nguyen Du acknowledges the decadence of the old order with the prominent role played by corrupt officials, dishonest scholars, and prostitutes throughout the *Tale of Kieu*. In 1771 a popular revolution known as the Tay-son broke out, characterized by "virtuous and charitable banditry." The character Tur Hai in the *Tale of Kieu*, "with sword and lute upon his shoulders slung" (Nguyen, *Tale* 113), strongly resembles the Tay-son leader Nguyen Hue. The movement eventually destroyed the government, climaxing in the defeat of an invading Chinese army in 1788–1789. The Tay-son were in turn suppressed by warlords affiliated with the Nguyen clan, leading to the establishment of the Nguyen dynasty (1802–1945) under the leadership of its first emperor, Gia Long (1802–1822), who built a fortified capital at Hue in 1802 with technical assistance from French engineers and soldiers, thereby laying the groundwork for subsequent French colonization,

Japanese occupation, partition, civil war, American intervention, and eventually reunification in 1975.

Born in 1766, Nguyen Du endured the upheavals surrounding the collapse of the Lê dynasty, the Tay-son revolution, and the early years of the Nguyen dynasty. He was born in northern Vietnam, a member of the scholar class, his father once a minister in the Lê empire. His mother, reportedly, was a singer, which may explain his intimate familiarity with rhythms and the themes of popular songs and tales that suffuse his poetry. It may also inform his portrait of Kieu as an accomplished musician. Like the character Kim, Nguyen Du was a scholar in the Confucian mode, fluent in Chinese as well as Vietnamese. Surviving the Tay-son, Nguyen Du and other northern scholars with affiliations to the old Lê regime were absorbed into the Nguyen bureaucracy, assuming various provincial offices. His service was honorable, but clouded with a wistful nostalgia for the Lê as a lost world. Because of his abilities in composing Chinese verse, he was sent on a diplomatic mission to China in 1813. He died in 1820, during preparations for another mission. His public persona was that of a shy, reserved, and even tongue-tied man, his private passions finding outlet in his poetry.

It was probably on his embassy to China that Nguyen Du become familiar with the Chinese novel *Chin Yün Ch'iao chuan* (*The Tale of Chin, Yün, and Ch'iao*), which became the basis of the *Tale of Kieu*. In reworking this sprawling Chinese prose novel into a Vietnamese verse romance, he did not slavishly translate and versify the prose, but used elements of the basic plot as the frame and foundation for his own very original contribution to literature. As with Shakespeare, who occasionally reworked the plays of others, Nguyen Du's borrowing represents the transformation of lead into gold.

There are few enduring verse novels in Western literature, the possible exceptions being Alexander Pushkin's Russian classic *Eugene Onegin* (1831) and perhaps Elizabeth Barrett Browning's *Aurora Leigh* (1856). The verse romance or *truyen nom* was, however, very popular in Vietnam, and Nguyen Du wished to demonstrate that in a culture dominated by classical Chinese, the Vietnamese vernacular was capable of serious art. Thus, he remade and concentrated the novel into a long narrative poem, using a popular verse form built on couplets formed out of a six-syllable line and an eight-syllable line. The rhythmic and auditory effects are distantly analogous to those of the English ballad stanza produced by the alternation of a line of four metrical feet with one of three, the three foot lines rhymed, or the linked interweaving terza rima that Dante sustains through the entire *Divine Comedy*.

Nguyen Du completed a version titled *Doan truàng tân thanh* (literally "Bowels in Torment, a New Style," or more figuratively "A Broken Heart, New Version"). He showed the work to his friend and colleague, the scholar

Pham Quy Thich, who was so impressed that with slight editorial revision, he arranged to have it engraved and printed in Hanoi. It appeared under the title *Kim Vân Kieu tân tryên* (A New Version of the Tale of Kim, Vân, and Kieu).

PLOT AND CHARACTER DEVELOPMENT

Running 3,254 lines of verse, the *Tale of Kieu* traces some 15 years of misadventure on the part of its heroine. The basic plot line is linear, but a recurrence of motifs in Kieu's misfortunes suggests the movement of a circle, related to the wheel of suffering in Buddhist thought *(samsara)*. In broad terms, her adventures can be divided into four or five parts that roughly correspond to a seasonal cycle.

The spring of Thuy Kieu's youth centers on her origins and family. She is the talented daughter of a scholar of modest rank and limited means. She has a brother and a younger sister, Thuy Vân. If Vân is marked by quiet grace, Kieu "possessed a keener, deeper charm" (Nguyen, *Tale* 3), achieving a high degree of cultivation in music, painting, and the composition of poetry. During the Spring Feast of Light, a time when people clean the graves of the dead and make offerings (part of a tradition of ancestor worship), Kieu notices a neglected grave. Her brother explains that it belonged to the courtesan Dam Tien, a woman of remarkable talent, but of questionable reputation, adding, "But fate makes roses fragile—in mid-spring / it broke the flower that breathed forth heaven's scents" (Nguyen, *Tale* 5). This introduces the image of the rose, combining delicacy and vulnerability with the precariousness of life and happiness, subsequently correlative of Kieu's own fate. In this Nguyen deploys a common motif in Vietnamese folklore, to speak of the "fragility" of "delight" (Le Huy Hap 9). Feeling profound sympathy and seized with poetic inspiration, Kieu composes a poem in Dam Tien's praise. There is a brief whirlwind and the scent of perfume, and Kieu believes that Dam Tien has manifested herself. Later, Dan Tien appears to Kieu in a dream, acknowledging their spiritual sisterhood, but also warning Kieu that she is condemned to suffer because of the sins of a prior life. Kieu meditates on her fate.

> Alone with her dilemma in deep night,
> she viewed the road ahead and dread seized her.
> A rose afloat. A water fern adrift. (Nguyen, *Tale* 13)

The image of the fragile rose is combined with that of the river, a complex metaphor that conflates a Buddhist motif of the river signifying the transience of life and its perpetual change with the prominent Vietnamese folk motif of water (rivers, lakes, the sea) linked to the Vietnamese origin myth as a people born from the union of the sea and the land, the Dragon Prince (Lac Long Quan) and the mountain goddess, Au Co.

At this time, a young scholar named Kim Trong, a friend of Kieu's brother, takes up residence in the district. Matching each other in talent and cultivation, Kieu and Kim soon fall in love, pledging themselves to each other under the light of the full moon:

> The stark bright moon was gazing from the skies
> as with one voice both mouths pronounced the oath.
> Their hearts' recesses they explored and probed,
> etching their vow of union in their bones. (Nguyen, *Tale* 19)

At Kim's invitation, Kieu then serenades him on a moon-shaped lute, singing sad songs of lost love and exile:

> Clear notes like cries of egrets flying past;
> dark tones like torrents tumbling in mid-course.
> Andantes languid as a wafting breeze;
> allegros rushing like a pouring rain. (Nguyen, *Tale* 27)

Thereafter, the combined image of the moon accompanied by the delicate music of the lute becomes a recurrent motif in Kieu's mind for their love and their vow, like Shakespeare's "ever fixéd mark, / That looks on tempests and is never shaken" (*Sonnet* 116). The moon is important throughout the *Tale of Kieu*, a full moon signifying clarity and truth, a moon obscured by trees or peeping through curtains, uncertainty or a dream state. Vietnam, like many other east Asian countries, observes the lunar calendar, with its weeklong New Year's festival, Tet, occurring in late January or early February, marking the advent of spring, so the moon in its various phases provides a constellation of images natural to the culture.

Leaving spring and entering into the harsher summer of her discontent, Kieu's difficulties now begin to multiply. First, before formal marriage rites can be performed, Kim is called away by his father to represent the family at the funeral of an uncle, a journey that takes him away for many months. Next, Kieu's father and brother are arrested on false charges, and lacking the necessary funds to bribe officials, she decides to put herself on the marriage market to raise money, an act of profound filial duty. Her bride price is met by a supposed scholar named Ma Giam-Sinh. "A wanton god, the Old Man of the Moon, / at random tying couples with his threads!" (Nguyen, *Tale* 37). Kieu accepts this arrangement, but makes her sister Vân promise to marry Kim when he returns to compensate for her broken vow. Ma turns out to be a scoundrel, procuring young women for a distant brothel keeper known as Tu Ba, "whose wealth of charms was taxed by creeping age" (Nguyen, *Tale* 43). Once he has satisfied his sexual desires, he abandons her to the old bawd. "Oh, shame! A pure camellia had to let / the bee explore and probe all ins and outs" (Nguyen, *Tale* 45). Betrayed and isolated from her family, Kieu first attempts suicide. She is persuaded to escape by a would-be savior named So Khanh: "over camellias peeped just half a moon" (Nguyen, *Tale* 57). During this escape, she is abandoned by him and returned to the brothel, where she is beaten by Tu Ba. Without hope, Kieu acquiesces to Tu Ba's instruction, taking up the life of a prostitute.

Among the regular clients at Tu Ba's establishment is a young gentleman named Ky Tam of the Thuc clan. Kieu plays the lute for him, much as she once played for Kim, but now with a real sense of melancholy and loss. Able to appreciate Kieu's talent, Thuc falls in love with her, taking her out of the brothel and making her his number 2 wife. Although the practice is sanctioned by custom, Kytam is a weak man and does not tell his powerful and jealous number 1 wife.

The prominent seasonal imagery begins to shift to autumn. Kieu is grateful to be away from the brothel, but worries about her fate in relation to Thuc's first wife, Hoan Thu, a woman of high status from a great clan. "A drifting cloud, a floating fern, am I / to drain your fond affection from your spouse?" (Nguyen, *Tale* 71). She tries to persuade Thuc to tell Hoan Thu about their relationship and to reassure her that she has no ambitions for wealth and power. Kieu's anxieties are well founded. But Thuc is a coward and cannot bring himself to tell Hoan Thu. She, however, has already learned of the relationship through gossip and has planned revenge. Under her instruction, thugs kidnap Kieu, burn down her house with a corpse inside to trick people into believing she has been killed, and bring her to Hoan Thu as a slave. "The ant's inside the cup—where can it crawl?" (Nguyen, *Tale* 81) the cruel Hoan Thu muses. Kieu and Thuc must pretend not to recognize each other for fear of incriminating the other, which allows Hoan Thu, who actually knows how things are, to play a sadistic cat and mouse game. One evening, she orders Kieu to play the lute.

> Four strings together seemed to cry and moan
> in tones that wrenched him who was feasting there.
> Both [Hoan and Thuc] heard the selfsame voice of silk and wood—
> she smiled and gloated while he wept within. (Nguyen, *Tale* 97)

Hoping to entrap the two, Hoan eventually lets Kieu become the attendant of a garden shrine to Kuan-yin, the Buddhist Bodhisattva of Compassion, an ironic gesture that underlines her own lack of compassion, but at the same time allows Nguyen Du to make explicit the Buddhist dimensions of the narrative. Fearing that she has been compromised by spies, Kieu flees the house when Thuc tries to visit her, eventually finding refuge in a Buddhist convent run by the saintly Giác Duyên. Sympathetic to her condition, the old nun entrusts her to the care of a woman named Bac Ba, who has in the past made offerings at the nunnery. Appearances are deceptive, and Bac Ba turns out to be a bawd like Tu Ba, and Kieu is forced to marry her nephew, a scoundrel much like Ma Giam-Sinh, again finding herself abandoned in a brothel. Trapped on the turning Buddhist wheel of fate, Kieu is back to where her misery started. Thus another cycle in Kieu's narrative comes to a close, and her winter begins.

One cold day, a handsome broad-shouldered young warrior-scholar enters the brothel. "Plying his oar, he roved the streams and lakes / with sword and lute upon his shoulders slung" (Nguyen, *Tale* 113). The romantic hero Tu Hai and Kieu quickly fall in love, and she joins him. Tu Hai soon leads a successful campaign against the Chinese authorities, becoming master of the country. Although the narrative is supposedly set at some earlier point in history, Nguyen Du has in mind the Tay-son revolution. Once in power, Tu Hai determines to vindicate and avenge the years of suffering that Kieu has had to endure, rounding up her various persecutors: Thuc, Hoan, Bac Ba and her nephew, So Khanh, Tu Ba, and Ma Giam-Sinh. Thuc is released in payment for his earlier kindnesses. In turn, so that she won't be thought mean-spirited, Kieu orders that the humiliated Hoan also be released. The rest are executed.

Life now seems to have rectified itself. Kieu, however, worries about Tu Hai's rebellion against the Chinese emperor, asking him to seek the emperor's clemency by disbanding his army. Reluctantly, Tu Hai complies with her wish, only to be betrayed and assassinated in a ruse concocted by the Chinese general Ho Ton Hien. Kieu is horrified that her moral impulse should be repaid by treachery from the moral authorities. This theme of trust betrayed by corrupt officers echoes Kieu's earlier act of selling herself in order to get her father and brother released from prison, marking the close of another cycle, another turn of the wheel of misfortune. She is captured and forced to play the lute for the Chinese general.

> It moaned like wind and rain—five fingertips
> dripped blood upon four strings. When gibbons howl,
> cicadas wail, they cannot match such grief. (Nguyen, *Tale* 133)

Ho is moved by the music, but decides to dispose of Kieu by marrying her off to a local tribal chief. On the wedding night, Kieu again tries to commit suicide, this time throwing herself off the wedding barge into the Tsien-tang River, and her body floats off downstream. Meanwhile, the saintly Giác Duyên, having been alerted by a prophetess about Kieu's fate, arranges with fishermen to stretch nets across the river to catch and rescue her when her body floats by. Kieu is revived and takes up a quiet life in a Buddhist temple.

The narrative now returns to the past, picking up the story of Kim and Vân. Having returned from the funeral that originally separated him from Kieu, Kim is desolate. Acquiescing to Kieu's wishes, he marries Vân, and they begin a life together. Over the years he proves a competent official, rising in the imperial bureaucracy. One spring night, Vân dreams of her sister and encourages Kim to inquire after her during his official travels. Bit by bit, he reconstructs her fate, but the trail ends with the account of her supposed drowning. In an act of remembrance, not unlike the poem that Kieu once wrote to memorialize Dan Tien many springtimes earlier, Kim posts a tablet by the river. "How queerly fortune's wheel will turn and spin! Giác Duyên now somehow happened by the spot" (Nguyen, *Tale* 153). Recognizing Kieu's name, Giác Duyên introduces herself to Kim and then leads him and his in-laws to the Buddhist shrine and to their reunion with Kieu. The emotions are profound, but in a minor key. Weeping at the knees of her mother, Kieu says,

> Since I set out to wander through strange lands,
> a wave-tossed fern, some fifteen years have passed,
> I sought to end it in the river's mud—
> who could have hoped to see you all on earth? (Nguyen, *Tale* 155)

Vân insists that Kieu and Kim should marry, she as younger sister becoming the number 2 wife. Only after persistent argument does Kieu finally relent to the marriage.

Here Nguyen Du's artistry transcends the conventional romantic formula of "they lived happily ever after." After 15 years of suffering and sorrow, Kieu has achieved an inner peace, a mature appreciation of the fragility of happiness, and an acceptance of her fate, avoiding bitterness or jaded cynicism. Though married, they decide to keep the relationship platonic. Kim then asks Kieu to play her lute one last time, to which she complies, singing a hymn to life and peace, the passion of their love transformed into music. "Was it a butterfly or Master Chuang?" alluding to the Daoist philosopher Chuang-tzu, who once asked whether he was a man dreaming he is a butterfly, or a butterfly dreaming he is a man. "And who poured forth this rhapsody of love?... Clear notes like pearls dropped in a moon-lit bay" (Nguyen, *Tale* 165). Finishing, Kieu says, "For you my lute just sang its one last song— / henceforth,

of the self, giving rise to an elaborate body of imagery and iconography. *The Tale of Kieu* picks up the theme of Buddhism explicitly in Kieu's attendance at the shrine of Kuan-yin, Bodhisattva of Compassion, and in the figure of saintly Buddhist nun Giác Duyên, herself something of a Kuan-yin figure. It is also stated in Kieu's dream warning from her spiritual sister Dam Tien that she is fated to suffer for sins performed in a previous life, a warning reiterated by Giác Duyên, who has consulted a shaman about Kieu's fate. The theme is expressed more implicitly in the various images related to the cycles of the season and in the recurrent pattern of her hardships, the recurrence of suffering for those who remain attached to the desires and illusions of the world and who therefore are self-condemned to repeat the same sins over and over, tied to the turning wheel of fate. It is also picked up in the water imagery. Kieu repeatedly describes herself as a fern drifting in the water, and her fate is continually associated with rivers, whether it is crossing rivers when first taken away by Ma or when she first encounters Tu Hai. Water is also related to her attempted suicide, when she tries to drown herself, only to be fished out eventually by Giác Duyên. In Mahayana Buddhist doctrine, the river is a metaphor signifying variously the transient nature of the self, the interaction and continuity of contingent events, and the barrier to be crossed in order to achieve enlightenment and liberation.

One more constellation of images, though not explicitly associated with Buddhism, is relevant to the theme. Throughout the narrative, the text plays on the metaphor of threads; spinning; knots; tangled, snarled, or raveled skeins; spun silk; and snares. Closely related to these are the mesh of a net and the silk strings of the lute. Such images are both ubiquitous and natural to Kieu's circumstances as a woman, who would include weaving among her domestic skills, but at the same time were used by Nguyen Du with a subtlety that make them fresh and evocative. Kieu speaks of her vow to Kim in terms of a knot, which related to the notion that the god of weddings weaves red silk threats for tying couples together, an image repeated ironically when Kieu is figuratively bound to the scoundrel Ma. These knots figurative and literal signify the attachments and entanglements that tie us to the suffering of life. In turn, Kieu repeatedly describes her perplexity or her suffering in terms of tangles and snarled threads or skeins of silk. Again it is these perplexities, her confusion over the appearance of things, that snare and tangle her in the web of attachments. "My heart's near bursting, for it's caught / in love's own webs and tangles yet unsnarled" (Nguyen, *Tale* 39), she laments. Finally, the images of the web in silk weaving, long threads, and the net by which Giác Duyên saves Kieu from the river offer metaphorical representations of the interconnection of events (dependent origination) that undergirds Buddhist notions of karma, reincarnation, and fate. Finally, this metaphorical play of threads informs the full significance of Kieu's resolution to renounce the lute: "henceforth, I'll *roll its strings* [my emphasis] and play no more" (Nguyen, *Tale* 165). Her detaching the strings is correlative to her struggle to detach herself from the entanglements of her life, to break the threads that bind her to the cycles of suffering.

As with many mystical traditions, both Eastern and Western, the goal of Buddhist enlightenment is nirvana, the taming and ultimately the obliteration of selfhood. Kieu's suffering and humiliation, culminating in her acceptance of things, is a version of this. Indeed, the arc of Kieu's 15 years of trials moves from attachment to liberation, from pride in her abilities, her love vows rooted in her romantic passions, and her fears to a calm acceptance, a sense of happiness from a platonic love detached from goal or purpose, whether from sensual pleasure or from procreation. "I've made my peace with my own fate," she tells Kim on their long delayed wedding night. "What can this cast-off body be good for?" (Nguyen, *Tale* 161).

Of equal importance are the themes that can be read in terms of Confucianism. Confucianism is one of the defining traditions of China, Japan, Korea, and Vietnam, persistent even down to the present, shaping both social structure and personal identity. At its worst, it can become puritanical, officious, and inflexible. The conditions of women under a rigid, traditional Confucianism are circumscribed by submission and obedience, and indeed, much of Kieu's passivity can be attributed to such a tradition. Nevertheless, at its best, it nurtures self-realization within the values of the human community. "Only Confucianism among the Three Teachings," writes the contemporary Confucian philosopher Tu Wei-Ming, "unequivocally asserts that society is both necessary and intrinsically valuable for self-realization. Daoism and Ch'an [a Chinese sect of Buddhism; Zen in Japanese] do not seem to have attached much importance to human relations" (Tu 26). Confucianism (*ruxue*—"the doctrine of the scholars") derived from the teaching of Confucius (Kong Fuzi, 551–479 B.C.E.) and followers such as Mencius (Menzgi, 371–289 B.C.E.) and Hsün-tzu (Xunzi, 310–211 B.C.E.), seeking to reestablish political and social harmony (*he*), the way of people with the way of heaven, during the turbulent decline and collapse of the Zhou Dynasty, the so-called Spring and Autumn period (770–476 B.C.E.), and the Warring States period (475–221 B.C.E.). "I set my heart on the Way," says Confucius in the *Analects*, "base myself on virtue, lean upon benevolence for support and take my recreation in the arts" (Confucius 7.6). The doctrine evolved from practical philosophy to state ideology, with knowledge of the five Confucian "classics" and the "Four Books" becoming the basis of civil service examinations and placement in the state hierarchy. The central concern of philosophical Confucianism is the cultivation of human-heartedness and virtue (*jen*), to create the ideal of the "gentleman" or virtuous man *(junzi)*, often contrasted with the grasping and vulgar "small man" *(xiaoren)*. "The gentleman" observes Confucius, "understands what is moral. The small man understands what is profitable" (Confucius 4.16). It seeks to achieve this end through a combination of the development of the individual's talents and the ritualization of human behavior and social interaction. This ritualized behavior in turn codifies human relationships, filial piety *(xiao)*, and fraternal love *(ti)*, the mutual obligations between parents and children and between siblings.

It entered Vietnam with Chinese colonization, becoming fully entrenched by 900 to 1000 C.E. Nguyen Du, as already mentioned, was fully a scholar and gentleman in the Confucian mode, and the *Tale of Kieu* quotes or paraphrases the Confucian *Classic of Songs* (*Shih Ching*) some 50 times. Several Confucian themes are central to our appreciation of Kieu's motivation and character. This plays out in two ways: first, Kieu's desire to be a virtuous person by the cultivation of her talents and by her sense of duty to both her parents and Kim and second, in an implied critique of those who ought to be virtuous but who are not, the sign of a world out of harmony with heaven. If Kieu upholds a Confucian ideal that forces her into passivity, she does so with more fidelity than anyone else in the *Tale*, a standard that underlines the failure and faithlessness of almost everyone else. She is a true Confucian gentlewoman in a realm of small men.

Kieu's behavior exemplifies the Confucian ideal. Within the realms open to women in her world, she has developed her talents with regard to music and poetry. "By Heaven blessed with wit, she knew all skills: / she could write verse and paint, could sing and chant" (Nguyen, *Tale* 3). In turn, her sympathetic family, as part of its reciprocal obligations, nourishes her creativity and self-actualization. More significant is her act of profound filial piety, when she puts herself on the marriage market in order to raise the money to rescue her father from prison. Confucian literature abounds with stories of children who sacrifice themselves to help a parent in distress. The gentlemanly ideal also underlines Kieu's benevolence toward the evil Hoan Thu. The dishonor of being thought "small" outweighs any satisfaction that might derive from revenge. It similarly informs her vow to Kim and her desire that Vân should marry and thereby redeem their vow. She begs her father to approve the arrangement. "Father, help me fulfill my pledge to him— / then I shan't mind a slave's own lot or care / if I should leave my bones in alien soil" (Nguyen, *Tale* 41). Better to sacrifice personal happiness than break a vow. Correspondingly, Vân's willingness to accommodate her sister by sacrificing her own heart's desires in order to honor the dignity of her sister's word is consistent with the spirit of *ti*, as is her later willingness to step aside and assume the role of number 2 wife, when Kieu and Kim are at long last reunited.

This Confucian theme of fraternal (or sororal) loyalty that characterizes the relationship between Kim and Vân strongly resonates with the Vietnamese spirit. Among the oldest and best-known Vietnamese legends is a story titled "The Betel and the Areca Tree," about brothers Tân and Lang. Though Tân is a year older, their appearance is identical. Both are in love with a beautiful girl. In deference to age, Lang lets his older brother marry the girl. Later, Tân seems to have grown distant from his brother. One day when Tân's wife mistakenly embraces Lang, confusing him for his brother, Lang decides to steal away into the forest rather than risk any appearance of impropriety. Exhausted and grieving, he dies at the edge of the sea, where he turns into limestone. When Tân learns that his brother has left, he is ashamed of himself for his own lack of proper attention to fraternal obligations. Going in search of his brother, he also succumbs to grief and exhaustion at the very spot where Lang died. Tân, however, turns into an areca tree. Finally, the wife, observing the proper duty for her husband, also travels into the forest, also dying at the same spot. She is transformed into the twining vine of a betel plant, wrapping itself around the areca tree next to the limestone. Thereafter the place is commemorated with the motto "Brothers united, spouses faithful" (*Vietnamese Legends* 82; see also Thich Nat Hanh 41–50). It is later learned that a bit of betel nut with a sprinkle of limestone, and wrapped in areca leaf, produces a blood-red stain on the lips and a pleasant taste. The king therefore decrees that the combination of betel, limestone, and areca leaf replace salt as the wedding offering, adding, "They shall be symbols of love and fidelity" (Thich Nat Hanh 50). In the *Tale of Kieu* the sisters show a fidelity like that of Tân and Lang; each has remained faithful to the spirit of Kieu's vow, despite circumstances that force her into prostitution. Despite her apparent guilt, she retains her innocence, the victim of duress.

A second legend, known variously as "The Supernatural Crossbow" (*Vietnamese Legends*) or "Blood Pearls" (Thich Nhat Hanh) makes the point of Kieu's innocence even more strongly. Once upon a time, King An Duong Vuong, fearing for the safety of his country, prays for help. He has a vision of a golden tortoise who gives him one of its claws. The king is instructed that if attached to a crossbow as a trigger, the claw will impart magical powers that will defeat any enemy. It proves so potent that An Duong Vuong easily defeats the army of the king Trieu Da. Realizing that he cannot win by force of arms, Trieu Da decides to employ deceit. He sues for peace, offering his son Prince Trong Thuy in marriage to An Duong Vuong's daughter My Chau to seal the bargain. The marriage takes place, and the newlyweds fall in love. Time passes, and Trieu Da reminds his son of his filial duties. The prince coaxes the secret of the magic crossbow from My Chau, who suspects no treachery from her husband. Trong Thuy surreptitiously replaces the magic tortoise claw with a forgery, informing his father of what he has done. Delighted with this intelligence, Trieu Da mounts another attack. Facing capture and defeat because the magic crossbow no longer works, An Duong Vuong flees his capital, taking My Chau with him on the back of his horse. In turn, Trong Thuy follows at a distance. When the king and his daughter reach the sea, An Duong Vuong calls to the golden tortoise. It appears but warns him, "Beware of the treacherous enemy who sits behind you" (*Vietnamese Legends* 34). The tortoise refers to the pursuing Trong Thuy, but the king misunderstands, supposing that he has been betrayed by his daughter. In anger, he cuts her head off (in other versions, she stabs herself). With her dying words, My Chau asserts her innocence: "Father, if it was my intention to betray you, let my dead body turn to dust. Otherwise, may my drops of blood turn to precious gems to prove my heart was ever faithful to you and our people" (Thih Nhat Hanh 120). An Duong Vuong disappears into the sea, Trong Thuy arrives to see what his actions have produced. In the end, King Trieu Da combines the kingdoms to form "Nam Viet," but Trong Thuy, despairing the death of My Chau, drowns himself. Finally, the blood from My Chau's body is washed into the water, where it is absorbed by oysters, resulting in beautiful pearls, an affirmation of her innocence.

The echoes in the *Tale of Kieu* are readily apparent. Kieu, like My Chau, has kept faith, despite all appearances. She is the victim of the deceit of others. Indeed, both prefer humiliation and death to being thought to have betrayed a trust. In turn, Kieu's story, as with that of My Chau, offers the promise that eventually the suffering of the person whose heart has remained true will be redeemed, that something precious will emerge from it. But their circumstances point to another theme as well, a political one. Both My Chau and Kieu are the victims of larger political and social forces outside their control. Both are pawns, caught up in the machinations and deceptions of others. Both have been betrayed by people and institutions that they trusted, that should have been the guardians of their well-being.

Central to Confucian political doctrine is the "mandate of heaven" (*tian ming*): that people and nations that live up to the heavenly ideal will prosper, and those that do not will suffer. Conversely, a corrupt society is a sign that the mandate has been lost, an augury of disaster. Throughout the *Tale*, Kieu's troubles are the consequence of corrupt officials or the betrayal of supposed "gentlemen." Her problems began when she needed to raise the money to bribe a judge, in order to rescue her father and brother from false charges brought by a crooked businessman. "This wrong / could they appeal to Heaven far away?" asks the narrator, adding, "Lawmen behaved that day as is their wont, / wreaking dire havoc just for money's sake" (Nguyen, *Tale* 33). The matter-of-factness of tone underlines Nguyen Du's sad irony. In this society, Heaven and its mandate seem remote. Later, the Chinese general Ho Ton Hien reciprocates Tu Hai's gesture of peace and honor with lies and treachery. Again the sad irony is that Kieu has naively supposed that the Chinese emperor or his representative would exemplify the Confucian ideal. On a more personal level, Kieu is deceived and betrayed at the hands of a succession of false scholar-gentlemen, from Ma and So Khanh to Bac Ba's nephew. Similarly, though Thuc possesses the cultivation of the gentlemen, he lacks the strength of character. Confucius repeatedly warns of the gentleman whose words outstrip his deeds (e.g., Confucius 14.27). Given such a society and such corrupt institutions, it is not surprising that rebellion, such as that led by Tu Hai, should follow. In couching the state of social and political corruption from the perspective of a woman, critic Nathalie Nguyen points out, Nguyen Du follows a convention in Vietnamese literature that uses the tribulations of women to represent the nation (Nguyen, *Classical* 455). In the end, it is precisely this epic quality—the power to articulate and remember the values and aspirations of the culture, its sense of itself and its complex history—that endears the *Tale of Kieu* to so many Vietnamese, that makes it the national poem; at the same time, it possesses a quality of humane sympathy that makes it a part of world literature.

SUBSEQUENT INFLUENCE

Tale of Kieu has enjoyed general popularity from the beginning, transmitted through inexpensive printings and public recitations. It is not surprising to find people who have memorized long sections or who use selected passages to punctuate a statement. Its critical reception has been more complex. Both critics and general readers are unanimous in their praise of Nguyen Du's aesthetic achievement, his perfection of the popular idiom and his creation of an enduring work that can hold its own against any work of world literature. Nevertheless, some critical circles were less sympathetic to the content of the poem, especially among orthodox Confucians who complained of what they took to be Kieu's lack of moral propriety. They may also have sensed its implicit political and social critique directed against themselves.

The period after World War I marked a resurgence of interest and attention among intellectual circles as various nationalist groups vied to assert a Vietnamese identity against the cultural and political hegemony of French Indochinese colonialism. The *Tale* was especially championed by the moderate nationalists associated with the periodical *Nam Phong*. This position was well summarized by the following 1924 statement: "While 'The Story of Kieu' endures, our language will endure, and while our language endures, our country will endure" (qtd. in Durand and Nguyen 91). They were criticized by the Confucians and more independence-minded nationalists. When the Indochinese Communist Party formed the Viet-minh in 1943, party intellectuals argued that the *Tale* represented a decadent world, the last vestiges of a dying feudalism. Critics such as Truong Tuu (Ngyuen Bach Khon) suggested, for instance, that the theme of karma in the *Tale* was ripe for Freudian analysis and that Kieu exemplified the neurotic personality created by social forces. Whatever the diagnosis of Kieu's difficulties, the *Tale* remains popular. In a speech celebrating the foundation of the Vietnamese Communist Party, Ho Chi Minh referred to Tu Hai's victory, quoting Kieu's lines: "It's only now we see it all come true, / yet from the first I felt it in my bones" (Nguyen, *Tale* 119). Over the years, the *Tale* has enjoyed some 10 translations into French and two into English, in addition to translations in a variety of other languages.

In 1970, during the Vietnam War, East German novelist and playwright Peter Weiss (most noted for his play *Marat/Sade*) traveled to then North Vietnam as part of a cultural delegation. Visiting a bomb shelter and hospital facility cut deep into a mountain, he observed a guard. "The guard at the entrance, a young girl with helmet and rifle, sits bent over a dog-eared copy of *Kieu*" (Weiss 120). In the midst of war, and maybe especially because of the war and its aftermath, Nguyen Du's *Tale of Kieu* remains a potent and beloved book.

The *Tale* has exercised a profound effect on modern Vietnamese, postcolonial Vietnamese Francophone, and Vietnamese diasporan literature. Hoang Ngoc Phach's 1925 *To Tam* (*Pure Heart*), regarded as the first modern Vietnamese novel, plays extensively off of the *Tale*, while challenging and complicating many of its values. A number of Vietnamese Francophone works also play on the *Tale*, of note Trinh Thuc Oanah and Marguerite Triaire's 1939 *En s'écartant des ancêtres* (*In Distancing Oneself from the Ancestors*), Tran Van Tung's 1946 *Bach-Yên ou la fille au coeur fidèle* (*Bach-Yên or the Girl with the Faithful Heart*), Ly Thu Ho's 1962 *Printemps inachevé* (*Unfinished Spring*), and Kim Lefevre's 1990 *Retour à la saison des pluies* (*Return of the Rainy Season*). The work of five South Vietnamese feminist writers who emerged in the 1960s (known collectively as the "Five She-Devils"—*Ngu Quai*) is also of note. These include Nguyen Thi Hoang (1942–), Nguyen Thi Thy Vu (1932–), Tuy Hong, writer and composer Trung Duong, and Nah Ca (1939–), whose 1968 *At Night I Hear the Cannons* (*Dem nghe tieng dai bac*) is available in translation. Also of relevance are the memoirs of Le Ly Hayslip, *When Heaven and Earth Changed Places* (1989) and *Children of War, Women of Peace* (1993). Assessing the place of Kieu in modern Vietnamese literature, Nathalie Nguyen writes, "Writers transpose the classical figure of Kieu to a modern setting as a means of both asserting the centrality of Vietnamese identity and culture and simultaneously questioning many of the assumptions carried within the symbolic persona of this acme of Vietnamese female protagonists" (Nguyen, *Vietnamese* 176).

The *Tale* has also found its way onto film. It was the basis for the first feature-length film made in Vietnam (1924), albeit under French direction. More recently, director Nguyen Dinh Chieu produced a musical version of *Kim-Vân-Kieu* (1990–1994). There have also been several fine independent films, though these are hard to come by. These translate the suffering and heroic endurance of Kieu to the modern experience of the refugee and the immigrant. Trinh T. Minh-Ha touched on Kieu in her 1989 *Surname Viet Given Name Nam* and more fully and explicitly in her *A Tale of Love* (1995), which she describes as "an open 'haiku' of *The Tale*" (*Cinema Interval* 257). Director Vu T. Thu Ha's 2006 *Kieu* casts the story into a day in the life of a young woman working in a massage parlor in San Francisco.

Trinh T. Minh-Ha's comments on her *A Tale of Love* are relevant to our general appreciation of Kieu and her enduring qualities. Rather than a character attached to a story, T Minh-Ha Trinh suggests that Kieu be seen "as a *situated multiplicity*, a mirror that reflects other mirrors" (*Cinema Interval* 267). By this she takes on a mythic dimension, speaking to anyone who seeks to preserve her dignity in difficult circumstances or dangerous times.

SUGGESTED READINGS

Cao Thi Nhu-Quynh and John C. Schafer. "From Verse Narrative to Novel: The Development of Prose Fiction in Vietnam." *The Journal of Asian Studies* 47.4 (November 1988): 756–777.

Chan, Wing-tsit, ed and trans. *A Source Book in Chinese Philosophy*. Princeton: Princeton University Press, 1969.

Chesneaux, Jean, and Daniel Hemery, eds. *Tradition et révolution au Vietnam*. Paris: Editions Anthropos, 1971.

Confucius. *The Analects*. Trans. D. C. Lau. London: Penguin Books, 1979.

Durand, Maurice M., and Nguyen Tran Huan. *An Introduction to Vietnamese Literature*. Trans. D. M. Hawke. New York: Columbia University Press, 1985.

Durand, Maurice M. ed. *Mélanges sur Nguyen Du: Réunis à l'occasion du bi-centenaire de sa naissance (1765)*. Paris: École Française d'Extreme-Orient, 1966.

Elman, Benjamin A., John B. Duncan, and Herman Ooms, eds. *Rethinking Confucianism: Past and Present in China, Japan, Korea, and Vietnam*. Los Angeles: UCLA Asian Monographs, 2002.

Fingarette, Herbert. *Confucius: The Secular as Sacred*. Prospect Heights, IL: Waveland Press, 1972.

Kelley, Liam C. *Beyond the Bronze Pillars: Envoy Poetry and the Sino-Vietnamese Relationship*. Honolulu: University of Hawai'i Press, 2005.

Keyes, Charles F. *The Golden Peninsula: Culture and Adaptation in Mainland Southeast Asia*. New York: Macmillan Publishing, 1977.

Ko, Dorothy, JaHyum Kim Haboush, and Joan R. Piggott, eds. *Women and Confucian Cultures in Premodern China, Korea, and Japan*. Berkeley: University of California Press, 2003.

Le Huy Hap. *Vietnamese Legends*. Rev. ed. Saigon: Khai Tri, 1976.

Nguyen Du. *The Kim Vân Kieu*. Trans. Vladislav Zhukov. Canberra: Pandanus, 2004.

———. *The Tale of Kieu: A Bilingual Edition of Truyen Kieu*. Trans. Huynh Sanh Thong and Alexander B. Woodside. New Haven: Yale University Press, 1983.

Nguyen, Nathalie. "A Classical Heroine and Her Modern Manifestation: *The Tale of Kieu* and Its Modern Parallels in *Printemps inachevé*." *French Review* 73.3 (February 2000): 454–462.

———. *Vietnamese Voices: Gender and Cultural Identity in the Vietnamese Francophone Novel*. DeKalb: Southeast Asia Publications, Northern Illinois University Press, 2004.

Nhat Hanh, Thich. *A Taste of Earth and Other Legends of Vietnam*. Trans. Mobi Warren. Berkeley: Parallax Press, 1993.

Phung, Vu Trong. *Dumb Luck*. Ed. Peter Zinoman. Trans. Nguyen Nguyet Cam and Peter Zinoman. Ann Arbor: University of Michigan Press, 2002.

Schultz, George F. *Vietnamese Legends*. Rutland, VT: Charles E. Tuttle Co., 1965.

Trinh T. Minh-ha. *Cinema Interval*. New York: Routledge, 1999.

———. *Women, Native, Other Writing Postcoloniality and Feminism*. Bloomington: Indiana University Press, 1989.

Tu, Wei-Ming. *Confucian Thought: Selfhood as Creative Transformation*. Albany: State University of New York Press, 1985.

Vietnamese Legends and Folk-Tales. Hanoi: The Gioi Publishers, 1997.

Weiss, Peter. *Notes on the Cultural Life of the Democratic Republic of Vietnam*. Trans. from German. New York: Dell, 1970.

Yao, Xinzhong. *An Introduction to Confucianism*. Cambridge: Cambridge University Press, 2000.

10

Quetzalcoatl

All the days of my life I have seen nothing that rejoiced my heart so much as these things [artifacts from Mexico], for I saw amongst them wonderful works of art, and I marveled at the subtle *Ingenia* of men in foreign lands.

—Albrecht Dürer (101–102)

And as for their [Inca and Aztec] piety, observance of the laws, goodness, liberality, loyalty and frankness: well, it served us well that we had less of that than they did; their superiority in that ruined them.

—Michel de Montaigne (343)

Celestial creator god, cultural hero, figure of regeneration, and symbol of the priest-king, Quetzalcoatl was the most powerful and pervasive religious and mythic figure among the gods of Mesoamerican cultures. He is often known as or identified with Ehécatl, the Aztec wind god; Topiltzin Quetzalcoatl, the Toltec ruling prince and founder; Ce Acatal Topiltzin ("our dear prince"); and Nacxitl Topiltzin (the "Lord of the Four Directions"). In Nahuatl, the language of the Aztecs, the name *quetzal [li]-coatl* means "quetzal feather snake," sometimes translated "feathered serpent" or "plumed serpent." The name may also be glossed "precious twin," punning on *coatl*, which may signify either "snake" or "twin" (Bierhorst, *Four*4). In the Yucatec Mayan culture, he is known as Kukulkán, and in the Guatemalan Highlands, Gucumatz. He also shares parallels among the Navajo as Nayénezgani. Our understanding of Quetzalcoatl derives from about 70 surviving written, painted, and archeological sources. At the same time his presence continues to exercise an influence in art and literature. The Mexican author and diplomat Octavio Paz (winner of the 1990 Nobel Prize in Literature) writes, "The image of the serpent is repeated with obsessive frequency: the visions do not come forth from individual imagination but have been codified into a ritual....The serpent is a true archetype. A channel of communication between the world of humans and the infernal world, gods and ancestors appear between its jaws" (Paz, *Essays* 76). This chapter will look at four surviving literary fragments. Each was translated from Nahuatl by the anthropologist John Bierhorst and included in his anthology, *Four Masterworks of American Indian Literature*. Although by no means exhausting the rich variety of material, they are works of literary merit that express the nature and character of Quetzalcoatl. These works also give some indication of the enduring power of Quetzalcoatl to move the imagination of later writers and artists.

MESOAMERICA

Historians and archeologists broadly define the historical boundaries of the Mesoamerican world from about 2500 B.C.E. to the Spanish Conquest in 1521. Geographically, this world extended from the southern half of Mexico to parts of Nicaragua and Costa Rica. Central to its formation was the transformation of various nomadic peoples into a sedentary agricultural society based on the domestication of maize. Indeed, despite local, ethnic, and linguistic differences (there are 16 language families and some 65 different indigenous languages), all of these cultures shared a set of core traditions related to maize cultivation on which they built their intellectual and religious framework. "This unity derives from a history shared by societies at different levels of development, an evolution based on intensive relationships that converted this heterogeneous group of peoples into joint producers of a cultural substrate," writes the historian Alfredo López Austin (López Austin and López Luján 52). Thus, though particular societies, such as the Olmecs, Teotihuacans, Totecs, or the Mexicas, at different times played the role of "lead actor," imposing certain styles, knowledge, or institutions over the whole, there remained an underlying unity related to the myths of origin, the major deities, the symbolism, the calendar, and the cycles of rituals sustained by a similar cosmology. In turn the development of intensive agriculture permitted the development of large sophisticated urban centers with a stratified social structure. It is also relevant to add that though the Spanish Conquest destroyed the social superstructure, it did not eliminate the core, much of which still informs native Christianity. As López Austin points out, "indigenous religions and myths are not just the remains of past traditions and beliefs. They are living, contemporary processes" (*Myths* 307).

Despite cultural and ethnic differences, there is a remarkable similarity in the cosmology, religious practice, and mythology of the pre-Columbian peoples, building on a series of polar, but complementary dualities. Some of these seem universal: sky–earth, male–female, father–mother, heat–cold. Others seem more local: eagle–ocelot, flower–flint, number 13–number 9, stream of blood (life)–night stream (death) (López Austin, *Human* 53). The primal nature of these dualities is symbolized by the figure of Ometeotl (literally "Twice God" or "Two Gods in One"), Lord of Dualities, the supreme deity, and the creator of the cosmic forces. He is also known by the names Yohualli Echecatl, "Invisible and Intangible"; Tlacatl, "The Person"; and Moyocoyani, "The Arbitrary One" (López Austin and López Luján 244). In turn, he has four sons, who divide the horizontal plane of the earth into five regions, the four cardinal points of the compass and the central space at the intersection of the polarities, the point of order or equilibrium. Each direction is named and associated with its characteristic cosmic elements and colors. North is known as Flint and associated with death and the color black, whereas its opposite, South, is known as Rabbit and associated with life and the color blue The East is known as Reed and associated with the male and red, and West is House and associated with female and white. (The great four-sided pyramids with their crowning platform or temple are emblematic of the cosmic archetype.) The world, associated with the color green, represents a dynamic steady state, an epoch of balance or temporary harmony created by the tension of competing elements, each seeking ascendancy and dominance. The title of Wilson Harris's novel *The Four Banks of the River of Space,* deeply influenced by this cosmology, nicely expresses the interconnection among flux, time, and space. The loss of balance releases cataclysmic forces that end the world until a new order is achieved. These epochs or periods of harmony were called Suns, and the Aztecs thought that they lived in the Fifth Sun (*Nahui Ollin*), four previous worlds having preceded them.

The figure of Quetzalcoatl as the Plumed Serpent is a hybrid, an attempt to represent the unity of opposed dualities. As a bird in this cosmic lexicon, he contains aspects of the male, heaven, and light, but as a serpent, he contains the opposite corresponding aspects of the female, earth, and darkness. This underlines the basis of the pun in his name, *coatl*, which may signify "twin" as well as "snake." This is also related to the mythic motif of putting Quetzalcoatl in opposition and conflict with his brother Tezcatlipoca ("Smoking Mirror"), a trickster sorcerer and the spirit of opposition, part of the conceptual framework of paired dualities central to the cosmology. Tezcatlipoca is, say Miller and Traube, "the embodiment of change through conflict" (164). Tezcatlipoca is also known by the name Ome Ácatl or "Two-Reed." In one myth he is the sun, but jealous Quetzalcoatl, as the incarnation of Venus, knocks him out of the sky with a stick, whereupon Tezcatlipoca takes the form of a jaguar.

The horizontal plane of the earth is suspended within a vertical dimension, consisting of 13 heavens or celestial regions over the earth, and 9 subterranean below (the binary opposition 13–9 mentioned above.) The heavens were held up by the branches of five trees, corresponding to the five regions, and roots penetrated the subterranean realms. The trees also represented the route of passage from one realm to another. The lowest of the celestial realms is inhabited by the moon; the second by the stars; the third by the sun; the fourth, Venus; the fifth, comets ("smoking stars," *citlanin popoca*); and the sixth through the eighth, night, day, and storms. The ninth, tenth, and eleventh are the places of the gods and known respectively as the God who is White, the God who is Yellow, and the God who is Red. (These gods relate to the divine personification of maize.) The last two heavens are the abode of Ometeotl. The nine lower realms are the source of water, winds, and the places where the dead reside in various stages of death. In the context of mythic narratives, Quetzalcoatl is often represented as passing through subterranean passages or tunnels dug by moles, or descending from heaven through an opening in the sky, or in the Aztec legend, emerging at Tula from the cloud-covered peak of the highest mountain (a volcano).

It is important not to lose sight of the dynamic character of the Mesoamerican cosmos. Their classification of nature also served to spatialize time or temporalize space, orienting years and days according to their four corresponding directions. It became the basis of the complex geometry of the sacred calendars with their 52-year cycle, tracking the relative positions of the sun, moon, and Venus and shaping their ritual practice, divination, and their sense of the synchronization of events. Past dates and events gave meaning to present and future dates to which they corresponded. Quetzalcoatl was said to be born on the date One Reed, which associates him with the East, water, and by extension the planet Venus, which rises from the East. He was sometimes associated with Tlahuizcalpantecuhtli ("Lord of the House of Dawn"). More fatefully, this thinking led many Aztecs to suppose that Hernán Cortés, who arrived out of the water in the East, on a date that corresponded to One Reed, must be an emissary of Quetzalcoatl, if not the god himself. The dynamic relationship between time and space also served to put the Aztecs on the path of what León-Portilla terms "mystical imperialism," the belief that they could control nature and put off the end of their Sun period by sustaining the forces of nature with the fluid of life (blood), leading to the practice of sacrificing victims to Huitzilopochtil, their sun god. Thus, they became great warriors, conquering neighbors in order to provide themselves with a supply of victims—ironically, a practice that helped to undermine the Fifth Sun (León-Portilla, *Aztec* 61).

The earliest representations that suggest elements of Quetzalcoatl are found among artifacts of the Olmec civilization (1500 B.C.E. to1150 C.E.). Little is known of this civilization aside from its development of agriculture. A surviving relief sculpture (the so-called Monument 19) shows a man wearing a hooded Jaguar mask, cradled by a giant snake. Next to them are two long-tailed Quetzal birds. Quetzalcoatl played a prominent role among the peoples who formed the urban complex, Teotihuacān, which flourished between 100 B.C.E. to 600 C.E., a major population center dominating the basin of Mexico and the major trade routes stretching north to the Zuni in New Mexico and the Hopi in Arizona. Tradition claimed that the city was founded at the start of the Fifth Sun. The Temple of Quetzalcoatl, partly an architectural representation of the myth of time, includes a pyramid elaborately decorated with recurrent images of the Plumed Serpent. After a period of unrest caused by the invasion of various nomadic peoples, the Toltecs assumed the role of "lead actors" from about 800 C.E. until 1150, when its urban center Tula was abandoned. The Toltec religious center, Tula (or Tollán in Nahuatl), "The Place of Reeds," was supposedly the earthly expression of the cosmic archetype, and subsequent peoples styled themselves the descendants of the Toltecs. "At Tula stood the beamed sanctuary, / only the snake columns still stand, / our prince Nacxitl [often identified with Quetzalcoatl] has gone, has moved away," says the poet Ten Flower, recorded in the *Cantares mexicanos* (qtd. in Brotherston, *Book* 158). The poet adds, "The pyramid burst apart hence my tears / the sacred sand whirled up hence my desolation. / My fine-plumed lord has gone away / has left me, Ten Flower, an orphan" (qtd. in Brotherston, *Book* 159). Aztec legend claimed that this was the result of a self-imposed exile caused by Quetzalcoatl's transgressing his ascetic vows by getting drunk and sleeping with a priestess. The decline of Tula contributed to an eastward migration and conquest, resulting in strong connections between the Toltec and Mayan cultures.

On the religious and mythic levels, the Toltecs worshiped the "Lord of the Dawn," Tlahuizcalpantechutli, who was identified with the Plumed Serpent. In a union of the cosmic and earthly, the Toltecs were ruled by a priest-king named Quetzalcoatl. In this form, he typically held the title Ce Ácatl Topiltzin ("Our Dear Prince One-Reed [Quetzalcoatl]"). One of Sahagun's informants in the *Florentine Codex* recollected that "this Quetzalcoatl also did penances. He bled the calf of his leg to stain thorns with blood. And he bathed at midnight" (*Florentine* 4.14). The informant also explains that the mythic pattern of the god informed the ritual practice of the priests. "Him each of the fire priests imitated, as well as the offering priests. And the offering priests took their manner of conduct from the life of Quetzalcoatl. By it they established the law of Tula. Thus were customs established here in Mexico" (*Florentine* 4.15). In the role of founder, priest-king Quetzalcoatl was the creator of civilization and prosperity, a role found among many native American traditions in the figure of the great teacher or bringer of "first things."

The Aztecs were late to the scene, following a nomadic life until they established their capital in Tenochlitlan around 1325. Claiming descent from the Toltecs to legitimize their authority, they asserted political hegemony over the region, building an empire. They worshiped Huitzilopochli, god of war and the sun. His name means "Hummingbird of the South," or "God of the Left." South and left were considered synonymous, both signifying the way to the Palace of the Sun. Souls of dead warriors were thought to return to the earth from the Sun in the form of hummingbirds or butterflies. Blending their cosmology with that of the Toltecs and preserving the underlying motif of paired contraries, they identified Huitzilopochli as one of the four sons of Ometeotl, the four cosmic forces. Each is known by a representative color: Quetzalcoatl is white; Tezcatlipoca, black; Huitzilopochli, blue; and Xipe Totec ("Our Lord the Flayed One"), red.

TEXTS AND CONTEXTS

In the pre-Colombian world, literary transmission involved picture signs and oral interpretation. The writing system was largely based on a combination of pictographs and ideographs. In the former, the images of objects represented the objects; thus, a pictograph of a bird or a skull would represent a bird or a skull. In the latter, images represented ideas or concepts associated with the object. Thus, the bird might represent the soul, or the skull might represent death. These images were sculptured into reliefs or painted in storybooks, known as *amoxtli* (from *ama(tl)* and *oxitl*—"glued sheets of paper") (León-Portilla, *Fifteen* 15). These storybooks were made of cloth, native papers, or stripes of animal hides and were then sewn or glued together in the form of rolls or pleated screens *(tira)* that would unfold like an accordion to reveal a sequence of pictures. Others were simply large sheets of cloth sewn together *(lienzos)* (Carrasco 24). These were then painted with black and red inks, and the sage, the *tlamatini* ("one who knows"), was characterized as "he who possesses the *amoxtli* and the black and red inks" (quoted León-Portilla, *Fifteen* 15). The pictographs and ideographs served as mnemonics to trigger the memory of an oral interpreter, the *tlamatinime* (literally "those who know something"), who had been trained in *calmécac* priestly schools how to read the images and their metaphorical complexity. A Nahuatl poem recorded in a sixteenth-century compilation, *Cantares Mexicanos*, gives some idea of the relationship between pictographs and oral performance:

> I sing the pictures of the books
> and see them widely known,
> I am a precious bird
> for I make the books speak,
> there in the house of the painted books. (qtd. in León-Portilla, *Fifteen* 5)

At the same time, there was room for variation. The Spanish translator of the *Codex Mendoza* reported that his native informants often disagreed and argued heatedly over the interpretation of a number of images.

Our knowledge of Quetzalcoatl and his world derives from seven types of "document." First are pre-Columbian storybooks that escaped destruction from zealous conquerors determined to stamp out the old culture. Only 16 are extant. Second are post-Columbian storybooks copied from pre-Columbian storybooks or recreated by Indians in the native style, but under Spanish patronage. The images were often glossed with Spanish annotations. Among the most important are the *Codex Vaticanus A*, the *Codex Vienna*, and the *Codex Telleriano-Remensis* (the name generally signifies either the library that houses the extant volume or the sponsoring patron who commissioned its compilation). The third are early prose works written in Nahuatl, transliterated with a Latin alphabet, and including a Spanish translation. These offer narrative accounts that in many cases would have accompanied the storybooks. Among these is the *Codex Chimalpopoca*, which includes the *Anales de Cuauhtitlán* and the *Leyenda de los Soles*, both important sources on Quetzalcoatl. The fourth are prose works written by the descendants of the old Indian elites, among the most significant being those of Alvarado Tezozomoc and Juan Bautista Pomar. The fifth are letters and historical accounts written by Spanish witnesses of the conquest and what they saw of the Aztec culture. The sixth are the ethnographic accounts made by priests, derived from their observations and conversations with the natives. Here the most important is the *Florentine Codex*, which contains the monumental and encyclopedic ethnographic study the *Historia general (universal) de las cosas de (la) Nueva España* [*The General History of the Things of New Spain*] by Fray Bernardino de Sahagún (1499–1590). Finally, the seventh consists of the surviving archaeological evidence, from potsherds and low-relief sculpture such as wall friezes and calendar stones to the temple complexes of ceremonial centers.

Because of the nature of the pre-Colombian system of literary transmission, and because of the consequence of the Spanish conquest and colonization of Mexico, many of these documents must be read with what historian David Carrasco terms a "combination of suspicion, synthesis, and tolerance" (Carrasco 13). The surviving pre-Columbian storybooks offer the images, but not the interpretations that the images were to recall. The post-Columbian books reflect problems derived from reading metaphors removed from their original contexts, whether this is the consequence of a faulty memory on the part of the native informants, no longer part of a living culture, or of the selection of materials to appeal to a European audience, or of an attempt to make the materials conform to European paradigms.

PLOT DEVELOPMENT AND THEMES

The first two fragments that Bierhorst translates and we shall examine derive from the *Leyenda de los Soles* (*Legends of the Suns*). The first treats the origins of the Fifth Sun. It begins after the destruction of the Fourth Sun by a cataclysmic flood. "The skies have dried, the Earth Lord has dried. But who, O gods, shall live?" (Bierhorst, *Four* 17). There are eight gods, paired into four groups, suggesting the primal forces and the four directions: Skirt-of-Stars/Light of-Day, Lord-Drawn-to-the-Water/Lord-Issuing-Forth, Who-Firms-the-Earth/Who-Tills-the-Earth, and Quetzalcoatl/Titlachuan. Each of the names is applied to Ometeotl, and each pairing represents a duality, a complex series of oppositions that will give rise to the new world.

Quetzalcoatl travels to the realm of the dead, Mictlan ("Dead Land"), where he gathers the bones of the dead. In trying to achieve this, he is challenged by the Lord of the Dead Land, who tells him to perform a ritual and then has a trap dug to stop him. Quetzalcoatl falls into this pit or crypt, and the bones he has gathered are scattered and then nibbled by quail. The motif of falling into a hole or crypt or being buried underground is frequently associated with the mythic account of the disappearance of Venus below the western horizon in the evening, followed by its morning appearance out of the East. It is also frequently connected to the theme of recurrent death and resurrection. Weeping, he asks his soul (*nahual*) what is to be done, a move that indicates a duality within the person. His soul answers, "How will it be? It will be undone. But let it be as it will" (Bierhorst, *Four* 19). In other words, because the bones have been damaged, humans are imperfect and must be mortal ("be undone") and accept it as a part of the human condition. That said, Quetzalcoatl again gathers and bundles the bones, finally taking them to Tamoanchan, thereafter known as the original abode of humans and, by extension, the surface of the earth.

The bones are ground to powder by Quilaztli ("Serpent woman"), the Mother Earth, and put into a jadestone (bowl). That done, Quetzalcoatl pierces his penis with a spine and bleeds into the powder, thereby fertilizing the mixture. From this the human race is born, the bowl symbolic of the womb, and humans a combination of blood and bone. Quetzalcoatl's act of penance, conflating sexual union with blood sacrifice, brings into balance the four competing elements—male-red-East, female-white-West, life-blue(day)-South, and death-black(night)-North—to produce the green realm, the earth.

The gods now ask a second question: what will the humans eat? Quetzalcoatl sees a red ant carrying kernels of maize. Confronting the ant, he learns that the maize comes out of Food Mountain. Changing into a black ant, he calls upon the red ant to show him the passage, by which he is able to bring maize to the gods, who then feed it to the primal humans, Oxomoco and his wife Cipactonal. To assure a permanent supply of nutrition, Quetzalcoatl tries to truss up and carry Food Mountain to Tamoanchan. He is, however, unable to budge it. As with his earlier fall into the pit, this misfortune marks the limits of the human condition. Oxomoco and Cipactonal ask Nanahuatl the thunder god to break open the mountain that they might get at the food. "But suddenly rain gods came forth: blue rain gods, white rain gods, yellow rain gods, red rain gods. Then Nanahuatl broke open the mountain, and then the rain gods stole the food" (Bierhorst, *Four* 20). The story of the Food Mountain dramatizes the precarious relationship between humans, the weather, and agriculture. The gods help, but humans must also provide, breaking the Food Mountain open themselves by tilling the soil in order to extract maize, beans, and other foods from the land. Rains are necessary, but too much can sweep away crops.

The second fragment under consideration also comes from the *Leyenda de los Soles*. Here, throughout, Quetzalcoatl is known by the epithet Ce Acatl, literally "One Reed," which identifies him both with Venus and with the astronomical appearance of Venus on the ritual calendar. It seems to have grown out of an earlier account of the god Mixcoatl, "Cloud Serpent," and provides a mythical explanation of the origins of the morning fire ceremony. The story explains that Ce Acatl was born after the four-day hard labor of his mother, who died in the process. He is thereafter reared by Quilaztli, "Serpent Woman." Ce Acatl becomes a warrior, accompanying his father the Sun in battle. His father, however, is murdered by Ce Acatl's uncles, the four hundred Mimixcoa, who bury the corpse in the sand in the west.

Ce Acatl retrieves his father's body, placing it within the Cloud Serpent Mountain temple. He next wishes to make a sacrifice at the temple, but is blocked by his uncles (now reduced from four hundred to three, related to the struggle among the four cosmic elements parts), who demand that the sacrifice should include a jaguar, an eagle, and a wolf. They suppose that this is an impossible challenge. Ce Acatl, however, convinces the jaguar, eagle, and wolf to pretend that they have been captured, in order to divert and turn the tables on the three uncles. Ce Acatl calls on the moles to tunnel a passage into the temple. By this route he emerges at the temple's summit. With the aid of the animals, he subdues his uncles, making them the sacrificial victims: "*and* as the animals blew *on the fire*, then he put them [the uncles] to death: he spread them with chili *and* slashed their flesh; and when he had tortured them, then he cut open their breasts" (Bierhorst, *Four* 23). The sacrifice made, Ce Acatl continues his path of conquest, moving eastward until he reaches Tlapallan, the "Red Place," the mystical land of the rising sun, whereupon he dies after a five-day illness and is consumed in flames.

The narrative allegorizes astronomical phenomena. The Mimixcoa are thought to represent the stars in the sky, the four hundred a rhetorical figure to suggest vast numbers, and their jealousy relates to the way the sun outshines and obscures the stars in the day. Analogously, Ce Acatl's consumption by flames ritualizes the morning star's disappearance after sunrise. The representation of sunset in terms of the murder and burial of the sun is a common motif in many myths in the West. It must then pass through the earth to be resurrected the following morning. As the brightest object in the sky after the sun at sunset and sunrise, the planet Venus is thought to be either the harbinger of the sun or, in this case, what kindles it back to life in the morning. Similarly, Ce Acatl's four-day birth and five-day death may suggest a way of describing and sacralizing the period when Venus is not visible in the sky. Whether an expression of sympathetic magic or ritual reenactment of the divine sacrifice, the narrative informs the priestly practice of ceremonial fires, the passage that connects the earthly with the divine.

The third fragment is from the *Anales de Cuauhtitlán*, intertwining the story of Quetzalcoatl with the semi-legendary chronicle of the Cuauhtitlán. Quetzalcoatl is said to have been born in One-Reed and called Topiltzin Priest One-Reed Quetzalcoatl. The cosmic creator of the earlier fragments now becomes the earthly benefactor of humankind. Reaching maturity in the year Nine-Reed, he learns that his father has died and been buried. Thereupon, he opens the earth and gathers his father's bones, reburying them in the shrine of Quilaztli. Synchronous with these events is the death of Huactli, the king of the Cuauhtitlán, a people who still exist in a hunter-gatherer state, ignorant of maize, still dressing in animal hides and still gathering their food from birds, snakes, rabbits, and deer while traveling from place to place. Their development is marked and made meaningful by its parallels with Quetzalcoatl, underlining his role as the bringer of civilization.

In the year Five-House, it is explained, the Toltecs install Quetzalcoatl as priest-king. Here he builds his four-fold house, a spatial reconstruction of the cosmogony: the house of turquoise, the house of red shell, the house of white shell, and the house of precious feathers. He also makes sacrifices, but limits the practice to snakes, birds, and butterflies, "crying out to the Place of Duality, which lies above the ninefold heavens" (Bierhorst, *Four* 27). It is also explained that he discovers great riches, including cacao and cotton: "And truly in his time he was a great artisan in all his works, in the blue, green, white, yellow, and red painted earthenware from which he drank and ate, and in many other things" (Bierhorst, *Four* 27).

During this period, he dwells deep within his house, separate and inaccessible, where he observes priestly asceticism, an expression of his personal sacrifice for the benefit of the community. Three sorcerers (one of whom is identified as Tezcatlipoca), unhappy that there is no human sacrifice, plot to destroy Quetzalcoatl. As with the earlier account with the three uncles, the three sorcerers form with Quetzalcoatl the pattern of the four cosmic elements in opposition to each other. In order to upset the balance, they formulate a complex plot. "Let us make pulque. We will have him drink it, to corrupt him, so that he will no longer perform *his* sacraments" (Bierhorst, *Four* 29). To achieve this end, Tezcatlipoca approaches Quetzalcoatl with a mirror, explaining to his confederates, "We must give him his body to see" (Bierhorst, *Four* 29). This odd challenge has deeper metaphysical implications. Initially, Quetzalcoatl responds to Tezcatlipoca's challenge with, "What is this body of mine?" (Bierhorst, *Four* 30). When he sees it, however, he is filled with fear. In "giving" Quetzalcoatl his body with the mirror, Tezcatlipoca shatters the unity of his self, revealing its duality, alienating him from his body. The sorcerers then arrange for an artist to create an elaborate mask for him, made of plumes and turquoise and decorated with serpents' teeth. Pleased with this new image in the mirror, Quetzalcoatl emerges from his refuge. The sorcerers first offer him the pulque, an alcoholic drink made from the fermented sap of the maguey plant, which he refuses. They then entice him to eat some spicy food, thereby making him thirsty. This time he does not refuse the drink. "[He] tasted it with the tip of his finger *and* finding it good said, 'I would drink *more* grandfather. Three more *draughts!*'" (Bierhorst, *Four* 32). *Five* draughts later, the throughly drunk Quetzalcoatl calls for his sister Quetzalpetlatl to be brought that they might drink together. It is then implied that Quetzalcoatl has sexual relations with his sister. "And at dawn they were filled with remorse, their spirits were heavy" (Bierhorst, *Four* 34).

Having broken his priestly vows, Quetzalcoatl leaves the city in an act of self-sacrifice and atonement, ordering that everything be buried, that all the Toltec treasures be concealed. Traveling east toward Tlapallan, the Red Land (place of sunrise), he puts on his mask and regalia and sets himself on fire. "And they say as he burned, his ashes arose. And all the precious birds appeared *and* were seen rising upward into the sky" (Bierhorst, *Four* 36). It is explained that he was transformed into a star and thus received the title Lord of the House of Dawn. It is also explained that his death and transformation were in the year One-Reed, completing one cycle of the calendar since his birth in the year One-Reed 52 years earlier. In turn, this sacrifice of the god assumes an archetypal character, establishing the practice of human sacrifice.

The fourth fragment under examination contains stories related to Quetzalcoatl in Sahagún's *Florentine Codex,* based on accounts collected from various Nahua informants. The materials are diverse. Some read like ethnographic reports, others like trickster tales, and others like "just so" stories, explaining the origin of place names. Nevertheless, they follow the broad trajectory of Quetzalcoatl's achievements, followed by his abandonment of Tollan, his self-imposed exile, and his journey toward Tlapallan. Central to this narrative are two interconnected themes, relevant to the Aztec appropriation of the Toltecs. The first derives from the lament "O Toltecs! All things now, *and* even we, *must* pass" (Bierhorst, *Four* 55). Closely related to this is the theme of moral laxness and the failure to observe the ritual practices rigorously. As in other narratives, Quetzalcoatl is the source of knowledge. In turn, his behavior sets the moral tone of sacrifice and purity. "[He] did penance also. He bled the flesh of his shinbone, he stained maguey thorns with blood" (Bierhorst, *Four* 40). Correspondingly, when he grows lax, so also do the Toltecs. It is under these circumstances that the three sorcerers appear and contrive to destroy Tollan, indicating the imbalance of the four elements. Here they are identified as Titlachuan, "He to Whom We Are Slaves," an alternative name for Tezcatlipoca; Huitzilopochtli, the Aztec sun god; and Tlacahuepan, "Human Log," also known by the name Cuexcoch, sometimes glossed as the embodiment of human guilt.

A shape-shifter, Titlachuan/Tezcatlipoca approaches Quetzalcoatl in the form of a little old man. The narrative repeats and underlines "indeed a little old-white-headed man" (Bierhorst, *Four* 41). This description makes a subtle allusion that conflates him with the figure of the opossum, who signifies both an aged grandfather, with his snaggled teeth and grey hair, and the god of the dying year. "In Mayan texts, even in the *Popol Vuh* and the *Chilam Balam of Tizimin,*" writes López Austin, "the opossum appears as lord of the half-light preceding dawn, or as a representation of the gods who hold up the sky at each of the four corners of the world" (López Austin, *Myths* 6). The opossum is one of the oldest figures in native American legends, a fire thief, manipulator, and happy drunk (see Munn; Lévi-Strauss). The identity between opossum and Titlachuan portents the senility of the Toltec and the dawn of a new epoch. As in other versions, the trickster tempts Quetzalcoatl into getting drunk on a potion made of maguey, violating his sacraments.

The fragment now offers a series of trickster tales in which the sorcerers wreak havoc on the Toltecs. In one instance, Titlachauan comes disguised as a Toueyo, literally "Our Neighbor," implying a crude, uncivilized people. He sits naked in the marketplace, selling peppers, "his penis dangling" (Bierhorst, *Four* 44). When the daughter of King Huemac sees this sight, she becomes physically sick from sexual desire. When the king tells the Toueyo to put on a loincloth, the latter replies, "But we truly are thus" (Bierhorst, *Four* 46)—that is, humans are sexual by nature. The king therefore orders the Toueyo to marry his daughter. In a move strikingly similar to the domestication of the wild man Enkidu from the Babylonian epic *Gilgamesh*, the Toueyo's hair is trimmed, and he is bathed and anointed, becoming the king's son-in-law. The people, however, mock the king for marrying his daughter to a Toueyo, so he instructs them to go into battle and there abandon the Toueyo in the middle of the fight. This happens, but the Toueyo joins forces with the dwarves and hunchbacks, destroying the Toltec enemy. The figure and pairing of dwarves and hunchbacks is a frequent motif in Mesoamerican culture, sometimes signifying tricksters, sometimes the children of gods. When King Huemac learns that his son-in-law has been victorious, he tells the Toltecs to put on their regalia of quetzal feathers and sing the praises of the Toueyo. They do this, but the sorcerer (Toueyo) sings and drums until the people are whipped into a feverish rapture, causing them to fall into a gorge. "The Toltecs indeed were destroyed" (Bierhorst, *Four* 51).

After a succession of similar disasters, Quetzalcoatl realizes that he must abandon everything and go into exile, ordering, as in other versions of the story, that the treasures of the Toltecs be hidden. He then leaves the Toltecs' sacred city of Tollan, beginning his pilgrimage toward Tlapallan. On this trek he is preceded by his flute-playing dwarves and hunchbacks. The figure of Kokopelli, the hunchbacked flute player venerated by the Native American culture in the southwestern United States, especially the Hopi, may owe something to Mesoamerican culture. The narrative chronicles a succession of stories, explaining place names. For instance, where Quetzalcoatl slept is now known as Cocatacan, "Where He Lay Sleeping" (Bierhorst, *Four* 61). In another place he left a handprint, thereafter known by the name Temacpalocos, "Where the hand prints Are" (Bierhorst, *Four* 59). In the end, Quetzalcoatl arrives at the seashore. In this version, instead of immolating himself, he sets sail in a snakeskin boat, seeking to reach Tlapallan. Thus he disappears, but with the promise of an eventual return, a promise that has fatal consequences for the Aztecs, but rich potential for later developments in Latin American culture.

SUBSEQUENT INFLUENCE

Despite the efforts of Hernán Cortés, the conquistadores, and the subsequent missionaries and colonizers of Mesoamerica, the figure and spirit of the Plumed Serpent has remained a presence, albeit subterranean and transformed. In 1531, only 10 years after the conquest, the Indian Juan Diego, a Christian convert, had a vision of a dark-skinned lady wreathed in light, a figure eventually known as the Virgin of Guadalupe. This vision played an important role in the conversions of the Indians, and the shrine built to the Virgin has since become central to Mexican Catholicism. Some scholars have noted that the site of the shrine at Tepeyac was once the place of veneration for Tonatzin, "Wife of the Serpent," a female counterpart to Quetzalcóatl, and that the name Guadalupe in Mexico may be the Spanish equivalent of the Nahuatl, *coatalopia*, built on *coatl*, meaning "serpent"; *tealoc*, "goddess"; and *tlapia*, "watch over" (Demarest and Taylor 30–31; see also Warner 302–303 and 390n). In other words, it is possible that Juan Diego read and conceptualized his Christian vision in term of the old traditions. One way or the other, it suggests how Quetzalcóatl has become naturalized into the popular imagination, both colonial and postcolonial.

There have also been more deliberate attempts to evoke the Mesoamerican past and Quetzalcoatl. As Mexico struggled to break colonial ties in the nineteenth century, many in the Mexican intelligentsia turned to the figure of Cuauhtémoc, the nephew of Montezuma, as a symbol of national identity and resistence. It was, however, in the era of creative ferment of the 1920s and 1930s, after the Mexican Revolution (1910–1917), that Quetzalcóatl reemerged as a major cultural icon, part of a reexamination and resurrection of the native past in the service of a socialist present. This is found, for instance, in the poetry of Alfonso Reyes, but most prominently in the visual arts, especially the work of Los Tres Grandes, the three great muralists of Mexican modernism: Diego Rivera (1886–1957), Jose Clemente Orozco (1883–1949), and José David Alfaro Siqueiros (1896–1974). Inspired by Renaissance frescoes, they considered the mural an expression of "public, socialized art" (Rochfort 25). Four works are of special note. Among the most famous is Rivera's triptych, *The Ancient Indian World* (1929–1935) from his *History of Mexico* fresco in the Palacio Nacional. Here Quetzalcóatl is represented heroically in four aspects. At the center of the panel he is the pale, bearded Topiltzin ("Our Dear Prince"), aspect of the earthly ruler. To the left is shown the fiery birth of the god, emerging from an erupting volcano.

To the right is Tlahuizcalpantecuhtli ("Lord of the House of Dawn"), the aspect of Venus. Finally, above is Tzontémoc, the setting sun. Another of Rivera's murals featuring Quetzalcoatl is his 1940 *Marriage of the Artistic Expression of the North and South on This Continent*, also known as *Pan American Unity*, painted in San Francisco. The focal point of the composition is a colossal Goddess of Life, "half Indian, half machine," wrote Rivera, adding, "she would be to the American civilization my vision of what Quetzalcoatl, the great mother of Mexico, was to the Aztec people" (Rivera 244).

Although Rivera's treatment of Quetzalcóatl is triumphant, that of Siqueiros is more ambiguous. His *Cuauhtémoc Against the Myth* (1944) plays on Cuauhtémoc's rejection of the claims that Cortez was the reincarnation of Quetzalcóatl to evoke an anti-colonialist and anti-imperialist theme. The mural represents the Spaniards as a writhing, rearing centaur, with the Aztecs in the form of a tortured (almost Christlike) Cuauhtémoc with a diminutive, open-armed, and blindfolded Montezuma. At their base is the sculpted head of the Plumed Serpent.

Perhaps the most powerful representation comes from Jose Clemente Orozco's 21-panel cycle *American Civilization—The Epic of Culture in the New World* (1930–1934), painted on the wall of the Baker Library at Dartmouth College. Here he conceptualizes the idea of America from the dual perspective of the historical experience of the Europeans and the Indians. "The great American myth of Quetzalcoatl is a living one," Orozco declared, "embracing both elements [European and indigenous] and pointing clearly by its prophetic nature, to the responsibility shared equally by the two Americas of creating here an authentic American civilization" (qtd. in Rochfort 103). Within the historical sweep is the cyclic pattern of doom and rebirth. The panel, *The Departure of Quetzalcoatl*, portrays a bearded Quetzalcoatl, a John the Baptist or Old Testament prophet in the wilderness. His departure signals the destruction of the Aztec epoch and the rise of the European. Similarly, the panels of the *Modern World* section point to the inevitable demise of the Western epoch. The blood sacrifices of the Aztecs are compared with the modern sacrifices caused by war and industrial capitalism. In the larger conception, the figure of Quetzalcóatl is juxtaposed to that of an angry Christ who has chopped the cross down with an axe, the ruins of a military-industrial complex and other civilizations in the background. Both are symbolic of destruction and renewal.

Since that period, a number of Latin American writers have been drawn to the indigenous cultures for inspiration. In his 1949 novel *Hombres de maíz* (*Men of Maize*), the Guatemalan Miguel Ángel Asturias, winner of the 1967 Nobel Prize in Literature, combined European surrealism and Mayan mythology to create one of the foundational works of Latin American "magical realism." The poets Octavio Paz and Ernesto Cardenal also exploit imagery and themes related to the Plumed Serpent. Paz's classic essay "The Labyrinth of Solitude" and its sequel explore the Mexican psyche with enduring subterranean elements that include the Hispanic, Mediterranean, and Moslem as well as the pre-Columbian. "In the popular imagination, many of our heroes are only translations of Quetzalcoatl. They are, in fact, unconscious translations. This is significant because the theme of the Quetzalcoatl myth is the legitimation of power" (Paz, *Labyrinth* 335). Politics also informs Cardenal's treatment. A Catholic priest long associated with revolutionary politics in Nicaragua, he blends myth, history, and quantum mechanics in his long poem *Quetzalcóatl* along with the themes of self-sacrifice with a liberation theology. By contrast, other writers look at the problems of recovering authentic spiritual roots. Several examples include Mexican novelist Carlos Fuentes's *A Change of Skin* (1967) and his monumental *Terra Nostra* (1975) and Peruvian writer Mario Vargas Llosa's *The Storyteller* (1987). Fuentes's *A Change of Skin* (*Cambio de peil*) is a particularly interesting postmodernist treatment that links the main narrative to the myth of Quetzalcoatl through a complex web of associations. Fuentes plays with Tezcatlipoca's use of the mirror to fragment Quetzalcoatl's identity by "giving him his body." Thus identities are dissolved in an infinite reflection of signifiers. Similarly, in his influential essay "Quetzalcoatl and the Smoking Mirror," Guyanese novelist Wilson Harris sees an epic quality underlying the best of Latin American literature, a quality that he attributes to the cultural complexity constructed from its many competing layers (what he terms a "medium of transitive density") (Harris 3). This is evident in many of his own novels, most notably *Carnival* (1985), *Infinite Rehearsal* (1987), and *The Four Banks of the River of Space* (1990), known collectively as the *Carnival Trilogy* (1993), and his *Resurrection at Sorrow Hill* (1993).

Straddling several cultures, the self-proclaimed Neo-Mayan playwright Luis Valdez writes from the perspective of the Chicano experience in the United States. Looking at both the spiritual and the revolutionary valences of the pre-Columbian traditions, Valdez declares in his narrative poem *Pensamiento Serpentino* (1971),

not Thomas Jefferson nor Karl Marx
will LIBERATE the Chicano
not Mahatma Ghandi nor Mao Tze Tung
IF HE IS NOT LIBERATED FIRST BY
HIS PROPRIO PUEBLO
BY HIS POPOL VUH
HIS CHILAM BALAM

HIS CHICHEN ITZA
KUKULCAN, GUCUMATZ, QUETZALCOATL. (Valdez, *Early* 173)

His 1978 play and subsequent 1981 film *Zoot Suit* is deeply informed by the creative opposition between Quetzalcoatl (the character Henry Reyna) and Tezcatlipoca (the character El Pachuco). Also of interest is Leslie Marmon Silko's 1991 *Almanac of the Dead: A Novel*, which looks at the 500-year history of the Americas from a Native American perspective.

The influence of Quetzalcoatl and Mesoamerican culture on art and literature outside the Latin orbit is more scattered. Some Spaniards, such as the Dominican priest Diego Duran, thought that Quetzalcoatl was really Saint Thomas the Apostle (Carrasco 57), others thought he was a Viking, and in the nineteenth century, some Mormons explained him as the New World appearance of Jesus. The Prussian naturalist Alexander Von Humboldt (1769–1859) was among the first Europeans interested in assessing the indigenous art on its own terms in his *Personal Narrative of Travels to the Equinoctial Regions of America During the Years 1799–1804* and his *Vues des cordillères et monuments des peuple indigènes de l'Amérique* (1810). Although he acknowledged some hypothetical plausibility of various external explanations of Quetzalcoatl, Humboldt concluded that the priests following the conquistadores "were naturally inclined to exaggerate the analogies, which they fancied they had recognized between the cosmology of the Aztecks [sic], and the dogmas of the Christian religion" (Humboldt, *Researches* 1.198). He added that the ancient Romans had made the same error with regard to the Germans and Gauls. In 1873 the American soldier and writer Lew Wallace, most famous for his novel *Ben Hur* (1880), published his first novel, *The Fair God, or The Last of the 'Tzins: A Tale of the Conquest of Mexico*. Inspired by what he saw during the 1846 American war with Mexico (coupled with intensive reading), Wallace recounts the world of the Aztecs and its collapse narrated from the perspective of a young Aztec warrior. Also of note is the suite for percussion ensemble *Los Dioses Aztecas* (1959), an impressionistic composition by the American composer Gardner Read.

Like Los Tres Grandes, a number of European and British writers and artists were attracted to Mexico's indigenous culture, partly inspired by the Mexican Revolution and partly in search of a cultural and spiritual alternative to the West. In many instances there is an element of exoticism in what results. Among the most famous literary responses is D. H. Lawrence's novel *The Plumed Serpent* (1927), about a 40-year-old Irish woman, Kate Leslie, seeking spiritual rebirth, repelled equally by American materialism and European decadence. Kate becomes involved with two men, Don Ramon, a Mexican intellectual of Spanish descent, who assumes the role of Quetzalcoatl, and Don Cipriano, a full-blooded Indian and officer in the Mexican army, in the role of Huitzilopochtli. They hope to replace the Christian and Western worldview with a phallic cult based on pre-Columbian traditions. In the end, she is unable to relinquish her sense of individuality, eventually returning to Europe. Like Lawrence, the French surrealists Georges Bataille (1897–1962) and Antonin Artaud (1896–1948) were fascinated by the myth of Quetzal-coatl as a spiritual alternative. Although their work influenced various Latin American writers such as Paz, Asturias, and Fuentes, there is a sense that as with the character of Kate Leslie, Bataille and Artaud focused primarily on the surface of the myth and failed to grasp its redemptive character. For Bataille, the Aztec gods were transgressive tricksters, "deified nightmares, ter-rifying phantasms " (Bataille 3). He adds, "*Bogeyman* or *mute* are the words as-sociated with these violent characters, evil pranksters, brimming with wicked humor, like the god Quetzalcoatl sliding down slopes of the high mountains on a little board" (Bataille 7). Artaud saw the Mexican revolution and the Mesoamerican culture as authentic expressions of surrealism, "an affirmation of life against all its caricatures," adding, "and the revolution invented by Marx is a caricature of life" (Artaud 357). Eventually he turned to the Peyote cult of the Tarahumara.

In the end, the lesson to be gleaned from Quetzalcoatl is part of the same lesson to be gained from the study of world literature in general, both the terror and the exhilaration that comes from recognizing someone beyond ourselves, from acknowledging traditions other than our own. It is the realiza-tion that we can only truly know ourselves in the reflections of others. Wilson Harris's comments on the terror seen by Quetzalcoatl in Tezcatlipoca's mirror are appropriate: "The Smoking Mirror brings through and beyond cosmic terror a sensation of being plural, of a capacity within ourselves to wear many masks, each mask possessing its *partial* eye that glances into a core of mystery at the heart of complex traditions" (Harris 2).

SUGGESTED READINGS

Anaya, Rudolfo A. "The Myth of Quetzalcoatl in a Contemporary Setting: Mythical Dimensions/Political Reality." *Western American Literature* 23.3 (November 1988): 195–200.

Anderson, Arthur J.O., and Charles E. Dibble, eds. and trans. *Florentine Codex*. 12 vols. Salt Lake City: University of Utah, 1950–1982.

Artaud, Antonin. *Selected Writings*. Ed. Susan Sontag. Trans. Helen Weaver. New York: Farrar, Straus and Giroux, 1976.

Asturias, Miguel Ángel. *Men of Maize*. Trans. Gerald Martin. Pittsburgh: University of Pittsburgh Press, 1993.

Baldwin, Neil. *Legends of the Plumed Serpent: Biography of a Mexican God*. New York: Public Affairs, 1998.

Bataille, Georges. "Extinct America." *October* 36 (Spring 1986): 3–9.

Bierhorst, John, ed. *Four Masterworks of American Indian Literature: Quetzalcoatl, the Ritual of Condolence, Cuceb, the Night Chant*. Tuscan: The University of Arizona Press, 1974.

———, trans. *History and Mythology of the Aztecs: The Codex Chimalpopoca*. Tucson: University of Arizona Press, 1992.

Boone, Elizabeth Hill. *Stories in Red and Black: Pictorial Histories of the Aztecs and Mixtecs*. Austin: University of Texas Press, 2000.

Brotherston, Gordon. *Book of the Fourth World: Reading the Native Americas through Their Literature*. Cambridge: Cambridge University Press, 1992.

———. *Images of the New World: The American Continent Portrayed in Native Texts*. London: Thames and Hudson, 1979.

Cardenal, Ernesto. *Cosmic Canticle*. Trans. John Lyons. Willimantic, CT: Curbstone Press, 2002.

———. *Quetzalcóatl*. Trans. Clifton Ross. Berkeley: New Earth Publications, 1993.

Carrasco, Davíd. *Quetzalcoatl and the Irony of Empire: Myths and Prophecies in the Aztec Tradition*. Boulder: University Press of Colorado, 2000.

Castillo, Debra A. "Postmodern Indigenism: 'Questzalcoatl and All That.'" *Modern Fiction Studies* 41.1 (Spring 1995): 35–73.

Coe, Michael D. *Mexico*. 2nd edition. London: Thames and Hudson, 1977.

Courlander, Harold. *The Fourth World of the Hopis: The Epic Story of the Hopi Indians Preserved in Their Legends and Traditions*. Albuquerque: University of New Mexico Press, 1971.

Demarest, Donald, and Coley Taylor, eds. *The Dark Virgin: The Book of Our Lady of Guadalupe: A Documentary Anthology*. Freeport, ME: Coley Taylor, 1956.

Dürer, Albrecht. *The Writings of Albrecht Dürer*. Trans. William Martin Conway. New York: Philosophical Library, 1958.

Florescano, Enrique. *The Myth of Quetzalcoatl*. Trans. Lysa Hochroth. Baltimore: Johns Hopkins University Press, 1999.

Fuentes, Carlos. *A Change of Skin*. Trans. Sam Hielman. London: Penguin Books, 1975.

Gingerich, Willard. "Quetzalcoatl and the Agon of Time: A Literary Reading of the *Anales de Cuauhtitlán*." *New Scholar* 10.1–2 (1986): 41–60.

Harris, Wilson. *The Carnival Trilogy*. London: Faber and Faber, 1993.

———. "Quetzalcoatl and the Smoking Mirror (Reflections on Originality and Tradition)." In *Sisyphus and Eldorado: Magical and Other Realisms in Caribbean Literature*. Ed. Timothy J. Reiss. Trenton, NJ: Africa World Press, 2002. 1–13.

Humboldt, Alexander Von, and Aime Bonpland. *Personal Narrative of Travels to the Equinoctial Regions of America During the Years 1799–1804*. 3 vols. Trans. Thomasina Ross. Charleston, SC: BiblioBazaar, 2006.

———. *Researches, Concerning the Institutions and Monuments of the Ancient Inhabitants of America*. 2 vols. Trans. Helen Williams. London: Longman, 1814.

Johnson, David. "The Messiah of Mesoamerica." *Arizona Quarterly* 38.3 (Autumn 1982): 241–250.

Lawrence, D. H. *The Plumed Serpent (Quetzalcoatl)*. New York: Vintage Books, 1959.

Le Clézio, J.M.G. *The Mexican Dream: Or, the Interrupted Thought of Amerindian Civilizations*. Trans. Teresa Lavender Fagan. Chicago: University of Chicago Press, 1993.

Lee, Jongsoo. "The Colonial Legacy in Ernesto Cardenal's Poetry: Images of Quetzalcoatl, Nezahualcoyotl, and the Aztecs." *Hispania* 87.1 (2004): 22–31.

León-Portilla, Miguel. *Aztec Thought and Culture: A Study of the Ancient Nahuatl Mind*. Trans. Jack Emory Davis. Norman: University of Oklahoma Press, 1963.

———. *Fifteen Poets of the Aztec World*. Norman: University of Oklahoma Press, 1992.

———. *Pre-Columbian Literatures of Mexico*. Trans. Grace Lobanov. Norman: University of Oklahoma Press, 1969.

Lévi-Strauss, Claude. "The Opossum's Cantata." *The Raw and the Cooked*. Vol. 1. *Introduction to the Science of Mythology*. Trans. Jon and Doreen Weightman. New York: Harper and Row, 1970. 164–195.

Llosa, Mario Vargas. *The Storyteller*. Trans. Helen Lane. New York: Farrar, Straus and Giroux, 1989.

López Austin, Alfredo. *The Human Body and Ideology Concepts of the Ancient Nahuas*. 2 vols. Trans. Thelma Ortiz de Montellano and Bernard Ortiz de Montellano. Salt Lake City: University of Utah Press, 1988.

———. *The Myths of the Opossum: Pathways of Mesoamerican Mythology*. Trans. Thelma Ortiz de Montellano and Bernard Ortiz de Montellano. Albuquerque: University of New Mexico Press, 1990.

———. *The Rabbit on the Face of the Moon: Mythology in the Mesoamerican Tradition*. Trans. Thelma Ortiz de Montellano and Bernard Ortiz de Montellano. Salt Lake City: University of Utah Press, 1996.

López Austin, Alfredo, and Leonardo López Luján. *Mexico's Indigenous Past*. Trans. Bernard R. Ortiz de Montellano. Norman: University of Oklahoma Press, 2001.

Malotki, Ekkehart. *Kokopelli: The Making of an Icon*. Lincoln: University of Nebraska Press, 2000.

Markman, Roberta H., and Peter T. Markman. *The Flayed God: The Mesoamerican Mythological Tradition: Sacred Texts and Images from PreColumbian Mexico and Central America*. San Francisco: Harper San Francisco, 1992.

Miller, Mary, and Karl Taube. *An Illustrated Dictionary of the Gods and Symbols of Ancient Mexico and the Maya*. London: Thames and Hudson, 1993.

Montaigne, Michel de. *The Essays: A Selection*. Trans. M. A. Screech. London: Penguin Books, 1991.

Munn, Henry. "The Opossum in Mesoamerican Mythology." *Journal of Latin American Lore* 10.1 (Summer 1984): 23–62.

Nicholson, H. B. *Topiltzin Quetzalcoatl: The Once and Future Lord of the Toltecs*. Boulder: University Press of Colorado, 2001.

Orozco, José Clemente. *An Autobiography.* Trans. Robert C. Stephenson. Austin: University of Texas Press, 1962.

Paz, Octavio. *The Collected Poems of Octavio: 1957–1987.* Trans. Eliot Weinberger. New York: New Directions, 1987.

———. *Essays on Mexican Art.* Trans. Helen Lane. New York: Harcourt Brace, 1993.

———. *The Labyrinth of Solitude and the Other Mexico, Return to the Labyrinth of Solitude, Mexico and the United States, the Philanthropic Ogre.* Trans. Lysander Kemp, Yara Milos, and Rachel Phillips Belash. New York: Grove Press, 1985.

Popol Vuh: The Mayan Book of the Dawn of Life. Trans. Dennis Tedlock. New York: Simon and Schuster, 1985.

Porter, Katherine Anne. "Quetzacoatl." *The Collected Essays and Occasional Writings of Katherine Anne Porter.* New York: Delacorte Press, 1970.

Rivera, Diego. *My Art, My Life: An Autobiography.* Ed. Gladys March. New York: Citidel Press, 1960.

Rochfort, Desmond. *Mexican Muralists: Orozco, Rivera, Siqueiros.* San Francisco: Chronicle Books, 1998.

Rothenberg, Jerome, ed. *Shaking the Pumpkin: Traditional Poetry of the Indian North Americas.* Garden City: Doubleday, 1972.

Séjourné, Laurette. *Burning Water: Thought and Religion in Ancient Mexico.* Berkeley: Shambhala, 1976.

Silko, Leslie Marmon. *Almanac of the Dead: A Novel.* New York: Simon and Schuster, 1991.

Townsend, Richard F. *The Aztecs.* London: Thames and Hudson, 2000.

Valdez, Luis. *Early Works: Actos, Bernabé and Pensamiento Serpentino.* Houston: Arte Publico Press, 1990.

———. *Mummified Deer and Other Plays.* Houston: Arte Publico Press, 2005.

———. *Zoot Suit and Other Plays.* Houston: Arte Publico Press, 1992.

Wallace, Lew. *The Fair God, or, the Last of the 'Tzins: A Tale of the Conquest of Mexico.* Boston: James R. Osgood, 1873.

Warner, Marina. *Alone of All Her Sex: The Myth and the Cult of the Virgin Mary.* New York: Vintage Books, 1983.

Williams, Shirley A. "*Cambio de piel:* The Quest for Quetzalcoatl and Total Fiction." *Hispanic Journal* 8.1 (Fall 1986): 109–124.

Zolbrod, Paul G. *Diné Bohane: The Navajo Creation Story.* Albuquerque: University of New Mexico

Selected Bibliography

Abbott, Justin E., and Narhar R. Godbole, eds. *Stories of Indian Saints: Translation of Mahipati's Marathi Bhaktavijaya*. Delhi: Motilal Banarsidass Publishers, 1933.

Adams, Laurie. *World Views: Topics in Non-Western Art*. New York: McGraw-Hill, 2003.

Aiken, Conrad. *A Letter from Li Po and Other Poems*. New York: Oxford University Press, 1955.

Aldridge, A. Owen. *The Reemergence of World Literature: A Study of Asia and the West*. Newark: University of Delaware Press, 1986.

Ali, Abdullah Yusuf, trans. *The Qur'an*. Elmhurst, NY: Tahrike Tarsile Qur'an, Inc, 2001.

Allen, Roger. *An Introduction to Arabic Literature*. Cambridge: Cambridge University Press, 2000.

Alter, Robert. *The Art of Biblical Narrative*. New York: Basic Books, 1981.

Alter, Robert, and Frank Kermode, eds. *The Literary Guide to the Bible*. Cambridge: Harvard University Press, 1987.

Ammons, A.R. *Collected Poems: 1951–1971*. New York: W. W. Norton, 1972.

Anderson, Arthur J. O., and Charles E. Dibble, eds. and trans. *Florentine Codex*. 12 vols. Salt Lake City: University of Utah, 1950–1982.

Appiah, Kwame Anthony. *Cosmopolitanism: Ethics in a World of Strangers*. New York: W. W. Norton, 2006.

Apter, Emily S. *The Translation Zone: A New Comparative Literature*. Princeton: Princeton University Press, 2006.

Aschcroft, Bill, Gareth Griffiths, and Helen Tiffin, eds. *Post-Colonial Studies: The Key Concepts*. London: Routledge, 2000.

'Attār, Farīd al-Dīn. *The Conference of the Birds*. Trans. Dick Davis. New York: Penguin Books, 1984.

———. *Muslim Saints and Mystics: Episodes from the Tadbkirat al-Auliya'*. Trans. A. J. Arberry. London: Arkana, 1990.

Attridge, Derek. *The Singularity of Literature*. London: Routledge, 2004.

Auerbach, Erich. *Mimesis: The Representation of Reality in Western Literature*. Trans. Willard R. Trask. Princeton: Princeton University Press, 1968.

Austen, Ralph A., ed. *In Search of Sunjata: The Mande Oral Epic as History, Literature, and Performance*. Bloomington: Indiana University Press, 1999.

Ayengar, N.S.R. *Gītagovindam: Sacred Profanities: A Study of Jayadeva's Gitagovinda*. Delhi: Penman Publishers, 2000.

Bakhtin, M. M. *Art and Answerability: Early Philosophical Essays*. Ed. Michael Holquist and Vadim Liapunov. Austin: University of Texas Press, 1990.

———. *The Dialogic Imagination: Four Essays*. Trans. Michael Holquist and Caryl Emerson. Austin: University of Texas Press, 1983.

Baldwin, Neil. *Legends of the Plumed Serpent: Biography of a Mexican God*. New York: Public Affairs, 1998.

Banham, Martin, ed. *A History of Theatre in Africa*. Cambridge: Cambridge University Press, 2004.

Barnstone, Willis. *The Poetics of Translation: History, Theory, Practice*. New Haven: Yale University Press, 1995.

Bartra, Roger. *Wild Men in the Looking Glass: The Mythic Origins of European Otherness*. Trans. Carl T. Berrisford. Ann Arbor: University of Michigan Press, 1994.

Bary, William Theodore de, and Irene Bloom, eds. *Approaches to the Asian Classics*. New York: Columbia University Press, 1990.

Bascom, William. *African Folktales in the New World*. Bloomington: Indiana University Press, 1992.

Basham, A. L. *The Wonder That Was India: A Survey of the History and Cuture of the Indian Sub-Continent before the Coming of the Muslims*. London: Sidgwick and Jackson, 1985.

Bataille, Georges. "Extinct America." *October* 36 (Spring 1986): 3–9.

Bauman, Richard. *A World of Others' Words: Cross-Cultural Perspectives on Intertextuality*. Oxford: Blackwell, 2004.

Bellah, Robert N. *The Japanese Tradition and Its Modern Interpretation*. Berkeley: University of California Press, 2003.

Ben Jelloun, Tahar. *Corruption*. Trans. Carol Volk. New York: The New Press, 1995.

Bennett, Bruce, and Dennis Haskell, eds. *Myths, Heroes, and Anti-Heroes: Essays on the Literature and Culture of the Asia-Pacific Region*. Nedlands: Centre for Studies in Australian Literature, University of Western Australia, 1992.

Bernheimer, Richard. *The Wild Men in the Middle Ages: A Study of Art, Sentiment, and Demonology*. Cambridge: Harvard University Press, 1952.

Bessinger, Margaret, Jane Tylus, and Susanne Wofford, eds. *Epic Traditions in the Contemporary World: The Poetics of Community*. Berkeley: University of California Press, 1999.

Bhabha, Homi. *The Location of Culture*. London: Routledge, 2004.

———, ed. *Nation and Narration*. London: Routledge, 1990.

Bharata Muni. *The Nātya Śāstra: English Translation with Critical Notes*. Trans. Adya Rangacharya. New Delhi: Munshiram Manoharlal, 1996.

Bierhorst, John, ed. *Four Masterworks of American Indian Literature: Quetzalcoatl, The Ritual of Condolence, Cuceb, The Night Chant*. Tuscan: University of Arizona Press, 1974.

Boas, Franz. *Primitive Art*. New York: Dover Publications, 1955.

Bohlman, Philip V. *World Music: A Very Short Introduction*. Oxford: Oxford University Press, 2002.

Borges, Jorge Luis. *Other Inquisitions, 1937–1952*. Trans. Ruth L. C. Simms. Austin: University of Texas Press, 1965.

———. *Seven Nights*. Trans. Eliot Weinberger. New York: New Directions, 1984.

Boubia, Fawzi. "Universal Literature and Otherness." Trans. Jeanne Ferguson. *Diogenes* 141 (1988): 76–101.

Bourdieu, Pierre. *The Field of Cultural Production: Essays on Art and Literature*. Ed. Randal Johnson. New York: Columbia University Press, 1993.

Bowring, Richard. *Murasaki Shikibu: The Tale of Genji*. Cambridge: Cambridge University Press, 2004.

Bradley, Linda, R. Barton Palmer, and Steven Jay Schneider, eds. *Traditions in World Cinema*. Brunswick, NJ: Rutgers University Press, 2006.

Brandon, James R., ed. *The Cambridge Guide to Asian Theatre*. Cambridge: Cambridge University Press, 1997.

Brazell, Karen, ed. *Traditional Japanese Theater*. New York: Columbia University Press, 1999.

Brook, Peter. *The Shifting Point: Theatre, Film, Opera, 1946–1987*. New York: Theatre Communications Group, 1987.

Brotherston, Gordon. *Book of the Fourth World: Reading the Native Americas through Their Literature*. Cambridge: Cambridge University Press, 1992.

Buck, William, trans. *Mahabharata*. New York: New American Library, 1973.

Burkert, Walter. *The Orientalizing Revolution: The Near Eastern Influence in the Early Archaic Age*. Trans. Margaret E. Pindar and Walter Burkert. Cambridge: Harvard University Press, 1992.

Bush, Susan, and Christian F. Murck, eds. *Theories of the Arts in China*. Princeton: Princeton University Press, 1983.

Bynner, Witter, trans. *The Jade Mountain: A Chinese Anthology*. New York: Vintage Books, 1972.

Caddeau, Patrick W. *Appraising Genji: Literary Criticism and Cultural Anxiety in the Age of the Last Samurai*. Albany: State University of New York Press, 2006.

Campbell, Joseph. *The Hero with a Thousand Faces*. Princeton: Princeton University Press, 1968.

Canguilhem, Georges. *The Normal and the Pathological*. Trans. Carolyn R. Fawcett and Robert S. Cohen. New York: Zone Books, 1989.

Carrasco, Davíd. *Quetzalcoatl and the Irony of Empire: Myths and Prophecies in the Aztec Tradition*. Boulder: University Press of Colorado, 2000.

Carroll, Michael Thomas, ed. *No Small World: Visions and Revisions of World Literature*. Urbana, IL: National Council of Teachers of English, 1996.

Caruth, Cathy. *Unclaimed Experience: Trauma, Narrative, and History*. Baltimore: Johns Hopkins University Press, 1996.

Casanova, Pascale. *The World Republic of Letters*. Cambridge: Harvard University Press, 2005.

Chan, Tak-hung Leo. *The Discourse on Foxes and Ghosts: Ji Yun and Eighteenth-Century Literati Storytelling*. Honolulu: Univeristy of Hawai'i Press, 1998.

Chan, Wing-Tsit, ed. *A Source Book in Chinese Philosophy*. Princeton: Princeton University Press, 1969.

Chang, Chung-yuan. *Creativity and Taoism: A Study of Chinese Philosophy, Art, and Poetry*. New York: Harper and Row, 1970.

Chang, Garma C. C. *The Buddhist Teaching of Totality: The Philosophy of Hwa Yen Buddhism*. University Park: Pennsylvania State University Press, 1971.

Chaudhuri, Shohini. *Contemporary World Cinema: Europe, the Middle East, East Asia and South Asia*. Edinburgh: Edinburgh University Press, 2006.

Cheah, Pheng, and Bruce Robbins, eds. *Cosmopolitics: Thinking and Feeling Beyond the Nation*. Minneapolis: University of Minnesota Press, 1998.

Chuang Tzu. *The Book of Chuang Tzu*. Trans. Martin Palmer. London: Penguin Books, 1996.

Cohen, Jeffrey Jerome, ed. *Monster Theory: Reading Culture*. Minneapolis: University of Minnesota Press, 1997.

Collins, Randall. *The Sociology of Philosophies: A Global Theory of Intellectual Change*. Cambridge: Harvard University Press, 1998.

Collon, Dominique. *First Impressions: Cylinder Seals in the Ancient Near East*. Chicago: University of Chicago Press, 1987.

Comrie, Bernard, Stephen Matthews, and Maria Polinsky, eds. *The Atlas of Languages: The Origin and Development of Languages Throughout the World*. New York: Facts On File, 1996.

Confucius. *The Analects*. Trans. DC Lau. London: Penguin Books, 1979.

Connah, Graham. *African Civilizations: An Archaeological Perspective*. Cambridge: Cambridge University Press, 2001.

Conrad, David C., ed. *Sunjata: A West African Epic of the Mande Peoples*. Indianapolis: Hackett Publishing Company, 2004.

Corbin Henry. *Alone with the Alone: Creative Imagination in the Sūfism of Ibn 'Arabī*. Princeton: Princeton University Press, 1969.

Crompton, Louis. *Homosexuality and Civilization*. Cambridge: Harvard University Press, 2006.

Damrosch, David. *The Buried Book: The Loss and Rediscovery of the Great Epic of Gilgamesh*. New York: Henry Holt, 2006.

———, et al., eds. *The Longman Anthology of World Literature*. 6 vols. New York: Longman, 2004.

————. *What Is World Literature?* Princeton: Princeton University Press, 2003.

Davis, Dick. "The Journey as Paradigm: Literal and Metaphorical Travel in 'Attār's *Mantiq al-Tayr.*" *Edebiyat: The Journal of Middle Eastern Literatures* 4 (2): 173–83.

Davis, Natalie Zemon. *Trickster Travels: A Sixteenth-Century Muslim Between Worlds.* New York: Hill and Wang, 2006.

Davis, Paul, et al., eds. *The Bedford Anthology of World Literature.* 6 vols. New York: Bedford/St. Martin's Press, 2003.

Derrida, Jacques. *Dissemination.* Trans. Barbara Johnson. Chicago: University of Chicago Press, 1981.

Dōgen. *Shobogenzo.* 4 vols. Trans. Gudo Wafu Nishijima and Chodo Cross. Tokyo: Dogen Sangha, 1996.

Doody, Margaret Anne. *The True Story of the Novel.* New Brunswick, NJ: Rutgers University Press, 1997.

Dorson, Richard M., ed. *African Folklore.* New York: Anchor Books, 1972.

Douglas, Mary. *Purity and Danger: An Analysis of Concept of Pollution and Taboo.* London: Routledge, 2002.

Dumezil, Georges. *The Destiny of a King.* Trans. Alf Hiltebeitel. Chicago: University of Chicago Press, 1988.

————. *Mythe et épopée.* Paris: Gallimard, 1995.

Dumoulin, Heinrich. *Zen Buddhism: A History.* 2 vols. Trans. James W. Heisig and Paul Knitter. New York: Macmillan Publishing Company, 1988.

Durand, Maurice M., and Nguyen Tran Huan. *An Introduction to Vietnamese Literature.* Trans. D.M. Hawke. New York: Columbia University Press, 1985.

Dürer, Albrecht. *The Writings of Albrecht Dürer.* Trans. William Martin Conway. New York: Philosophical Library, 1958.

Eisenstadt, S. N., ed. *The Origins and Diversity of Axial Age Civilizations.* Albany: State University of New York Press, 1980.

Eliade, Mircea. *A History of Religious Ideas.* 3 vols. Chicago: University of Chicago Press, 1978–1985.

————. *From the Stone Age to the Eleusinian Mysteries.* Vol. 1 of *A History of Religious Ideas.* Trans. Willard R. Trask. Chicago: University of Chicago Press, 1978.

————. *The Forge and the Crucible: The Origins and Structures of Alchemy.* Trans. Stephen Corrin. Chicago: University of Chicago Press, 1978.

————. *Patterns in Comparative Religion.* Trans. Rosemary Sheed. New York: New American Library, 1974.

————. *The Sacred and the Profane: The Nature of Religion.* Trans. Willard R. Trask. San Diego: Harcourt Brace Jovanovich, 1987.

Eliot, T. S. *Four Quartets.* New York: Harcourt Brace and Co., 1971.

Ellwood, Robert S., ed. *Discovering the Other: Humanities East and West.* Malibu: Undena Publications, 1984.

Emerson, Ralph Waldo. *Selected Writings of Ralph Waldo Emerson.* New York: New American Library, 1965.

Emigh, John. *Masked Performance: The Play of Self and Other in Ritual and Theatre.* University of Pennsylvania Press, 1996.

Falck, Colin. *Myth, Truth, and Literature: Towards a True Post-Modernism.* 2nd ed. Cambridge: Cambridge University Press, 1994.

Ferdowsi, Abolqasen. *Shahameh: The Persian Book of Kings.* Trans. Dick Davis. New York: Viking, 2006.

Figueira, Dorothy M. *The Exotic: A Decadent Quest.* Albany: State University of New York Press, 1994.

Fletcher, Peter. *World Musics in Context: A Comprehensive Survey of the World's Major Musical Cultures.* Oxford: Oxford University Press, 2001.

Foltz, Richard C. *Animals in Islamic Tradition and Muslim Cultures.* Oxford: Oneworld Publications, 2006.

Frédéric, Louis. *Buddhism: Flammarion Iconographic Guides.* Trans. Nissim Marshall. Paris: Flammarion, 1995.

Frye, Northrop. *The Great Code: The Bible and Literature.* New York: Harcourt Brace Jovanovich, 1982.

Fuchs, Barbara. *Mimesis and Empire: The New World, Islam, and European Identities.* Cambridge: Cambridge University Press, 2004.

Fung, Yu-Lan. *A Short History of Chinese Philosophy.* Ed. Derk Bodde. New York: Free Press, 1966.

Ganguli, Kisari Mohan, trans. *Mahabharata of Krishna-Dwaipayana Vyasa.* 4 vols. New Delhi: Munshiram Manoharlal Publishers, 2000.

Gasché, Rodolphe. *The Tain of the Mirror: Derrida and the Philosophy of Reflection.* Cambridge: Harvard University Press, 1986.

Gat, Azar. *War in Human Civilization.* Oxford: Oxford University Press, 2006.

al-Ghazālī, Abū Hamid. *The Niche of Lights (Miskhkat al-anwar).* Trans. David Buchman. Provo, UT: Brigham Young University Press, 1998.

Gelb, I. J. *A Study of Writing.* Chicago: University of Chicago Press, 1963.

Gilroy, Paul. *The Black Atlantic: Modernity and Double-Consciousness.* Cambridge: Harvard University Press, 2005.

Gladstone, William Ewart. *The Gladstone Diaries.* Vol. 8. Ed. H.C.G. Matthew. Oxford: Clarendon Press, 1982.

von Goethe, Johann Wolfgang. *West-Östlicher Divan. Gedichte.* Vol. 2. Ed. Erich Trunz. Hamburg: Fischer Bücheri, 1964.

Goodman, Felicitas D. *Ecstasy, Ritual, and Alternate Reality: Religion in a Pluralistic World.* Bloomington: Indiana University Press, 1988.

Grimes, John. *A Concise Dictionary of Indian Philosophy: Sanskrit Terms Defined in English.* Albany: State University of New York Press, 1989.

Griffith, Ralph T. H., trans. *Hymns of the Rgveda.* Ed. J. L. Shastri. Delhi: Motilal Banarsidass, 1973.

Guneratne, Anthony R., and Wimal Dissan, eds. *Rethinking Third Cinema.* London: Routledge, 2003.

Gurr, Andrew, and Pio Zirimu, eds. *Black Aesthetics: Papers from a Colloquium Heard at the University of Niarobi, June 1971.* Nairobi: East Africa Literature Bureau, 1973.

Haffenden, John, ed. *Selected Letters of William Empson,* Oxford: Oxford University Press, 2006.

Hale, Thomas A. *Griots and Griottes: Masters of Words and Music*. Bloomington: Indiana University Press, 1999.

Hamdun, Said, and Noël King. *Ibn Battuta in Black Africa*. Princeton: Markus Wiener Publishers, 1994.

Harré, Rom. *One Thousand Years of Philosophy: From Ramanuja to Wittgenstein*. Oxford: Blackwell Publishers, 2000.

Harris, Wilson. "Quetzalcoatl and the Smoking Mirror (Reflections on Originality and Tradition)." In *Sisyphus and Eldorado: Magical and Other Realisms in Caribbean Literature*. Ed. Timothy J. Reiss. Trenton, NJ: Africa World Press, 2002. 1–13.

Harrison, Jane Ellen. *Themis: A Study of the Social Origins of Greek Religion*. London: Merlin Press, 1963.

Hawkes, David, trans. *The Songs of the South: An Ancient Chinese Anthology of Poems by Qu Yuan and Other Poets*. London: Penguin Books, 1985.

Hays, Peter L. *The Limping Hero: Grotesques in Literature*. New York: New York University Press, 1971.

Hegel, Georg, and Wilhelm Friedrich. *The Philosophy of History*. Trans. J. Sibree. New York: Dover Publications, 1956.

Heine, Bernd, and Derek Nurse, eds. *African Languages: An Introduction*. Cambridge: Cambridge University Press, 2000.

Herbert, Mimi, and Nur S. Rahardjo. *Voices of the Puppet Masters: The Wayang Golek Theater of Indonesia*. Honolulu: University of Hawai'i Press, 2002.

Hilliard, Constance B., ed. *The Intellectual Traditions of Pre-Colonial Africa*. New York: McGraw-Hill, 1997.

Hiltebeitel, Alf. *Rethinking the Mahabharata: A Reader's Guide to the Education of the Dharma King*. Chicago: University of Chicago Press, 2001.

Hinsch, Bret. *Passions of the Cut Sleeve: The Male Homosexual Tradition in China*. Berkeley: University of California Press, 1990.

Hinton, David, trans. *The Selected Poems of Li Po*. New York: New Directions, 1996.

———, trans. *The Selected Poems of Tu Fu*. New York: New Directions, 1989.

Hopkins, E. Washburn. *The Great Epic of India: Its Character and Origin*. New York: Charles Scribner's Sons, 1901.

Hori, Ichiro. *Folk Religion in Japan: Continuity and Change*. Ed. Joseph M. Kitagawa and Alan L. Miller. Chicago: University of Chicago Press, 1968.

Hsieh, Ming. *Ezra Pound and the Appropriation of Chinese Poetry: Cathay, Translation, and Imagism*. New York: Garland, 1999.

Huang, Yunte. *Transpacific Displacement: Ethnography, Translation, and Intertextual Travel in Twentieth-Century American Literature*. Berkeley: University of California Press, 2002.

Huet, Marie-Hélène. *Monstrous Imagination*. Cambridge: Harvard University Press, 1993.

Humboldt, Alexander Von. *Researches, Concerning the Institutions and Monuments of the Ancient Inhabitants of America*. 2 vols. Trans. Helen Williams. London: Longman, 1814.

Hume, Nancy G., ed. *Japanese Aesthetics and Culture: A Reader*. Albany: State University of New York Press, 1995.

Humphries, Jeff. *Reading Emptiness: Buddhism and Literature*. Albany: State University of New York Press, 1999.

Irele, F. Abiola. *The African Imagination: Literature in Africa and the Black Diaspora*. Oxford: Oxford University Press, 2001.

Izutsu, Toshihiko. *Toward a Philosophy of Zen Buddhism*. Boulder, CO: Prajñā Press, 1977.

Jackson, Guida M. *Traditional Epics: A Literary Companion*. Oxford: Oxford University Press, 1994.

Jahn, Janheinz. *Muntu: African Culture and the Western World*. Trans. Marjorie Grene. New York: Grove Press, 1990.

James, William. *The Varieties of Religious Experience: A Study of Human Nature*. New York: Penguin Books, 1984.

Jameson, Fredric. *The Geopolitical Aesthetic: Cinema and Space in the World System*. Bloomington: Indiana University Press, 1995.

———. "Third-World Literature in the Era of Multinational Capitalism." In *The Jameson Reader*. Ed. Michael Hardt and Kathi Weeks. Oxford: Blackwell Publishers, 2000. 315–339.

Jasanoff, Maya. *Edge of Empire: Lives, Culture, and Conquest in the East, 1750–1850*. New York: Alfred A. Knopf, 2005.

Johnson, Charles. *Turning the Wheel: Essays on Buddhism and Writing*. New York: Scribner, 2003.

Johnson, William John, ed. *The Epic of Son-Jara: A West African Tradition*. Bloomington: Indiana University Press, 1992.

Joyce, James. *Finnegans Wake*. New York: Viking Press, 1959.

Kato, Shuichi. *Form, Style, Tradition: Reflections on Japanese Art and Society*. Trans. John Bester. Tokyo: Kodansha International, 1971.

Kearns, Cleo McNelly. *T. S. Eliot and Indic Traditions: A Study in Poetry and Belief*. Cambridge: Cambridge University Press, 1987.

Keene, Donald. *No and Bunraku*. New York: Columbia University Press, 1990.

Kelley, Liam C. *Beyond the Bronze Pillars: Envoy Poetry and the Sino-Vietnamese Relationship*. Honolulu: University of Hawaii Press, 2005.

Kenko, Yoshida. *Essays in Idleness*. Trans. G.B. Sansom. New York: Cosimo Classics, 2005.

Kim, Kichung. *An Introduction to Classical Korean Literature: From Hyanggr to Pansori*. Armonk, NY: M. E. Sharpe, 1996.

King, Bruce Alvin, ed. *New National and Post-Colonial Literatures: An Introduction*. Oxford: Clarendon Press, 1996.

Kirk, G. S. *Myth: Its Meaning and Function in Ancient and Other Cultures*. Cambridge: Cambridge University Press, 1973.

Kōjin, Karatani. *Origins of Modern Japanese Literature*. Trans. Brett de Bary. Durham: Duke University Press, 1993.

Koller, John M. *Asian Philosophies*. 5th ed. New York: Prentice Hall, 2006.

Komunyakaa, Yusef, and Chad Gracia. *Gilgamesh: A Verse Play*. Middletown, CT: Wesleyan University Press, 2006.

Kovacs, Maureen Gallery, trans. *The Epic of Gilgamesh*. Stanford: Stanford University Press, 1989.

Kramer, Samuel Noah, ed. *Mythologies of the Ancient World*. Garden City: Anchor Books, 1961.

Kundera, Milan. *The Curtain: An Essay in Seven Parts*. New York: HarperCollins, 2007.

Kurosawa, Akira. *Something Like an Autobiography*. Trans. Audie E. Bock. New York: Vintage Books, 1983.

Lach, Donald F. *Asia in the Making of Europe*. 5 vols. Chicago: University of Chicago Press, 1965–1977.

Laye, Camara. *The Guardian of the Word*. Trans. James Kirkup. New York: 1984.

Lawall, Sarah N., et al., eds. *The Norton Anthology of World Literature*. 2nd ed. 6 vols. New York: W. W. Norton, 2003.

Leaman, Oliver, ed. *Companion Encyclopedia of Middle Eastern and North African Film*. London: Routledge, 2001.

Lear, Jonathan. *Radical Hope: Ethics in the Face of Cultural Devastation*. Cambridge: Harvard University Press, 2006.

Lee, Peter H., ed. *A History of Korean Literature*. Cambridge: Cambridge University Press, 2003.

Le Huy Hap. *Vietnamese Legends*. Rev. ed. Saigon: Khai Tri, 1976.

Lem, Stanislaw. *Imaginary Magnitude*. Trans. Marc E. Heine. New York: Harcourt Brace Jovanovich, 1984.

———. *A Perfect Vacuum*. Trans. Michael Kandel. Evanston, IL: Northwestern University Press, 1979.

Lemming, David, ed. *The Oxford Companion to World Mythology*. Oxford: Oxford University Press, 2005.

León-Portilla, Miguel. *Aztec Thought and Culture: A Study of the Ancient Nahuatl Mind*. Trans. Jack Emory Davis. Norman: University of Oklahoma Press, 1963.

———. *Fifteen Poets of the Aztec World*. Norman: University of Oklahoma Press, 1992.

Leroi-Gourhan, André. *Gesture and Speech*. Trans. Anna Bostock Berger. Cambridge: MIT Press, 1993.

Lévi-Strauss, Claude. *Look, Listen, Read*. Trans. Brian C. J. Singer. New York: Basic Books, 1997.

———. "The Opossum's Cantata." In *The Raw and the Cooked*. Vol. 1 of *Introduction to the Science of Mythology*. Trans. Jon and Doreen Weightman. New York: Harper and Row, 1970. 164–195.

———. *Tristes Tropiques*. Trans. John and Doreen Weightman. New York: Atheneum, 1975.

———. *The Way of the Masks*. Trans. Sylvia Model. Seattle: University of Washington Press, 1982.

Leupp, Gary P. *Male Colors: The Construction of Homosexuality in Tokugawa Japan*. Berkeley: University of California Press, 1995.

Lewis, C. Day, trans. *The Eclogues and Georgics of Virgil*. New York: Anchor Books, 1964.

Lichtheim, Miriam, ed. *Ancient Egyptian Literature*. 2 vols. Berkeley: University of California Press, 1975–1980.

Lingis, Alphonso. *The Community of Those Who Have Nothing in Common*. Bloomington: Indiana University Press, 1994.

———. *Dangerous Emotions*. Berkeley: University of California Press, 2000.

Liu, Hsieh. *The Literary Mind and the Carving of Dragons*. Trans. Vincent Yu-chung Shih. New York: Columbia University Press, 1959.

Long, Charles H. *Significations: Signs, Symbols, and Images in the Interpretation of Religion*. Philadelphia: Fortress Press, 1995.

López Austin, Alfredo. *The Human Body and Ideology Concepts of the Ancient Nahuas*. 2 vols. Trans. Thelma Ortiz de Montellano and Bernard Ortiz de Montellano. Salt Lake City: University of Utah Press, 1988.

———. *The Myths of the Opossum: Pathways of Mesoamerican Mythology*. Trans. Thelma Ortiz de Montellano and Bernard Ortiz de Montellano. Albuquerque: University of New Mexico Press, 1990.

Lopez Austin, Alfredo and Leonardo López Luján. *Mexico's Indigenous Past*. Trans. Bernard R. Ortiz de Montellano. Norman: University of Oklahoma Press, 2001.

Lord, Albert. *Singer of Tales*. Cambridge: Harvard University Press, 1960.

Lott, Sandra Ward, Maureen S. G. Hawkins, and Norman McMillan, eds. *Global Perspectives on Teaching Literature: Shared Visions and Distinctive Visions*. Urbana, IL: National Council of Teachers of English, 1993.

Lundquist, Suzanne Evertsen. *Native American Literatures: An Introduction*. New York: Continuum Books, 2004.

Lüthi, Max. *The European Folktale: Form and Nature*. Trans. John D. Niles. Bloomington: Indiana University Press, 1986.

Majid, Anouar. *Unveiling Traditions: Postcolonial Islam in a Polycentric World*. Durham: Duke University Press, 2000.

Malak, Amin. *Muslim Narratives and the Discourse of English*. Albany: State University of New York Press, 2005.

Mann, Charles C. *1491: New Revelation of the Americas Before Columbus*. New York: Alfred A. Knopf, 2005.

Manuel, Peter. *Popular Musics of the Non-Western World: An Introductory Survey*. Oxford: Oxford University Press, 1988.

Mao Tze-tung. *The Poems of Mao Tze-tung*. Trans. Willis Barnstone. New York: Harper and Row, 1972.

Maurya, Abhai. *India and World Literature*. New Delhi: Indian Council for Cultural Relations, 1990.

McEvilley, Thomas. *The Shape of Ancient Thought: Comparative Studies in Greek and Indian Philosophies*. New York: Allworth Press, 2002.

Melentinsky, Eleazar M. *The Poetics of Myth*. Trans. Guy Lanoue and Alexandre Sadetsky. New York: Routledge, 2000.

Menocal, Maria Rosa. *The Arabic Role in Medieval Literary History: A Forgotten Heritage*. Philadelphia: University of Pennsylvania Press, 1987.

Miller, Barbara Stoler, ed. *The Gītagovinda of Jayadeva: Love Song of the Dark Lord*. New York: Columbia University Press, 1977.

———. *Masterworks of Asian Literature in Comparative Perspective: A Guide for Teaching*. Armonk, NY: East Gate Book, M. E. Sharpe, 1994.

———. *Theater of Memory: The Plays of Kalidasa*. New York: Columbia University Press, 1984.

Miller, Mary, and Karl Taube. *An Illustrated Dictionary of the Gods and Symbols of Ancient Mexico and the Maya*. London: Thames and Hudson, 1993.

Miner, Earl. *Comparative Poetics: An Intercultural Essay on Theories of Literature*. Princeton: Princeton University Press, 1990.

Miner, Earl, Hiroko Odagiri, and Robert E. Morrell. *The Princeton Companion to Classical Japanese Literature*. Princeton: Princeton University Press, 1985.

Minh-ha, Trinh T. *Cinema Interval*. New York: Routledge, 1999.

———. *Women, Native, Other Writing Postcoloniality and Feminism*. Bloomington: Indiana University Press, 1989.

Mobley, Gregory. "The Wild Man in the Bible and the Ancient Near East." *Journal of Biblical Literature* 116 (2): 217–233.

de Montaigne, Michel. *The Essays: A Selection*. Trans. M. A. Screech. London: Penguin Books, 1991.

Moran, William J. "Rilke and the Gilgamesh Epic." *Journal of Cuneiform Studies* 32 (4): 208–210.

Morette, Franco, ed. *The Novel*. 2 vols. Princeton: Princeton University Press, 2006.

Morgan, Kenneth W., ed. *The Religion of the Hindus*. New York: The Ronald Press, 1953.

Mori, Masaki. *Epic Grandeur: Toward a Comparative Poetics of World Epic*. Albany: State University of New York Press, 1997.

Moore, Charles A., ed. *The Japanese Mind: Essentials of Japanese Philosophy and Culture*. Honolulu: East-West Center Press, University of Hawai'i Press, 1969.

———, ed. *Philosophy and Culture—East and West: East-West Philosophy in Practical Perspective*. Honolulu: University of Hawaii Press, 1962.

Mote, Frederick W. *The Intellectual Foundations of China*. New York: McGraw-Hill, 1988.

Munn, Henry. "The Opossum in Mesoamerican Mythology." *Journal of Latin American Lore* 10 (1): 23–62.

Murray, Stephen O. and Will Roscoe, eds. *Boy-Wives and Female Husbands: Studies in African Homosexualities*. New York: St. Martin's Press, 1998.

———. *Islamic Homosexualities: Culture, History, and Literature*. New York: New York University Press, 1997.

Naficy, Hamid. *An Accented Cinema: Exilic and Diasporic Filmaking*. Princeton: Princeton University Press, 2001.

Nakamura, Hajime. *Ways of Thinking of Eastern Peoples: India, China, Tibet, Japan.* Trans. Philip P. Wiener. Honolulu: University of Hawai'i Press, 1964.

Narasimhan, Chakravarthi V., trans. *Mahabharata: An English Version Based on Selected Verses.* New York: Columbia University Press, 1998.

Narayan, R. K. *The Guide.* New York: Penguin Books, 1980.

Natsume, Sōseki. *My Individualism and The Philosophical Foundations of Literature.* Trans. Sammy I. Tsunematsu. Boston: Tuttle Publishing, 2004.

Ngũgĩ wa Thiong'o. *Penpoints, Gunpoints, and Dreams: Towards a Critical Theory of the Arts and the State in Africa.* Oxford: Clarendon Press, 1998.

Nguyen, Du. *The Tale of Kieu: A Bilingual Edition of Truyen Kieu.* Trans. Huynh Sanh Thong and Alexander B. Woodside. New Haven: Yale University Press, 1983.

Nguyen, Nathalie. "A Classical Heroine and Her Modern Manifestation: *The Tale of Kieu* and its Modern Parallels in *Printemps inachevé.*" *French Review* 73 (3): 454–462.

Nhat Hanh, Thich. *A Taste of Earth and Other Legends of Vietnam.* Trans. Mobi Warren. Berkeley: Parallax Press, 1993.

Niane, D. T. *Sundiata: An Epic of Old Mali.* Trans. G. D. Pickett. Harlow, Essex: Addison Wesley Longman, 1994.

Nowell-Smith, Geoffrey, ed. *The Oxford History of World Cinema.* Oxford: Oxford University Press, 1996.

Nunley, John W., et al., eds. *Masks: Faces of Culture.* New York: Abrams, 1999.

Nuttall, Sarah, ed. *Beautiful Ugly: African and Diaspora Aesthetics.* Cape Town: Kwela Books, 2005.

Obata, Shigeyoshi, trans. *The Works of Li Po.* New York: Paragon Books, 1965.

O'Flaherty, Wendy Doniger. *Other People's Myths: The Cave of Echoes.* New York: Macmillan Publishing, 1988.

Oinas, Felix J. *Heroic Epic and Saga: An Introduction to the World's Great Folk Epics.* Bloomington: Indiana University Press, 1978.

Okada, H. Richard. *Figures of Resistance: Language, Poetry, and Narrating in The Tale of Genji and Other Mid-Heian Texts.* Durham: Duke University Press, 1991.

Olney, James, ed. *Autobiography: Essays Theoretical and Critical.* Princeton: Princeton University Press, 1980.

Olson, Charles. *Collected Prose.* Ed. Donald Allen and Benjamin Friedlander. Berkeley: University of California Press, 1997.

Ong, Walter J. *Orality and Literacy: The Technologizing of the Word.* London: Routledge, 1982.

O'Riley, Michael Kampen. *Art Beyond the West: The Arts of Africa, India and Southeast Asia, China, Japan and Korea, the Pacific, and the Americas.* Boston: Abrams, 2002.

Otto, Rudolf. *Mysticism East and West: A Comparative Analysis of the Nature of Mysticism.* Trans. Bertha L. Bracey and Richenda C. Payne. New York: Collier, 1962.

Owen, Stephen. *The Great Age of Chinese Poetry: The High T'ang.* New Haven: Yale University Press, 1981.

Parmar, Arjunsinh K., ed. *Critical Perspectives on the Mahabharata*. New Delhi: Sarup, 2002.

Pasternak, Boris. *Selected Poems*. Trans. Jon Stallworthy and Peter France. New York: W. W. Norton, 1982.

Paz, Octavio. *Essays on Mexican Art*. Trans. Helen Lane. New York: Harcourt Brace and Co., 1993.

———. *The Labyrinth of Solitude and the Other Mexico, Return to the Labyrinth of Solitude, Mexico and the United States, the Philanthropic Ogre*. Trans. Lysander Kemp, Yara Milos, and Rachel Phillips Belash. New York: Grove Press, 1985.

Pelton, Robert D. *The Trickster in West Africa: A Study of Mythic Irony and Sacred Delight*. Berkeley: University of California Press, 1980.

Pine, Red, trans. *The Diamond Sutra: Text and Commentaries*. Washington, DC: Counterpoint, 2001.

———, trans. *The Heart Sutra*. Washington, DC: Shoemaker and Hoard, 2004.

Plaks, Andrew H. *The Four Masterworks of the Ming Novel: Ssu ta Ch'i-shu*. Princeton: Princeton University Press, 1987.

Poliakov, Léon, ed. *Hommes et bêtes entretiens sur le racisme*. Paris: Mouton, 1975.

Porter, Joy, and Kenneth M. Roemer, eds. *The Cambridge Companion to Native American Literature*. Cambridge: Cambridge University Press, 2005.

Prendergast, Christopher, ed. *Debating World Literature*. London: Verso, 2004.

Pritchard, James B., ed. *The Ancient Near East: An Anthology of Texts and Pictures*. 2 vols. Princeton: Princeton University Press, 1968.

Propp, Vladimir. *Morphology of the Folktale*. Trans. Laurence Scott. Ed. Louis A. Wagner. Rev. ed. Austin: University of Texas, 1968.

Proust, Marcel. *In Search of Lost Time*. 6 vols. Trans. C. K. Scott Moncrieff, Terence Kilmartin, and D. J. Enright. New York: Modern Library, 1993.

Puhvel, Jaan. *Comparative Mythology*. Baltimore: Johns Hopkins University Press, 1987.

Pye, Michael. *Skilful Means: A Concept in Mahayana Buddhism*. 2nd ed. London: Routledge, 2003.

Qian, Zhongshu. *Limited Views: Essays on Ideas and Letters*. Trans. Ronald C. Egan. Cambridge: Harvard University Press, 1998.

Radhakrishnan, Sarvepalli. *Indian Philosophy*. 2 vols. Delhi: Oxford University Press, 1989.

———, and Charles A. Moore, eds. *A Sourcebook in Indian Philosophy*. Princeton: Princeton University Press, 1957.

Rājaśekhara. *Kāvyamīmāṁsā: Original Text in Sanskrit and Translation with Explanatory Notes*. Ed. Sadhana Parashar. New Delhi: D. K. Printworld, 2000.

Radin, Paul, ed. *African Folktales*. New York: Schocken Books, 1983.

———. *The Trickster: A Study in American Indian Mythology*. New York: Schocken Books, 1972.

Rama, Angel. *The Lettered City*. Trans. John Charles Chasteen. Durham: Duke University Press, 1996.

Reiss, Timothy J., ed. *Sisyphus and Eldorado: Magical and Other Realisms in Caribbean Literature*. Trenton, NJ: Africa World Press, 2002.

Renfrew, Colin. *Archaeology and Language: The Puzzle of Indo-European Origins*. Cambridge: Cambridge University Press, 1988.

Richie, Donald. *A Hundred Years of Japanese Film*. New York: Kodansha, 2002.

Ricoeur, Paul. *The Rule of Metaphor: The Creation of Meaning in Language*. Trans. Robert Czerny. London: Routledge, 1977.

Rilke, Rainer Maria. *Duino Elegies*. Trans. Edward Snow. New York: North Point Press, 2000.

Rimer, J. Thomas. *Modern Japanese Fiction and Its Traditions: An Introduction*. Princeton: Princeton University Press, 1978.

———, and Yamazaki Masakuzu, trans. *On the Art of the Nō Drama: The Major Treatises of Zeami*. Princeton: Princeton University Press, 1984.

Ritter, Hellmut. *The Ocean of the Soul: Men, the World and God in the Stories of Farīd al-Dīn ʿAttār*. Trans. John O'Kane. Leiden: Brill, 2003.

Rivera, Diego. *My Art, My Life: An Autobiography*. Ed. Gladys March. New York: Citadel Press, 1960.

Rizui, Saiyid Athar Abbas, and A. L. Basham. *A Survey of the History and Culture of the Indian Sub-Continent from the Coming of the Muslims to the British Conquest, 1200–1700*. Vol. 2 of *The Wonder That Was India*. London: Sidgwick and Jackson, 1987.

Rochfort, Desmond. *Mexican Muralists: Orozco, Rivera, Siqueiros*. San Francisco: Chronicle Books, 1998.

Rodd, Laurel Rasplica, and Mary Catherine Henkenius, trans. *Kokinshū: A Collection of Poems Ancient and Modern*. Princeton: Princeton University Press, 1996.

Root, Deborah. *Cannibal Culture: Art, Appropriation, and the Commodification of Difference*. Boulder: Westview Press, 1996.

Rosenberg, Donna, ed. *World Mythology: An Anthology of Great Myths and Epics*. 3rd ed. New York: McGraw-Hill Humanities, 2001.

Rushdie, Salman. *Haroun and the Sea of Stories: A Novel*. New York: Penguin Books, 1990.

———. *Homelands: Essays and Criticism, 1981–1991*. London: Granta, 1991.

Safi, Omid. *The Politics of Knowledge in Premodern Islam: Negotiating Ideology and Religious Inquiry*. Chapel Hill: University of North Carolina Press, 2006.

Sandars, N. K., trans. *The Epic of Gilgamesh*. London: Penguin Books, 1972.

Sanders, Julie. *Adaptation and Appropriation*. London: Routledge, 2006.

Saussy, Haun, ed. *Comparative Literature in an Age of Globalization*. Baltimore: Johns Hopkins University Press, 2006.

Savanta, Sivaji. *Mrityunjaya, the Death Conqueror*. Trans. P. Lal and Nandini Nopany. Calcutta: Writers Workshop, 1989.

Schimmel, Annemarie. *And Muhammad Is His Messenger: The Veneration of the Prophet in Islamic Piety*. Chapel Hill: University of North Carolina Press, 1985.

Schulte, Rainer, and John Biguenet, eds. *Theories of Translation: An Anthology of Essays from Dryden to Derrida*. Chicago: University of Chicago Press, 1992.

Schwab, Raymond. *The Oriental Renaissance: Europe's Rediscovery of India and the East, 1680–1880*. Trans. Gene Patterson-Black and Victor Reinking. New York: Columbia University Press, 1987.

Schwartz, Benjamin I. *The World of Thought in Ancient China*. Cambridge: Harvard University Press, 1985.

Scruton, Roger. *The Aesthetic Understanding: Essays in the Philosophy of Art and Culture*. South Bend, IN: St. Augustine's Press, 1998.

———. *Art and Imagination: A Study in the Philosophy of Mind*. London: Methuen, 1974.

Sen, Amartya. *The Argumentative Indian: Writing on Indian History, Culture and Identity*. New York: Farrar, Straus and Giroux, 2005.

Shikibu, Murasaki. *Murasaki Shikibu: Her Diary and Poetic Memoirs*. Trans. Richard Bowring. Princeton: Princeton University Press, 1982.

———. *The Tale of Genji*. Trans. Royall Tyler. New York: Viking, 2001.

Shirane, Haruo. *The Bridge of Dreams: A Poetics of "The Tale of Genji."* Stanford: Stanford University Press, 1987.

———. *Traces of Dreams: Landscape, Cultural Memory, and the Poetry of Bashō*. Stanford: Stanford University Press, 1998.

Shohat, Ella. *Unthinking Eurocentrism: Multiculturalism and the Media*. London: Routledge, 1994.

Sidiqqi, Abdul Hamid, trans. *Sahim Muslim: Al-Jami-Us-Sahih*. 4 vols. New Delhi: Kitabbhavan, 2004.

Siegel, Lee. *Laughing Matters: Comic Tradition in India*. Chicago: University of Chicago Press, 1987.

———. *Sacred and Profane Dimensions of Love in Indian Traditions as Exemplified in the Gītagovinda of Jayadeva*. Delhi: Oxford University Press, 1972.

Smith, Huston. *Forgotten Truth: The Primordial Tradition*. New York: Harper and Row, 1985.

Smith, Jonathan Z. *Imagining Religion: From Babylon to Jonestown*. Chicago: University of Chicago Press, 1982.

Solomon, Robert C., and Kathleen M. Higgins, eds. *From Africa to Zen: An Invitation to World Philosophy*. Lanham, MD: Rowman and Littlefield, 1993.

Soyinka, Wole. *Art, Dialogue, and Outrage: Essays on Literature and Culture*. New York: Pantheon, 1988.

———. *Myth, Literature and the African World*. Cambridge: Cambridge University Press, 1976.

Spivak, Gayatri Chakravorty. *In Other Worlds: Essays in Cultural Politics*. New York: Methuen, 1987.

Steiner, George. *After Babel: Aspects of Language and Translation*. Oxford: Oxford University Press, 1975.

———. *Real Presences*. Chicago: University of Chicago Press, 1989.

Stetkevych, Jaroslav. *Muhammad and the Golden Bough: Reconstructing Arabian Myth*. Bloomington: Indiana University Press, 1996.

Stevens, Wallace. *The Collected Poems*. New York: Vintage, 1982.

Strich, Fritz. *Goethe and World Literature*. New York: Hafner Publishing, 1945.

Sullivan, Lawrence E. *Icanchu's Drum: An Orientation to Meaning in South American Religions*. New York: Macmillan Publishing, 1988.

Sullivan, Robert. *Star Waka*. Auckland: Auckland University Press, 1999.

Suzuki, Daisetz T. *Zen and Japanese Culture*. Princeton: Princeton University Press, 1959.

Suzuki, Shunryu. *Branching Streams Flow in the Darkness: Zen Talks on the* Sandokai. Ed. Mel Weitsman and Michael Wenger. Berkeley: University of California Press, 1999.

Tanizaki, Jun'ichiō. *In Praise of Shadows*. Trans. Thomas J. Harper. New Haven: Leete's Island Books, 1977.

Taussig, Michael T. *Mimesis and Alterity: A Particular History of the Senses*. London: Routledge, 1993.

Tedlock, Barbara, ed. *Dreaming: Anthropological and Psychological Interpretations*. Santa Fe, NM: School of American Research Press, 1992.

Thompson, Robert Farris. *Flash of the Spirit: African and Afro-American Art and Philosophy*. New York: Vintage Books, 1984.

Thoraval, Yves. *The Cinemas of India (1896–2000)*. Delhi: Macmillan India, 2000.

Tigay, Jeffrey H. *The Evolution of the Gilgamesh Epic*. Wauconda, IL: Bolchazy-Carducci Publishers, 2002.

Tonkinson, Carole. *Big Sky Mind: Buddhism and the Beat Generation*. New York: Riverhead Book, 1995.

Tu, Wei-ming. *Confucian Thought: Selfhood as Creative Transformation*. Albany: State University of New York Press, 1985.

Tuan, Yi-Fu. *Space and Place: The Perspective of Experience*. Minneapolis: University of Minnesota Press, 1977.

Ueda, Makoto. *The Master Haiku Poet Matsuo Bashō*. Tokyo: Kodansha International, 1982.

Underhill, Evelyn. *Mysticism: A Study in the Nature and Development of Man's Spiritual Consciousness*. New York: E. P. Dutton, 1961.

Valez, Luis. *Early Works: Actos, Bernabé and Pensamiento Serpentino*. Houston: Arte Publico Press, 1990.

van Buitenen, J.A.B., trans. *Bhagavadgītā: A Bilingual Edition*. Chicago: University of Chicago Press, 1981.

———. *Mahābhārata, Books 1–5*. 3 vols. Chicago: University of Chicago Press, 1973–1978.

Vanita, Ruth, ed. *Queering India: Same-Sex Love and Eroticism in Indian Culture and Society*. New York: Routledge, 2002.

Varsano, Paula M. *Tracking the Banished Immortal: The Poetry of Li Bo and Its Critical Reception*. Honolulu: University of Hawai'i Press, 2003.

Venkatraman, Leela, and Avinash Pasricha. *Indian Classical Dance: Tradition in Transition*. New Delhi: Roli Books, 2004.

Vietnamese Legends and Folk-Tales. Hanoi: The Gioi Publishers, 1997.

Visonà, Monica Backmun, ed. *History of Art in Africa*. New York: Abrams, 2001.

Waley, Arthur. *The Life and Times of Po Chü-I, 772–846 A.D.* London: George Allen and Unwin, 1949.

———, trans. *The Book of Songs: The Ancient Chinese Classic of Poetry.* New York: Grove Press, 1960.

Walkowitz, Rebecca L. *Cosmopolitan Style: Modernism Beyond the Nation.* New York: Columbia University Press, 2006.

Warner, Marina. *From the Beast to the Blonde: On Fairy Tales and Their Tellers.* New York: Vintage, 1994.

Weber, Max. *The Sociology of Religion.* Trans. Ephraim Fischoff. Boston: Beacon Press, 1963.

Wehrs, Donald D. *African Feminist Fiction and Indigenous Values.* Gainesville: University of Florida Press, 2001.

Weiss, Peter. *Notes on the Cultural Life of the Democratic Republic of Vietnam.* Trans. from German. New York: Dell, 1970.

Wexted, John Timothy. "Chinese Influences on the *Kokinshū* Prefaces." In *Kokinshū: A Collection of Poems Ancient and Modern.* Trans. Laurel Rasplica Rodd and Mary Catherine Henkenius. Princeton: Princeton University Press, 387–400.

Williams, David. *Deformed Discourse: The Function of Monsters in Medieval Thought and Literature.* Montreal: McGill-Queen's University Press, 1996.

Woolf, Virginia. *The Essays of Virginia Woolf.* Vol. 4. Ed. Andrew McNeillie. London: Hogarth Press, 1994.

Wu, Ch'êng-ên. *The Journey to the West.* Trans. Anthony C. Yu. 4 vols. Chicago: Chicago University Press, 1977.

———. *Monkey.* Trans. Arthur Waley. London: Penguin Books, 1961.

Yao, Steven G. *Translation and the Languages of Modernism: Gender, Politics, Language.* New York: Palgrave, 2002.

Yampolsky, Philip B., trans. *The Platform Sutra of the Sixth Patriarch.* New York: Columbia University Press, 1967.

Yip, Wai-lim, ed and trans. *Chinese Poetry: An Anthology of Major Modes of Genres.* Durham: Duke University Press, 1997.

Yu, Pauline. *The Reading of Imagery in the Chinese Poetic Tradition.* Princeton: Princeton University Press, 1987.

Zhang, Dainian. *Key Concepts in Chinese Philosophy.* Trans. Edmund Ryden. New Haven: Yale University Press, 2002.

Index